The Maltreatment of
the School-Aged Child

The Maltreatment of the School-Aged Child

Edited by
Richard Volpe
and
Margot Breton
Judith Mitton
University of Toronto

LexingtonBooks
D.C. Heath and Company
Lexington, Massachusetts
Toronto

Library of Congress Cataloging in Publication Data
Main entry under title:

The Maltreatment of the school-aged child.

Includes bibliographies and index.
1. Child abuse—United States—Addresses, essays, lectures. 2. Child abuse—Canada—Addresses, essays, lectures. I. Volpe, Richard. II. Breton, Margot. III. Mitton, Judith.
HV741.M34   362.7'044   79-3581
ISBN 0-669-03463-0

Copyright © 1980 by D.C. Heath and Company

Published simultaneously in Canada

Printed in the United States of America

Clothbound International Standard Book Number: 0-669-03463-0

Paperbound International Standard Book Number: 0-669-04151-3

Library of Congress Catalog Card Number: 79-3581

*To the memory of Ludwig von Bertalanffy,
teacher, scholar, and father of the General
Systems Theory tradition.*

Contents

Foreword *David G. Gil*   ix

Acknowledgments   xiii

Part I   *The Problem of Child Maltreatment*   1

Chapter 1   **Schools and the Problem of Child Abuse: An Introduction and Overview** *Richard Volpe*   3

Chapter 2   **The Behavioral and Ecological Syndrome of the High-Risk Child** *Vladimir de Lissovoy*   11

Chapter 3   **The Effect of Child Abuse and Neglect on the School-Aged Child** *Diane D. Broadhurst*   19

Chapter 4   **The Effects of Schools upon Families: Toward a More Supportive Relationship** *Robert M. Friedman* and *Paul A. D'Agostino*   27

Part II   *Recognition of Child Maltreatment*   43

Chapter 5   **Child Abuse and Neglect: A Medical Priority** *Robert P. Bates*   45

Chapter 6   **Emotional Child Abuse and Neglect: An Exercise in Definition** *Paul G.R. Patterson* and *Michael G.G. Thompson*   59

Chapter 7   **Is Physical Punishment of an Adolescent Abuse?** *Patricia Libbey*   69

Chapter 8   **Sexual Victimization of Children** *Ann Wolbert Burgess* and *Nicholas Groth*   79

Chapter 9   **Outraged: What It Feels Like to Be an Abused Child** *J. Zemdegs*   91

Part III   *Professional and Interprofessional Response*   109

Chapter 10   **The School's Role in the Coordination of Child-Protection Efforts** *Margot Breton*   111

Chapter 11   The Use of Interdisciplinary Problem-Solving
                  Groups in Educational Settings   *Bill Lee*   121

Chapter 12   Using Natural Helping Networks to Meet the
                  Problem of Child Maltreatment   *James Garbarino*   129

Chapter 13   Abuse in School-Aged Children: The Role of the
                  Community-Health Nurse   *Judith Mitton*   137

Chapter 14   The Relationship between the Schools and a Multi-
                  disciplinary Diagnostic Team   *Margaret M. Bailey*
                  and *Susan L. Scheurer*   145

Part IV   *Current Issues in the Study and Treatment of*
                  Child Abuse   155

Chapter 15   Child-Abuse Law in Canada and the United States
                  Bernard M. Dickens   157

Chapter 16   Metatheories of Child Abuse   *Norman W. Bell*   171

Chapter 17   Abused as a Child, Abusive as a Parent: Practitioners
                  Beware   *Michael Benjamin*   187

                  Index   203

                  About the Editors   209

                  About the Contributors   209

Foreword

Although my reflections on this book appear as a foreword, they were actually written as a "last word" with the advantage of hindsight gained from reading the entire work. Hence this foreword might more appropriately be viewed as a postscript by a reader who has studied over many years the roots and dynamics of societal, institutional, and domestic violence, and who has developed a particular perspective on these phenomena.

Maltreatment of children has been widely recognized during recent decades as a social problem of major proportions. Many books and articles have been written from diverse perspectives on various aspects of this destructive phenomenon. The present volume is, however, as far as I know, the first book-length publication concerning maltreatment of school-aged children and the responsibilities and opportunities of school personnel in relation to this. The objectives of the book are stated by Professor Volpe as spreading awareness of maltreatment of school children; helping school personnel to identify maltreated children among their pupils; and suggesting responses to maltreatment involving collaboration between schools and other agencies, and coordination of communitywide efforts on behalf of children identified by schools as maltreated.

Readers will find that the book attains its objectives reasonably well, provided they share the conception of child maltreatment of most of its authors. According to this conception, child maltreatment occurs mainly in the homes of children or in some other location, but not in schools. Also, child maltreatment usually involves some acts or inaction by parents or other caretakers. When these notions are accepted, it is valid for school personnel to view their responsibilities in relation to child maltreatment mainly as identification and protection of pupils who were maltreated outside the schools, and as activities designed to enhance parenting capacities of their pupils' parents and of their pupils as future parents.

In my view, however, the book's conception of child maltreatment is too narrow. It is a myth that schools are always acting in the best interest of children and their development and that they do not maltreat children. I am thinking not only of widespread use in schools of abusive and arbitrary methods of discipline such as corporal punishment and other demeaning, punitive measures, but also of the "normal," massive, educational failure of our schooling system and the consequences of this for the life experience of the "failing" students. The myth that locates child maltreatment outside the schools and makes scapegoats out of parents may offer comfort to school personnel and school authorities. Yet this myth creates obstacles to understanding and overcoming child maltreatment at its roots. By making school personnel aware only of child maltreatment outside the schools, rather than sensitizing them to the hidden dimensions of maltreatment that tend to permeate the milieu of contemporary schools, the book can attain its stated objectives only on the surface, but not in depth. I hope, therefore, that the editors will soon publish a sequence to the present volume in which they will address child maltreatment *in* schools as an intrinsic, though covert, function of schooling under prevailing societal conditions.

To support the assertion that maltreatment of children is widespread in our schools and is now actually an intrinsic, though covert, function of schooling as an institutional process requires clarification of the concept of child maltreatment (Gil, 1975). When testifying in 1973 before a committee of the United States Senate on the Child Abuse Prevention Act, I suggested defining child abuse as *acts or inactions by individuals, institutions, or society, and conditions resulting from such acts or inaction, which inhibit development in accordance with a child's innate capacities.* Drs. Patterson and Thompson suggest a similar definition in the present volume but do not explore the logical implications of a "developmental-deficit" conception of child maltreatment for a critique of schooling. Such an exploration and critique are necessary, however, if we are truly committed to the fullest possible development of every child.

Many observers of contemporary schools in North America have noted that large numbers of children fail to develop their innate intellectual, emotional, and physical capacities in the course of their schooling. A major reason for this seems to be that the established social and economic order of our countries, and especially our system of work and production, has little room for fully developed, creative, imaginative, and self-directing individuals. Rather, what is expected of most adults throughout their work life is to submit to authority without question or challenge, not to think and act independently and creatively, and to be ready to perform meaningless routine tasks or, even worse, accept unemployment without complaints. Schools and other agents of socialization, including families, in any society through history have always prepared the young for the tasks they are expected to undertake as adults rather than for nonexisting tasks. When the quality of adult tasks does not require individuals whose innate capacities are fully developed, then schools and other instruments of socialization tend to obstruct selectively the development of these capacities for children from different segments or classes of society. This is exactly what seems to happen in our countries, given the prevailing division of labor of industrial capitalism into manual and mental functions, the endless subdivisions of "blue-collar" and "white-collar" tasks, the effects of authoritarian bureaucracy, racism, and sexism on work allocation, and the large number of marginally and partially employed and unemployed persons.

This all too sketchy analysis, which is available more thoroughly elsewhere (Bowles and Gintis, 1976; Gil, 1979b), is not offered here in order to blame school personnel as individuals for massive maltreatment of large numbers of children whose capacities tend to atrophy in our schools. It is merely intended to stimulate awareness of certain normal, though covert, institutional dynamics of schooling in our societies and of the abusive and dehumanizing consequences of these dynamics for children and adults.

Once we realize that social and economic forces can transform potentially life-enhancing processes such as education into development-obstructing, abusive processes, we can perhaps also accept that the maltreatment of children in their own homes by their parents is also linked to these forces. Indeed, thorough study of interpersonal violence tends to reveal its multiple links with social structural violence such as poverty and alienation originating at work (Gil, 1978). Erich Fromm, a keen observer of social reality throughout much of the twentieth century, interpreted individual violence as follows:

> It would seem that the amount of destructiveness to be found in individuals is proportionate to the amount to which expansiveness of life is curtailed. By this we do not refer to individual frustrations of this or that instinctive desire, but to the thwarting of the whole of life, the blockage of spontaneity of the growth and expression of man's sensuous, emotional, and intellectual capacities. The more the drive toward life is thwarted, the stronger is the drive toward destruction; the more life is realized, the less is the strength of destructiveness. Destructiveness is the outcome of unlived life. (Fromm, 1941, pp. 183-184)

Understanding maltreatment of children by individuals and by schools in a societal context has far-reaching implications for child protection. These implications do not invalidate the suggestions for ameliorative measures in this book. However, quite different measures are required beyond the ones suggested here when one's objective is prevention of future maltreatment through elimination of its societal sources, rather than merely amelioration of the consequences of past maltreatment. Real prevention of maltreatment will require political action aimed at transforming prevailing social structures and dynamics in which abuse of people has become a normal condition into egalitarian and democratic ones. In such societies the needs and rights of all people would be acknowledged, and social, economic, and political institutions would be compatible with everyone's development (Gil, 1979a).

In concluding this foreword I should like to thank the editors for their broad-mindedness in giving me the opportunity to raise some critical questions concerning their book's approach to the maltreatment of school-aged children. I hope that these questions will assist readers in exploring the painful issues this volume urges them to confront.

David G. Gil
Brandeis University

References

Bowles, S., and Gintis, H. 1976. *Schooling in capitalist America.* New York: Basic Books, Inc.

Fromm, E. 1941. *Escape from freedom.* New York: Holt, Rinehart and Winston, Inc.

Gil, D.G. 1975. Unravelling child abuse. *American Journal of Orthopsychiatry* 45(3):346-356.

Gil, D.G. 1978. Societal violence and violence in families. In J.M. Eckelaar and S.N. Katz, eds. *Family violence.* Toronto: Butterworths; also in D.G. Gil, ed. 1979. *Child abuse and violence.* New York: AMS Press.

Gil, D.G. 1979b. The hidden success of schooling in the United States. *Humanist* 39(6):32-37.

United States Senate. 1973. Hearings before the Subcommittee on Children and Youth of the Committee on Labor and Public Welfare, Ninety Third Congress, First Session on S.1191, Child abuse prevention act. Washington, D.C.; U.S. Government Printing Office, pp. 13-48.

Acknowledgments

The preparation of this volume would not have been possible without the support of the Ontario Ministry of Community and Social Services and the suggestions and many hours of help provided by Kent Campbell, Patty Muñoz, Barbara Brodie, and Hazel Ross.

Part I
The Problem of Child Maltreatment

1

Schools and the Problem of Child Abuse: An Introduction and Overview

Richard Volpe

The erroneous notion exists that most maltreated children are infants and pre-schoolers. As early as 1969, however, Gil related that almost half of the reported cases in his national survey involved school-aged children. Subsequent studies have upheld this finding (Lebsack, 1976; Kline, 1977).

Schools should be playing a greater part in the recognition and provision of services to the abused child and his family; such a contribution would be in keeping with the school's ostensible concern for the well-being of the whole child (Volpe, 1976). In chapter 3 of this volume Broadhurst examines the educational needs, circumstances, and consequences of child maltreatment. Delays in language and motor development may limit the educability of the abused school-aged child. Positive school experience and good peer relations are depicted as ways to overcome the deficits. Zemdegs, chapter 9, presents a young woman's description of her childhood experience of emotional and physical abuse by her parents. She compares the life of the maltreated child to that of a prisoner of war. Her statement dramatically portrays the isolation and hopelessness of a child who should have been assisted by her school.

As the major social institution concerned with the development of children, it seems natural that schools should assume a major responsibility in facilitating, reporting, and participating in the delivery of services to the abused. Living up to the responsibility has been easier said than done. Although, as Drews (1972) pointed out, the school may be the only recourse for the abused school-aged child, the needed help is not usually available.

School personnel are often reluctant to get involved in family problems. They are often overburdened with community demands to be all things to all students. As social institutions have changed, the school has been asked to provide additional services. At the same time, as Friedman and D'Agostino indicate in chapter 4, distrust and hostility have also been characteristic of the new relationship between the school and the family. The expectations may be contradictory and unrealistic, but they do indicate a recognition of the importance and potential of the school in fostering the welfare of children, an awareness of the strategic opportunity school personnel, especially teachers, have for long-term contact with children and consequent knowledge of their needs.

The possibility of developing effective services for abused and at-risk children has also been limited by the traditional approach of professions to operate as

3

independent practitioners. The school's obligation to respond to child maltreatment is a responsibility shared among associated professionals such as teachers, nurses, and social workers. The expertise represented by these groups of professionals has seldom been brought together in such a way that information and knowledge is passed from one to the other.

There are communities in which schools are increasingly involved in the delivery of service to the abused child and abusive family. The forms these services may take include before- and after-school activities, day care, health and nutrition counseling, meals offered at reduced prices, educational and psychological testing, vocational guidance and counseling services (Lauderdale, 1977). Recognition that the abused child is disproportionately in need of special services because of educational and psychological problems (Kline and Christiansen, 1975) has meant that special-education programs have provided service to these children even if only by default (Martin, 1976). Most schools, boards, departments, and ministries do not, however, have policies, let alone programs, in the area of child abuse (Drews, 1972; Fox, 1977). The real consequences of this lack are dramatized by the consistent observation that even when schools do no more than find ways to facilitate reporting suspected cases of child abuse, the number of actual identifications increases significantly (Martin, 1976; Murdock, 1970).

Many of the first school-based programs began as an attempt to improve reporting procedures. These programs were then expanded to involve more school personnel and school-based activities. The Syracuse City School Project is one of the oldest and best known. Five years after its inception in 1964 it became the center of the child-abuse-prevention activities and the greatest single referral source in the city (Drews, 1972). The School Children Abused and Neglected Project carried on in the Bedford Stuyvesant area of Brooklyn made more than 170 referrals in the first two months of operation in 1974.

Schools and social-service agencies assumed mutual responsibility for reporting through an interprofessional Child Abuse and Neglect Team in Jefferson County, Colorado. The team designed reporting procedures and referral evaluation guidelines. Moreover, they provided in-service training for school personnel in their district. As a result of this program there was a substantial increase in the number of children referred and families receiving services (Nicholson, 1977).

Also in Colorado, the Adams County Department of Social Services established a service program for suspected and confirmed cases of child abuse through the district's school system. This referral program became effective only after two sources of resistance were overcome. First, school personnel had to be trained and made aware both of the nature and problem of child abuse and the legal necessity for reporting it, and of the legal protection available for those who report suspected cases. Second, school personnel had to be shown that the community supported their involvement in the detection and prevention of abuse (Broadhurst, 1977).

The desirability of providing educational programs for school personnel is further illustrated by Maryland's Project Protection in Montgomery County. Begun by the U.S. Office of Education in this district's public-school system to train school personnel to recognize and refer children suspected of being abused, the project involved three phases: policy revision, staff training, and curriculum development. School policy was redrafted to require all school personnel to report and refer children. Staff training involved countywide conferences and workshops. New and existing curricula were expanded to inform students about normal human development, child abuse, and ways to prepare for parenthood (Broadhurst, 1975).

These programs suggest that efforts to mobilize school resources to deal with child abuse can loosely be divided into three areas of concentration: awareness, identification, and response. These areas are the basis of three sections that organize the chapters in this volume. Two common themes, collaboration and coordination, bring together the ideas presented in the compilation. Collaboration involves school personnel and representatives from other helping agencies working toward the common goals of protecting children and supporting families. Collaboration must be based on an understanding of the problem of child maltreatment, an ability to recognize abuse, and a means of reporting and securing help for the child and his family. Lissovoy, chapter 2, attends to some of the taken-for-granted assumptions and unicausal explanations that may distort professional understanding of child abuse. He asserts that school personnel need to be aware of both behavioral and ecological indicators if collaborative efforts are to be effective.

In the framework provided here, collaboration involves the decisions that go into strategies for dealing with child maltreatment. Coordination is the concerted action that may result from collaboration. Coordination involves school personnel and other helping professionals acting together to implement the delivery of services to children and their families.

Garbarino, chapter 12, draws attention to the school in fostering natural helping networks in the community. The challenge of parenting and the lack of adequate resources can be reduced if families are assisted in developing existing interpersonal relationships among friends, neighbors, and extended family.

The challenge, then, appears to be to mobilize and coordinate existing services within the community and school system. The assumption is made that the quality of care provided will be improved through these efforts. As yet this assumption has not been evaluated. Bailey and Scheurer, however, report in chapter 14 their personal experiences working in a school-based team. They suggest that their efforts to mobilize and coordinate professionals to act as a team paid off because the team educated school personnel, assessed suspected cases, developed treatment plans and referrals, and reviewed results to see if programs were effective.

An important point is that resources to provide comprehensive services are seldom available to schools. Even if resources were adequate, establishing all the services that could assist children and their families would be an unnecessary duplication of the activities of other agencies. In chapter 11 Lee points out that multidisciplinary groups are necessary primarily because necessary professional and personal resources are seldom available to any one agency or institution. He delineates specific guidelines for organizing and training team members.

Coordination of services on the scale suggested here is difficult. Existing agencies have usually grown up in response to specific problems. Each tends to have its own area of expertise, objectives, and criteria for evaluating and prioritizing services. This development eventually comes to reflect the needs of staff as much as those of the groups to be served. Although coordination may be a reasonable way of increasing the efficiency of services, it is also problematic and potentially frustrating.

The issues of leadership, division of labor, and delegation of responsibility create problems in any interdisciplinary team. In most situations, however, one person must have authority and decision-making power. Ultimately one person must be recognized as the responsible team leader. By distinguishing leadership from accountability no one group should assume leadership by virtue of a particular professional competence. Where leadership is required, leaders should be chosen because of their ability to lead and their flexibility. Because much of what constitutes team functioning can be carried out by consensus, leadership functions may vary with the problems at hand. In chapter 10 Breton outlines the role of team leader or coordinator. She argues that to ensure the effectiveness of the team's effort, the coordinator should have consultation and group-leadership skills. As depicted by Breton, this role requires that community participation be encouraged, helping networks be developed, and child and family advocacy be advanced.

More fundamentally, collaboration of any sort between professionals and agencies, like any form of collaboration, is a matter of meaningful communication. Underlying this simple statement are complex problems. Even when helping professionals are from the same disciplines communication is difficult. Lack of communication between schools and helping agencies is even more problematic. Although these professionals presumably share a common commitment to helping children and families, they and their respective professions have their own value and belief systems. These factors often make for grave communication problems.

The solution to these problems does not mean that schools' teachers, nurses, and social workers are expected to become all things. Nor does it mean a blurring of role functions. Rather, the potential to provide services to children and their families inherent in existing roles needs to be developed.

The teacher is on the front line. Seeing the child everyday the educator may be the first to detect the signs of abuse. Teachers must learn the symptoms of child abuse; they must know when to be suspicious. The kind of information made available by Bates in chapter 5 regarding indicators of abuse and some of the nuances of medical examination and diagnosis should be more commonly known. This sort of information is important because only in school does the child regularly come into contact with a professional trained in observation and assessment. The child whose basic needs for security and safety are unmet may be unable to function optimally in the classroom. Maltreatment may foster retarded development and competence. Concomitant low self-esteem may be manifest in learning and behavior problems. In chapter 6 Patterson and Thompson provide a working definition of the most profound assault on self-esteem, emotional abuse. They advocate the use of the term emotional neglect, any act which inhibits a child from reaching his maximum potential. The functional definition derived from this term points to manifestations of dysfunction that the child experiences in coping and adaptation. Teachers, all school personnel, and administrators are challenged by this definition to examine their programs and the extent their classrooms and institutions contribute to this form of child maltreatment.

This issue is highlighted by Libbey's discussion, chapter 7, of the differentiation of physical punishment and adolescent abuse. This issue is complicated by the belief that the adolescent may have provoked punishment and is partially responsible for his injuries. The uncertainty surrounding this area is seen as advantageous at this time because it has enabled inquiry into the problem to remain open and empathy to be shown both to caretakers and to adolescents. This uncertainty has unfortunately made self-scrutiny, reporting, and response more difficult for school personnel. Teachers must, however, go beyond merely identifying and reporting abuse and should be prepared to assist in treatment, remediation, and prevention.

Community-health nurses link schools, hospitals, and the home. Mitton, chapter 13, portrays the nurse in this role as a nonthreatening helper acceptable both to parents and to children. Community-health nurses also provide liaison among health-care professionals, families, and schools. She can do clothes-off examinations and make routine home visits. Moreover, the nurse, with her knowledge of health promotion, can play a continuing and essential part on the school-based child-abuse team.

Although the nurse has access to the homes of students and can observe family life, the school social worker is the member of the school team who reaches out to the family and community agencies. The social worker can help the teacher and nurse by providing information about a child's family life. Moreover, the social worker can draw attention to any special circumstances and needs of family members. Burgess and Groth, chapter 8, point out the circumstances in which sexual victimization occurs and the particular fears and vulnerabilities of the victimized child. In these and other cases of abuse the social worker can provide assistance to the entire family that parallels the treatment arranged for the child.

Experience with schools suggests that there is and should be overlap in the roles of team members. All school personnel need to do whatever is necessary to detect, report, help, and follow up the treatment of abused children and their families. Where gaps exist and vacuums are created by ignorance, politics, or inefficiency, school personnel need to feel confident of their position to step in and help. The school team can act as a professional support system to both the child and his family. All parties involved can be assisted to develop coping strategies and supports within their own communities when schools effectively develop their potential to orchestrate and contribute to the provision of services.

Traditionally when school personnel suspected that a child was suffering from abuse they called in another institution and assumed that their responsibility ended there. A better alternative, one that can be encouraged through specialized training, is for schools to go beyond this point and take responsibility for mobilizing natural parenting networks for the child in trouble. In most neighborhoods there are individuals available to care for children in crisis situations (Lauderdale, 1977); school personnel can be effective in locating and expanding this network. This is a more active role for the school in which reporting is just one step. Ultimately the role of the schools needs to be further expanded to include prevention through the sponsoring of such programs as education for parenthood, forums on discipline, groups for adolescents, premarital and parenting seminars, and courses for the community on child abuse. One educator has noted that "child abuse and neglect have been the concern of social work for 80 years, of medicine for 15 years, and education for 10 years" (Lauderdale, 1977). Ascribing a decade of concern about child abuse to education appears optimistic. Attention paid to the problem of child abuse in professional education and inservice training is fragmented and almost nonexistent. It is difficult to speak of the result of ten years of concern when the development and evaluation of widespread child-protection training programs for school-based professionals are badly needed, yet not in place.

The concluding section of this volume deals with current legal, conceptual, and methodological problems that confound efforts to understand, treat, and combat child maltreatment. One major obstacle to dealing effectively with abuse is insufficient knowledge. The priorities and values that are reflected in legislation, policy, and the operations of the helping professions reflect what is thought to be known and knowable in an area. In chapter 15 Dickens provides a survey of child-abuse legislation in Canada and the United States. He finds that laws generally require school personnel both to observe the health of children in attendance and to safeguard their welfare. Although commonalities exist in child-abuse legislation, variations in emphasis, definition, and professional judgment require additional research consideration.

School personnel need to participate in research areas that affect them. This means that research must be generated, advanced, and utilized by school-based professionals. Rather than being seen as something alien, research can be conceived as a systematic attempt to solve problems. These problems almost always have scientific, technical, and practical aspects. Because they also have political and ideological components their resolution through research is complicated. Bureaucratic execution of research without the participation of those affected by it creates a gap between research findings and everyday information needs. These factors obscure the intent of problem-solving efforts and become covertly imbedded in the conceptualization of problems. Bell observes in chapter 16 that existing conceptions of child abuse can function as preconceptions which may influence what facts are investigated and how they are interpreted. He examines four conceptions of abuse—the legal, mental, social construction, and family systems—and makes their assumptions explicit.

Myth and ideology often exist together and impair the mobilization of resources to solve problems and obscure the inseparability of theory (the distilled experience of others in problem solving) and practice (Volpe, 1975, 1978). In chapter 17 Benjamin deals with these issues by examining the proposition widely held by both professionals and the public that the abused child is likely to grow up to be an abusive parent. He finds the data used to support this notion inconsistent, methodologically flawed, and theoretically weak. A General System Theory approach is offered as a more accurate way to picture the process of functional and dysfunctional family life.

Hopefully the chapters in this volume will be a source of insight into the maltreatment of the school-aged child and the potential of interprofessional efforts to deal with the problem. Child abuse will not succumb merely as a result of legislation and government policy. The personal decision of school personnel to extend their responsibilities is required in order for them to take full advantage of their strategic involvement in the lives of children. This decision ultimately depends on whether or not the commitment necessary is perceived as another idealistically based burden or a more efficient utilization of existing competencies.

References

Broadhurst, D. 1975. Project protection: a school program to detect and prevent child abuse and neglect. *Children Today* 4(3): 22-25.

Broadhurst, D. 1977. When I see an abused or neglected child, what do I do about it. In M. Thomas, ed. *Children alone: what can be done about abuse and neglect.* Reston, Va.: Council for Exceptional Children.

Drews, K. 1972. The child and his school. In C.H. Kempe and R.E. Helfer, eds. *Helping the battered child and his family.* Philadelphia: J.B. Lippincott.

Fox, P. 1977. How do we get started. In M. Thomas, ed. *Children alone: what can be done about abuse and neglect.* Reston, Va.: Council for Exceptional Children.

Gil, D.G. 1969. What schools can do about child abuse. *American Education 5*, 2-4.

Kline, D.F. 1977. *Child abuse and neglect: a primer for school personnel.* Reston, Va.: Council for Exceptional Children.

Kline, D.F., and Christiansen, V. 1975. *Educational and psychological problems of abused children.* Logan, Utah: Utah State University Department of Special Education.

Lauderdale, M. 1977. Family structure and professional roles. In M. Thomas, ed. *Children alone: what can be done about abuse and neglect.* Reston, Va.: Council for Exceptional Children.

Lebsack, J. 1976. *Highlights of 1975 national data.* Denver: American Humane Association.

Martin, H.P., ed. 1976. *The abused child: a multidisciplinary approach to developmental issues and treatment.* Cambridge, Mass.: Ballinger Publishing Co.

Murdock, G. 1970. The abused child and the school system. *American Journal of Public Health 60,* 105-109.

Nicholson, M. 1977. Policies and procedures for reporting. In M. Thomas, ed. *Children alone: what can be done about abuse and neglect.* Reston, Va.: Council for Exceptional Children.

Volpe, R. 1975. Behavioral science theory in medical education. *Social Science and Medicine 9,* 493-499.

Volpe, R. 1976. The role of the educator in the provision of adolescent health services. *School Guidance Worker 32*(2): 48-54.

Volpe, R. 1978. Genetic epistemology and the content of professional education. In R. Weizmann, R. Brown, P. Levinson, and P. Taylor, eds. *Piagetian theory and its implications for the helping professions.* Los Angeles: University of Southern California.

The Behavioral and Ecological Syndrome of the High-Risk Child

Vladimir de Lissovoy

Investigators, long active in the area of child abuse and neglect, agree that, in spite of laws that mandate reporting, "hot-lines" to facilitate contacts with investigative agencies, and programs aimed at public awareness, a great many child-abuse/neglect cases go undetected. Since the introduction of compulsory public-school education, teachers have been in a particularly favorable position to identify and to report suspected cases of abuse or neglect among school-aged children. Teachers are with almost all these children on a day-to-day basis. It is true that their contact is limited to children over six (although an increasing number of kindergarten children in the United States enter kindergarten at the age of five). It is also true that one-half of reported cases of abuse/neglect involve children of school age. Detection of the problem, however, rests upon sensitivity, a knowledge of normal as well as problem behavior, and an ability to recognize the syndrome of the abused or the high-risk child.

Theoretical Approaches to Child Abuse and Neglect

Extensive theoretical research has been carried on since the medical profession first became concerned with "the battered-child syndrome." There are many studies that document physical violence by parents or other caretakers (Martin, 1977; Helfer and Kempe, 1974; Fontana, 1973; Gil, 1970; Elmer and Gregg, 1967). Excellent review articles enable the practitioner to grasp the significance of past efforts (Spinetta and Rigler, 1972; Parke and Collmer, 1975; Burgess, 1977; Belsky, 1977). Three major theoretical approaches are evident in the research results now available.

The *psychiatric model,* sometimes defined as the psychopathological model (Gelles, 1973), views the parents as the causal factors. In this model, the parent is seen as deficient in character or in some way abnormal. To date, research has failed to produce findings that link distinct personalities or character disorders with abusing parents (Spinetta and Rigler, 1972), The *sociological model* identifies the etiology of abuse with the social system. The model includes, for example, the belief systems that see societal violence reflected in a violent family milieu (Maurer, 1974). Social structure with its inequalities and resulting frustrations is seen by Gil (1970) as stress producing. Poverty, isolation, unemployment, and the general quality of life are regarded as stress producing and linked to abuse. The third model is defined by Parke and Collmer (1975) as the *social-situational* or the *social-interactional* (Burgess, 1977). In this model interaction patterns within the family may be rooted in a tradition of physical discipline. In some families, parental approaches to childrearing might tend to be inconsistent and capricious, but physical violence produces results: it gets obedience. It may also be the case that the child's traits or behaviors may be of such a nature that they serve to provoke abuse (de Lissovoy, 1978).

The models noted demonstrate that child abuse is a multicausal phenomenon and that it is a transactional phenomenon within the family system. The teacher should be aware of the multiplicity of variables involved, but one must also be pragmatic in one's effort. It is the child who is closest to the teacher, and it is from the child that the teacher's information comes. By becoming aware of behavioral cues and by being informed regarding the child's ecological systems (that is, structure of the family, sociocultural milieu, parent-child relationships), the teacher can recognize some abused children or become aware of those who may be "at risk." Before examining in more depth the family transactional system it is appropriate to review very briefly the developmental highlights of the school-aged child.

The School-Aged Child: One-half of the Abused Children

For many years development of the six- to 12-year-old child was neglected in research efforts. Latency may have been accepted too literally and, in fact, the slow, steady growth characteristic of these years belies the more dramatic psychodynamic changes taking place. At this age the child must make a transition from the primary group of the family to the world outside. Cognitive structures undergo changes and there is less egocentrism, more objectivity and social cognition. Most children of this age have a high energy level, and their activities are marked by noise, boisterous behavior, and motion.[1]

It is not possible to discuss developmental imperatives of this age group in depth but two central themes that are particularly relevant to family and school behavior merit attention. Erikson (1963) refers to this time of development as the stage of industry versus inferiority. The central problem to be solved at this time is to learn the rules of society. If the child feels he cannot measure up to the standards held for him by family or society (school), feelings of inadequacy and inferiority may develop. Children who feel inadequate and frustrated often translate such feelings into negative behavior.

In an article that has become a classic Redl suggests that preadolescence is ". . . the phase when the nicest children behave in a most awful way" (1966, p. 619). Much of the behavior is irritating to parents and is manifested in acts of rebellion, distrust, ingratitude, lack of consideration for others, disobedience, crudeness, and a general downgrading of parental contributions. The transition from preschool dependence to the new world of peers and society is often accompanied by traumatic side effects. Redl's explanation suggests that such behavior is the result of the loosening up of well-knit patterns of the child's personality in preparation for adolescent changes and modification into the personality of an adult. The forgotten impulses of early childhood come to the fore while the already-learned standards of behavior and self-control tend to become ineffectual.

In fact, research indicates that children from six to twelve tend to show a considerable amount of "problem" behaviors. This is not to say that these behaviors in themselves indicate psychopathology; rather, they tend to be noted and, in some cases, may be annoying to the adults around them. LaPouse and Monk (1964) studied emotional problems among a nonpsychiatric sample of 482 children representative of a child population six to twelve. As reported by mothers, some of the most frequent behaviors were as follows: bed-wetting once a month or more, 8 percent of children; nightmares, 28 percent; temper loss once a month or more, 80 percent; temper loss twice a week or more, 48 percent; twitching or jerking, 12 percent; biting nails, 27 percent; picking nose, 26 percent. Peterson, (1961) used a statistical approach in which he studied 427 referral problems. These were reduced to fifty-eight inclusive categories, and teachers were asked to rate 831 kindergarten and elementary-school children on these problems on a scale of three degrees of severity. A factor analysis by four age groups resulted in two invariant factors. The first suggested a tendency to express impulses (conduct problems). These included such behaviors as disobedience, disruptiveness, boisterousness, fighting, attention-seeking, restlessness, negativeness, impertinence, destructiveness, irritability, temper tantrums, hyperactivity, uncooperativeness, distractability, and inattentiveness. These are behaviors that are easily seen. The second factor was labeled "personality problem" and contained traits suggesting low self-esteem, withdrawal, and "dysphoric mood." Examples include feelings of inferiority, lack of self-confidence, self-consciousness, anxiety, hypersensitivity, clumsiness, tension; this type of behavior is more difficult to note. Boys displayed more severe conduct problems than girls. In the younger age groups boys showed more severe personality problems than girls but at the older ages (grades three to six) girls displayed more personality problems than did boys. A number of other studies show similar results.

It is safe to conclude that the school-aged child is a very active and labile individual with propensities for potentially disruptive and annoying behaviors.

The Ecology of Abusive Behavior

A number of social variables have been shown to be associated with child abuse. It is tempting to generalize these as predictors but it is important to remember that, although such variables may show statistical significance in comparative study samples, their predictive accuracy is generally low. Evidence of child abuse can be encountered by any teacher; while the results of abusive behavior are more visible among the less privileged, research has shown that neither money nor education makes parents completely immune. Nevertheless, teachers should be aware that existing social factors play a role in child abuse. This suggests that teachers should become familiar with the ecological background of their pupils. A number of research investigations have provided information in this regard. The conclusion of a current study will serve to identify these issues. Straus (1979) related social factors that were associated with abuse of children ages three to seventeen and concluded that the following are among the factors which contribute to child abuse: (1) mothers bear almost complete responsibility for childcare; (2) parental stress is increased by poverty and an uncertain economic situation; (3) social isolation separates people from the help which they need; and (4) cultural approval of physical punishment. In short, abuse is the result of society and societal changes are the best way to reduce abuse (Straus, 1979).

The Abuse-Provoking Child

The social variables so ably defined by Straus help to identify the potential for abuse, but they give an incomplete description. As long as the child is viewed solely in the role of victim it will be difficult to change parental abusive behavior. The child is an active member of the family transactional system and his behavior, innocent in terms of motivation and, in some cases, instigative, may serve as an abuse-provoking stimulus. It has already been noted that school-aged children manifest a number of disrupting and annoying behaviors. Teachers are well aware that there are children whose appearance, habits, and modes of activity are unpleasant and frequently beyond tolerance limits. Indeed some children, whatever the reason, may be thoroughly disliked, and this response is not limited to one specific teacher; it is as though the child has a propensity to evoke negative reactions.

Gil by statistical analysis identified a factor he labeled "child-originated abuse" in which behavioral descriptions included "persistent behavioral atypicality of child . . . hyperactivity . . . high annoyance potential . . ." (1971, p. 643). Johnson and Morse (1968) investigated child abuse utilizing caseworkers' reports. The data led these investigators to conclude that children who were most likely to be abused were overactive and difficult to supervise. The reality of a child's abuse-provoking potential is revealed in reports of repeated abuse of the same children in different foster homes (Milowe and Lourie, 1964), Friedrick and Boriskin (1976) suggested in a review article that abusive parents perceive their children as "different." In an ongoing prospective study, de Lissovoy (1978) obtained descriptions of abused children by mothers who were identified as primary participants in abusive acts. Modal descriptions included "never slept; cries a lot; always sick; does not stay still; gets into everything." In comparison with their other children these mothers stated that the abused child was "sick more than others; cries a lot; takes more time; just different." Using an adjective checklist both abused boys and girls were described as alert, aggressive, bossy, demanding, excitable, high strung, and restless (partial listing).

These findings suggest that the child can be an abuse-provoking stimulus. The recognition that the child can be an active instigator of abuse is imperative in order to understand this phenomenon beyond the limited model of "deprived parent" and the "victimized child."

This review of abuse-provoking variables is not meant as a defense of abusing parents. It is recognized that the great majority of parents are faced with many of these same problems without resorting to abuse. The teacher can have little effect on the parents' personal characteristics and the social milieu. The teacher, however, can be supportive of the parents by explaining normal development, by assisting in the formation of realistic expectations, and in guiding the parents to cope with behaviors that are particularly annoying.

The teacher is in an excellent position to understand child behavior that is provocative. It should be clear, however, that such behavior cannot, in itself, be interpreted as causal. The transactional family system within its sociocultural milieu is fundamental in the identification of potential child abuse. Awareness of the *behavioral* and *ecological* syndrome can assist the teacher to integrate the behavioral cues of the child with the salient variables of the family-situational milieu. At the risk of redundancy it is imperative to emphasize that behavioral cues may have limited predictive value, but, in the ecological analysis that considers poverty, isolation, size of family, parental attitudes and behavior, and family support systems, it is possible to identify children at risk. The identification of high-risk children, when it involves an awareness of so many factors, seems an impossible task for teachers already burdened with professional responsibilities of the classroom. A recent development in medical practice shows that doctors have begun to see themselves in a comparable situation. "Family medicine" is a specialization that treats the family as a system and the patient as more than a collection of symptoms. Although the patient receives direct medical or surgical intervention, the process of healing has a much more encompassing gestalt. Thus the physician is more involved in understanding the total family situation of the patient whether it be in supportive counseling, education, or more direct guidance.

For many years there have been pronouncements about education of the whole child. Guidance counselors, school psychologists, and home visitors (truant or attendance officers) are now part of many school systems and such functionaries often perform nobly despite arduous demands for their time. However, their service is primarily ameliorative and oriented to the most pressing concerns. Although parental guidance programs have been instituted in some school systems in the United States, more often than not it is the parent who least needs this service who responds to such programs. The same can be said for participation in parent-teacher organizations or special events such as Education Week.

What is sometimes not recognized is the fact that the unstable, isolated, economically deprived family may see the school as a threat rather than as a potentially helpful institution. Teachers, on the other hand, are sometimes much too prone to blame the parents for the child's appearance, unkempt dress, or disruptive behavior, without any awareness of family circumstances. Sheridan, (1979) a guidance counselor in a middle-class community who conducts an innovative program for children whose parents are separated or divorced, suggests that most teachers are not aware as to whether a child has one or both parents in the home.

In order to become better acquainted with the family background of a high-risk child a home visit could be productive. During such a visit, the teacher could establish a positive relationship on the parents' home ground. A few well-put questions could bring out the most salient information about the child's family and the teacher could emphasize that family and school are equally important in education. More important, the teacher could extend a personal invitation for parental visits to learn about the child's progress or to ask such questions as may occur. It is this "psychological bridge," if established and carried on from teacher to teacher, that could do much to foster confidence in the school's ability to help. Indeed, the perceptive teacher cognizant of atypical behavior or appearance and aware of potentially disruptive influences in the child's family system is more likely to be receptive to the child's or to the parents' "cries for help" before abuse takes place.

Note

1. One of the most understated but one of the most valuable books dealing with children of this age is A.W. Blair and W.H. Burton, *Growth and Development of the Preadolescent* (New York: Appleton-Century-Crofts, Inc., 1951).

References

Belsky, J. 1977. *Child abuse: from research to remediation.* Paper presented at the Groves Conference on Marriage and the Family. Liberty, N.Y., May.

Burgess, R.L. 1977. Child abuse: a behavioral analysis. In B.B. Lahey and A.E. Kazdin, eds. *Advances in child clinical psychology.* New York: Plenum.

de Lissovoy, V. 1978. *Maternal descriptions of abused children.* Unpublished study.

Elmer, E., and Gregg, G.S. 1967. Developmental characteristics of abused children. *Pediatrics 40*, 596–602.

Erikson, E. 1963. *Childhood and society*. 2nd ed. New York: W.W. Norton and Company, Inc.

Fontana, U.J. 1973. *Somewhere a child is crying*. New York: Macmillan.

Friedrick, W.N., and Boriskin, J.A. 1976. The role of the child in abuse: a review of the literature. *American Journal of Orthopsychiatry 46*, 580–590.

Gelles, R.J. 1973. Child abuse as psychopathology: a sociological critique and reformulation. *American Journal of Orthopsychiatry 43*, 611–621.

Gil, D.G., 1970. *Violence against children: physical abuse in the United States*. Cambridge, Mass.: Harvard University Press.

Gil, D.G. 1971. Violence against children. *Journal of Marriage and the Family 33*, 637–648.

Helfer, R.E., and Kempe, C.H., eds. 1974. *The battered child*. 2nd ed. Chicago: The University of Chicago Press.

Johnson, G., and Morse, H.A. 1968. Injured children and their parents. *Children 15*, 147–152.

LaPouse, R., and Monk, M.A. 1964. Behavior deviations in a representative sample of children. *American Journal of Orthopsychiatry 34*, 436–446.

Martin, H., ed. 1977. *The abused child: a multidisciplinary approach to developmental issues and treatment*. Cambridge, Mass.: Ballinger Press, 1977.

Maurer, A. 1974. Corporal punishment. *American Psychologist 29*(8): 614–626.

Milowe, J.D., and Lourie, R.S. 1964. The child's role in the battered child syndrome. *Journal of Pediatrics 65*, 1079–1081.

Parke, R., and Collmer, C. 1975. Child abuse: an interdisciplinary analysis. In E. Hetherington, ed. *Review of Child Development Research* (Vol. 5). Chicago: The University of Chicago Press.

Peterson, D.R. 1961. Behavior problems of middle childhood. *Journal of Consulting Psychology 35*(3): 205–209.

Redl, F. 1966. Pre-adolescents—what makes them tick? In M.L. Haimowitz and N. R. Haimowitz, eds. *Human Development*. New York: Crowell.

Shanas, B. 1975. Child abuse: a killer teachers can help control. *Phi Delta Kappan 56*(7): 479–482.

Sheridan, J. 1979. Personal communication.

Spinetta, J.J., and Rigler, D. 1972. The child abusing parent: a psychological review. *Psychological Bulletin 77*, 296–304.

Straus, M.A. 1979. Family patterns and child abuse in a nationally representative American sample. *Child Abuse and Neglect 3*, 213–225.

The Effect of Child Abuse and Neglect on the School-Aged Child

Diane D. Broadhurst

School-aged children are subject to the same range of maltreatment as younger children: physical abuse, neglect, sexual abuse, and emotional maltreatment. Contrary to popular belief, however, few of the affected children tell of their trauma, though they are old enough to speak. Instead they protect their parents and cover up their injuries. Few run away, although they are old enough to walk. Instead they remain at home, trying to stay out of trouble and accepting their treatment as valid and just.

Maltreatment of school-aged children is less often life-threatening, though certainly more frequent, than maltreatment of very young children. Yet the effects may be both devastating and long term. Martin notes:

> . . . The morbidity of the syndrome is just beginning to be studied. We know that many children die. We see now that even larger numbers of children will be retarded, brain damaged, undernourished, and emotionally crippled. (1972, p. 111)

While the effects are only beginning to be studied, preliminary indicators give cause for concern: frequently the effects of child abuse and neglect include, for the school-aged child, problems in adjustment, development, peer relations, and learning. Inevitably these problems involve the school as well. A child who adjusts poorly to new situations or who does not relate well to his classmates or who is developmentally delayed or experiencing learning difficulties will likely have problems in school. Such a child may be in double jeopardy, a problem at home and in school, with his condition thought to be intrinsic. Unless the school is prepared to reach out, to understand, and to help the child, it may merely exacerbate his situation.

Indicators of Maltreatment

Indicators of child maltreatment are well documented and are treated elsewhere in this volume. However, it is worth noting that some indicators are particularly apparent in school-aged children. According to a recent publication from the National Center on Child Abuse and Neglect in Washington, D.C. (Broadhurst, 1979) these indicators may include sudden changes in school performance;

extremes in behavior; hoarding or stealing food; unexplained injuries which regularly appear after the child has been absent from school; a pattern of consistently poor hygiene, inappropriate dress, fatigue, or unattended medical problems; bizarre, sophisticated, or unusual sexual behavior or knowledge.

Howell notes that "the school-age child also shows a higher incidence of burns than younger children" (1977, p. 10). Lourie notes that physically abused adolescents may display "barroom brawl signs" including "bruises, black eyes, split lips, scratches, and other facial injuries." He states further that adolescents may react emotionally to physical abuse in ways that lead to "drug problems, school learning and truancy problems, and control (behavior) problems" (1977, p. 15).

Kline (1977) notes that young schoolchildren who have been sexually abused may regress into fantasy or infantile behavior. Older children may display delinquent or aggressive behavior, poor peer relationships, and abuse of alcohol or other drugs.

Development of Maltreated Children

The effects of maltreatment in school-aged children are perhaps less well known than the indicators, but data about this phenomenon are beginning to emerge. It must be emphasized that the data are not definitive; much more research needs to be done before conclusions can be drawn and cause-and-effect relationships established. However, some trends are apparent. Recent studies in the western United States, for example, indicate a relationship between maltreatment and certain learning problems. Blager and Martin reported delays in language development among the preschool- and elementary-aged children they studied. The younger children exhibited nine-to-ten-month delays in receptive and spoken language with "clear deficits in quantity and quality of speech" (1976, p. 85). The older children were about eleven months delayed in spontaneous language use. Both groups were "manipulative, clearly distrustful, and passive-aggressive in their resistance to being tested" (1976, p. 87).

Significantly, after six to twelve months of therapy, including speech therapy and psychotherapy, those children who were retested "became much more likable, easier to test, and more cooperative" (1976, p. 87).

Martin, in testing a group of abused preschoolers, noted that

> . . . these children performed gross motor tasks poorly. They were both delayed in the acquisition of specific skills, such as balancing, hopping, skipping, riding a tricycle, etc., and just as impressively demonstrated very poor quality of gross motor tasks. They were poorly coordinated, maladroit, dyssynchronous, awkward. (1976, p. 78)

Rozansky (1978) also reported delays in motor and language skills in addition to behavior problems among the preschool children she studied. It should be noted that the three studies cited dealt with only small numbers of children between the ages of three and eight. Thus the data are not definitive, but they are indicative. As Kempe and Kempe have pointed out, "without treatment between the ages of 3 and 6, earlier behavior patterns continue, but in more aggravated forms" (1978, p. 39).

The implications for schools are clear. Untreated, abused children may begin, or may have already begun, their formal education exhibiting behavior problems or deficiencies in language development and in the ability to perform routine gross motor tasks. According to Kempe and Kempe,

> . . . many of these children become academic and social failures almost immediately upon entering school. An additional complicating factor in older children is that their educational and behavioral difficulties are often seen as intrinsic, and the possibility of abuse as a major causative factor may not be entertained by the school. (1978, p. 125)

If only the symptoms, but never the cause, are recognized, help for the child will not be fully effective. Yet schools have available an array of professionals skilled in psychological services, special education, and speech and language therapy. Together they can and should offer a comprehensive therapeutic program for abused and neglected children identified as having specific learning or adjustment problems.

School Placement

Kline and Christiansen (1975) studied 138 Utah children referred to juvenile court as abused. Included in the definition of abuse were sexual abuse, neglect, and physical abuse. The researchers sought to determine the current school placement of these children, who had been referred over a six-year period. The results of the study were startling:

> 26.8 percent of the children were placed in special education classes, as compared to 8 percent of the school-district population not classified as abused;

> the largest number of abused children in special-education classes were placed in classes for the emotionally disturbed;

> 7 percent of the children were placed in residential psychiatric institutions;

> 25 percent of the children identified as sexually abused were placed in classes for the emotionally disturbed;

> the majority of the children studied were below grade level in reading, spelling, and mathematics;

sexually abused children had lower achievement levels than children who had been neglected or physically abused;

the children were frequently described as aggressive, withdrawn, fearful, and having poor social relationships.

Kline and Christiansen concluded that

> ... the abused population was different from the population of children who had not been reported as abused. They were placed in special education classes more frequently, more were found in institutions, and their academic achievement was generally below average. Further, they were found to exhibit behaviors indicative of psychological problems. On the basis of these findings, it was concluded that abuse is a multidimensional problem which extends beyond the immediate effects of the abusive act. ... Further, the data showed that some kinds of psychological problems were related to type of abuse. Aggressive destructive traits were found in association with injuries resulting from physical aggression. Hostility was documented only in those cases where sexual abuse had taken place. ... (1975, p. 107)

In a related study, Martin states, "It is clear that abused children are at considerably greater risk of having learning disorders in school than their non-abused peers. School personnel have reported to us that children assigned to EH classes (educationally handicapped) are overrepresented by abused and neglected children" (1976, p. 77).

Some researchers have suggested that abuse results in later learning or behavior problems for the child. Others have suggested that the presence of a problem may precipitate the abuse. Halperin (1979) writes:

> Every adult who works with children has encountered youngsters who seem to provoke hostility, aggression, and frustration. These children are infuriating, or at the very least, extremely irritating. It is difficult to determine what came first in such cases: maltreatment by the parent or provocative behavior by the child. (1979, p. 77)

Kline and Christiansen note that one cannot assume a cause-effect relationship between abuse and special education or institutional placement, and they call for additional research in this critical area.

Academic Achievement

Kent (1976), in the most comprehensive effort to date, studied 378 children adjudicated "dependent" in Los Angeles County, California. The children in the study had suffered injury resulting from either nonaccidental trauma or gross physical neglect. For a control group Kent chose 185 children receiving special services from the County Department of Public Social Services. Thus the study group and the control group were well matched with regard to the level of family functioning and socioeconomic status. Kent sought to measure the effectiveness of intervention in the form of removal from the home on children identified as abused or neglected. The baseline data Kent provides for children tested at intake is significant:

25 percent of the abused and 64 percent of the neglected children tested demonstrated delay in motor development;

39 percent of the abused and 72 percent of the neglected children tested demonstrated delay in language development;

78 percent of the neglected children tested had IQs below 90;

53 percent of the abused and 82 percent of the neglected children of school age were rated Below Average or Failing in academic performance, as compared to 28 percent of the controls;

67 percent of the abused and 60 percent of the neglected children of school age were rated Unsatisfactory with regard to school peer relations, as compared to 23 percent of the control group;

the abused children tested were rated as more aggressive toward peers and adults, as more disobedient, and as having more problems with peer relations than either the neglected children or the controls.

The children studied were retested at the time of follow-up, twelve months to three years after intake, when 80 percent were still placed outside the home. On almost every measure the abused and the neglected groups showed improvement, but

the abused child continued to be rated as more aggressive to adults and peers, more disobedient, and having more problems with peer relations than either the neglected children or the controls at the time of intake;

38 percent of the abused and 35 percent of the neglected children were still rated Unsatisfactory in school peer relations, higher than the control group at intake;

28 percent of the abused and 37 percent of the neglected children continued to be rated Below Average or Failing in academic performance;

23 percent of the abused and 40 percent of the neglected children still demonstrated delay in motor development;

30 percent of the abused and 49 percent of the neglected children continued to demonstrate delay in language development.

Clearly intervention by removal from the harmful environment was beneficial to these children. But just as clearly, removal alone was not sufficient. One wonders what help, if any, these children received from their schools in overcoming their significant academic, behavior, and peer-relationship problems.

The victim of sexual abuse and the physically abused adolescent may also exhibit a variety of problems and behavior which can have an effect on school performance. Forward and Buck note that the victim of incest

> . . . suffers a fundamental lack of self-confidence and self-respect; she feels undeserving of emotional, physical, or material satisfaction.

> She has feelings of betrayal and self-loathing. Because her first experiment with trust was such a painful failure, she cannot bring herself to trust again. . . . The victim may often manifest her guilt in psychosomatic symptoms—most often migraines. . . . Stomach ailments, skin disorders, and disabling aches and pains [may appear] . . . . Most victims experience periods of deep depression, often leading to attempted suicide. (1978, pp. 22–23)

Libbey and Bybee, in a study of twenty-five cases of adolescent abuse, noted that

> . . . where abuse had been chronic and ongoing since childhood we found retarded, emotionally disturbed, or hyperactive adolescents. . . . Half of the adolescents were of good or high intelligence but underachieving. Three had special educational needs. The rest were performing at expected levels. None were truant or acting out in the classroom. Ten had poor relationships with their peers. (1979, pp. 120, 122)

What Schools Can Do

The schools are in perhaps the best possible position to be of help to children like those described above. Schools are where children are every day, all day, year after year. School is the only place where children are routinely seen by professionals trained to interact with children. As McCaffrey (1978) has pointed out, schools already provide a number of special services, including

> diagnosis and assessment of specific problems including academic, behavior, health, learning, and social-adjustment problems;

> development of individualized educational plans;

> support services, including counseling, speech, hearing, and language therapy, behavior management, special education, and health care.

Most of these services can be provided on the spot. Many schools already routinely conduct pupil-services staffings at the local school level to assess and develop plans for children with special needs. These special services should be extended to abused and neglected children as well, for they too have special needs.

The regular school program can also have a significant impact by offering to an abused or neglected child positive experiences, a sense of achievement and self-worth, the chance to establish sound peer relationships, and the opportunity to see adults in a supportive, consistent, and caring role. More than other community institutions, schools are seen as caring for and about children; as readily accessible; and perhaps most important for troubled families, as "neutral ground" where help is offered and can be accepted in a nonthreatening, nonpunitive atmosphere.

There is little doubt that the schools have a significant part to play in the prevention and treatment of child abuse and neglect, a part that may already be thrust upon them, whether they are ready and willing or reluctant and unprepared. In their study of twenty-five cases of adolescent abuse Libbey and Bybee found

> . . . that the schools played a role both in identifying and in treating adolescent abuse. In 10 of the cases, adolescents told a school nurse, counselor, or teacher of an injury. School personnel reported the injuries as required by law. The laws do not require school involvement in treatment (or prevention) but in our data, in 17 of the cases, the school was directly involved in the intervention. *The school was indirectly involved in a total of 21 cases, because those adolescents were experiencing moderate or severe school problems.* (1979, p. 123; emphasis added)

By and large schools have not responded well to their abused and neglected students. Perhaps it is because schools do not recognize these children. Perhaps schools do not see that they have readily available resources to help them. That must change. Educators *can* learn to recognize abused and neglected children. Schools *do* have resources already in place which can be of great help to children at risk. In those few schools where child-abuse and child-neglect detection and prevention programs have been instituted, they have proven of great value in uncovering cases of child abuse and neglect and in bringing help to hundreds of children and families who might otherwise have gone unhelped.

It is time for school systems everywhere to do their part by establishing comprehensive child-abuse and child-neglect prevention programs and by helping to reduce the effects of abuse and neglect upon the children in their care.

References

American Humane Association. 1978. *National analysis of official child neglect and abuse reporting.* Denver: The American Humane Association.

Blager, F., and Martin, H.P. 1976. Speech and language of abused children. In H.P. Martin, ed. *The abused child. A multidisciplinary approach to developmental issues and treatment.* Cambridge, Mass.: Ballinger Publishing Company.

Broadhurst, D.D. 1979. *The educator's role in the prevention and treatment of child abuse and neglect.* Washington, D.C.: U.S. Department of Health, Education, and Welfare.

Forward, S., and Buck, C. 1978. *Betrayal of innocence.* Los Angeles: J.P. Tarcher, Inc.

Halperin, M. 1979. *Helping maltreated children.* St. Louis: C.V. Mosby Company.

Howell, D.A. 1977. The sensitive teacher. In M.A. Thomas, ed. *Children alone: what can be done about abuse and neglect.* Reston, Va.: The Council for Exceptional Children.

Kempe, R., and Kempe, C.H. 1978. *Child abuse.* Cambridge, Mass.: Harvard University Press.

Kent, J.T. 1976. A follow-up study of abused children. *Journal of Pediatric Psychology,* Spring, pp. 25–31.

Kline, D.F. 1977. *Child abuse and neglect: a primer for school personnel.* Reston, Va.: The Council for Exceptional Children.

Kline, D.F., and Christiansen, J. 1975. *Educational and psychological problems of abused children.* Logan, Utah: Utah State University Department of Special Education.

Libbey, P., and Bybee, R. 1979. The physical abuse of adolescents. *Journal of Social Issues 35*(2): 101–125.

Lourie, I.S. 1977. The abuse of adolescents. In M.A. Thomas, ed. *Children alone: what can be done about abuse and neglect.* Reston, Va.: The Council for Exceptional Children.

Martin, H.P. 1972. The child and his development. In C.H. Kempe and R.E. Kempe, eds. *Helping the battered child and his family.* Philadelphia: J.B. Lippincott Company.

Martin, H.P. 1976. Neurologic status of abused children. In H.P. Martin, ed. *The abused child. A multidisciplinary approach to developmental issues and treatment.* Cambridge, Mass.: Ballinger Publishing Company.

McCaffrey, M. 1978. Realistic expectations of children and families: maximization of education resources. In M. Lauderdale, N. Anderson, and S.E. Cramer, eds. *Child abuse and neglect: issues on innovation and implementation (vol. II).* Washington, D.C.: U.S. Department of Health, Education, and Welfare.

Rozansky, P. 1978. Family resource center: a family intervention approach in child abuse and neglect. In M. Lauderdale, N. Anderson, and S.E. Cramer, eds. *Child abuse and neglect: issues on innovation and implementation (Vol. II).* Washington, D.C.: U.S. Department of Health, Education, and Welfare.

The Effects of Schools upon Families: Toward a More Supportive Relationship

Robert M. Friedman and
Paul A. D'Agostino

Families and schools represent the two most significant socializing agents in the life of a child. They not only have an enormous impact upon children, but also upon each other. The present chapter will focus on the importance of schools as a critical element in the ecological network of families. While special attention will be paid to the problem of child abuse, the chapter will discuss the general area of family-school relationships.

The chapter is prepared by individuals whose main professional training and involvement has been directed toward the provision and development of services for dysfunctional families and not specifically in the field of education. As a result, the chapter will present a perspective (or set of biases) that in some cases may differ substantially from that of educators.

Meaning of School to Families

The starting point of this analysis is an examination of the meaning of schools for families in general. This will later be related specifically to families in which abuse has occurred, or who are at high risk for abuse. For many families, schools have characteristically been a stabilizing influence, almost an anchor. Parents have developed relationships with teachers and administrators over a period of years during which time more than one child from their family has attended the same school. However, as a result of the greater mobility of families in recent years, and the movement away from neighborhood schools in some communities, this stabilizing influence of the school has diminished. Instead, for some families schools have become formidable and distant institutions contributing more to a sense of alienation than identity. This change in the role and meaning of schools has come about as a response to sociological and political forces, as well as to varying educational influences.

Similarly for many families, teachers and school administrators have traditionally been looked up to as positive models, exemplary both in general character and behavior. Parents would admire and respect school personnel to the

27

point of trying to get their children to emulate them. While this is still the case in some communities, in others there has developed either an antagonistic relationship or simply an estrangement between the school and families. Now, rather than being the recipient of almost blind respect and obedience, schools are more likely to be met with resistance and criticism. While it may be argued that schools have done much to earn this increasingly harsh response, such a development is clearly consistent with a generally increased skepticism and concern regarding large social institutions.

Essentially the relationship between schools and families appears to be steadily moving from one of mutual support to one of mutual distrust. Parents are less likely to look to schools as important resources for family problems and as cooperative partners in the task of raising children; rather parents are more likely to view schools as being unconcerned about families and as generating part of the stress that contributes to family problems. This strain may be created when a child is unhappy in school, does not progress along with his/her peers, or receives bad reports from the school staff. Parents, often looking for support and assistance with their child, perceive the school staff as "blaming" them for the problems of the child in school. Parents, in turn, are less likely in recent years to work along with the school and quicker to place the responsibility for their child's problem on inadequate school staff or school procedures. The result is often a reciprocal negative interaction in which a problem with a child in school leads to negative feedback to parents, which in turn generates a negative response from parents to school.

System Approach to Parent-School-Student Relationships

The educational process involves at a minimum a triad of relationships—school staff, student, and parents. A social-systems approach is helpful in analyzing the types of interaction patterns that can develop within such a triad. Such an approach emphasizes the risk that a coalition between two elements of the triad will develop with harmful effects upon the third. Within family units, this occurs when a coalition develops across generational lines (parent and child) that excludes the other parent. The most constructive coalition within the family is parent to parent. This leads to consistent and clear actions being taken toward the child, who in turn does not get caught between two adults at conflict.

A parallel situation exists with the parent-school-student triad. If, for example, a cross-generational coalition develops between parents and student with school staff being excluded, then complaints from the school are likely to be ignored or discarded as invalid, or the child's negative behavior may even be positively reinforced by parents. Similarly, if a coalition develops between school personnel and student, then problems of the student are likely to be tolerated and perhaps even encouraged as another example of the type of parental inadequacy with which the school has to deal. The most desirable arrangement for the education of the child is the development of a strong coalition between parents and school staff, one which is characterized by mutual support. Such a coalition almost always results in positive, constructive school behavior by the student.

At the same time as relationships of mutual support between parents and school staff are becoming less frequent, each group is in greater need of such support. With the increase in single-parent homes, and the increased geographical distance between parents and the community in which they were raised, parents have a greater need for the extrafamilial supports that schools have the potential to provide. Similarly, with the growing pressures and demands on schools, school staff have a larger need for the extraschool support that parents individually and in groups have the potential to provide. Strategies for reversing this increasing trend toward greater isolation and antagonism between schools and families, with each blaming the other for its problems, will be presented in the concluding section of this chapter.

Parent-School Involvement

The existence of a strong relationship between the home environment and school functioning has been referred to by numerous authors (for example, Dinkmeyer, 1973; Eells, 1974; Karnes and Zehrbach, 1975; Landsberger, 1973; and McIntire and Payne, 1971). Also, there have been frequent calls in the educational literature to involve parents more closely in the education of their child in order to strengthen the effect of schools (Abbot, 1973; Cooke and Appolini, 1975; Larrick, 1976; Moore, 1973; and Pellegrino, 1973). However, within this literature there are very few clear and specific statements of objectives for schools (or school systems) concerning their impact upon families. Nor is there recognition of the very real ways in which schools impact upon families, whether that impact is intended or unintended, desirable or undesirable. An ecological orientation to social institutions would require that the impact of schools upon families be clearly considered in program planning and evaluation activities. To this point, "family-impact" statements for school programs have been minimal.

A recent review (Filipczak, Lordeman, and Friedman, 1977) broke down the types of parental involvement in school activities into four categories: (1) volunteerism, in which parents contribute time at the school; (2) special efforts to facilitate closer home-school communication; (3) involvement of parents in training and education programs; (4) parental involvement in policymaking roles. Of this group, policymaking involvement by parents has the greatest potential for creating more supportive home-school relationships. In a major study in this area, Schmuck has advocated joint decision-making involving teachers, administrators, parents, and students. He maintains that such processes "will lead to greater attractiveness between teachers and students, reduced absenteeism on the part of both, and an acceleration in the use of participative classroom methods" (1974, p. 210). To date, however, there has been more rhetoric than research on the parent-school issue, and with the exception of a group of studies in the parent-training area, there is a lack of data on the effects of parental involvement in the schools (Filipczak et al., 1977).

The chapter's focus to this point has been on the general area of home-school relationships. The emphasis will now switch to examine the potential impact of schools in relation to acts of abuse within families. This will begin with an examination of characteristics of abusive families, particularly as these families relate to groups and institutions outside of the home.

Characteristics of Abusive Families

Knowledge of the characteristics, problem areas, and response patterns of abusive families is one of the major keys in developing effective, comprehensive approaches to the problems of working with abusive families. It allows for the planning and implementation of effective remedial intervention with individuals during the time of stress following the occurrence of the violent behavior. Equally important, such knowledge allows for the early identification of problem situations and therefore assists in the prevention of abuse.

Statistical descriptions of the characteristics of a group can be misleading and do not define the personal characteristics of all individuals within that group. Nevertheless, they provide a basis for understanding the problem, particularly when combined with an understanding of the specific conditions, situations, and tasks which stress individual coping abilities.

Since the early 1960s, few groups have been studied as frequently or as intensively as abusive parents (Garbarino, 1976; Gil, 1970; Giovannoni and Billingsley, 1970; Kempe, 1973; and Parke and Collmer, 1975). Social scientists, researchers, educators, and practitioners from divergent fields have addressed themselves to the multifaceted aspects of this growing individual and social problem. This has resulted in a proliferation of literature in the areas of research, identification, clinical management, and individual and societal responsibilities. Beginning with the well-known early studies of child abuse in Denver, Colorado (Helfer and Kempe, 1968), the characteristics identified for abusive parents have, with few exceptions (Gil, 1970), remained relatively consistent, although the research supporting the characteristics remains somewhat shaky (Friedman, 1976).

General Characteristics

What, then, are these characteristics and how do they relate specifically both to the school system, as part of a family's total environment, and to school personnel as they individually interact with a child and his parents? The list of attributes which have been identified most frequently as characteristics of abusive parents include the following:

grew up in homes with frequent disruptions, high levels of tension, poor parenting, and violence between family members;

have unfulfilled childhood dependency needs;

are overwhelmed by the role of parent, and by child's needs;

generally have inappropriate expectations of children, including expecting children to satisfy their (parents') needs, and perceiving the inability of children to do so as rejection;

project their own hostilities onto child;

are socially isolated, and have limited ability to form relationships;

have difficulty in trusting others;

are still engaged in destructive relationships with own families;

have low impulse control;

make frequent use of denial as a psychological defense mechanism.

These characteristics affect not only the parent-child interaction, but also how the parent is perceived and responded to by school staff. The special significance of selected characteristics of these parents will now be discussed in greater detail.

Social Isolation

The social isolation of abusive parents, frequently but not always self-imposed, serves as a barrier toward the development of positive working relationships and inhibits mutual understanding between the parents and the school. When contacts do occur, they are usually by demand, precipitated by some real or perceived crisis, and are, therefore, negatively oriented. When these kinds of contacts occur, the school effectively becomes an external "stressor" for an already fragile family. Such contacts reinforce the parental perception of the school as threatening and powerful, and contribute to further isolation.

This negative cycle of interaction is all too easy for school personnel to step into. The absence of positive parent-school interactions only serves to reinforce the occurrence of negative ones. The difficulty of the abusive parents in identifying, initiating, and accepting supportive relationships, and their feelings of powerlessness in relationship to authority of the school, make it very difficult for this cycle to be broken. The first steps in breaking this cycle of school-parent isolation must be taken by the school. Supportive, non-crisis-oriented, non-demanding, and nonthreatening contacts are essential and can only be achieved through an outreach program on the part of school staff.

Unrealistic Expectations of Children

The tendency of abusive parents to have unrealistic emotional, behavioral, and academic expectations of their children is influenced and either reinforced or eased by the attitudes, expectations, and responses of the school. Abusive parents frequently perceive their child's actions as direct reflections of their own self-worth and ability to parent. To an anxious and insecure parent, a child's behavior, relationships with "outsiders" and ability to achieve become very important and often very threatening.

Some parents deal with these feelings by trying to deny and sabotage the role of the school with their child (Young, 1964), while others use the school as a direct measurement. Such a use of the school increases the importance of the parents of their child's performance in school. The teachers and other school staff need to be sensitive to this reaction on the part of the parent. Otherwise, it is easy to inadvertently reinforce the unrealistic and inappropriate expectations of the parent, and thereby also reinforce the meaning of the child's behavior for them.

This is one area in which teachers can frequently serve as subtle, informal, and nonthreatening parent educators. They can assist parents in the development of appropriate and more realistic expectations of their child and help to diminish personalized interpretation of the child's behavior.

Power-Oriented Disciplinary Procedures

Many abusive parents grew up in homes where power-oriented negative and abusive disciplinary procedures were used as childrearing practices. Through vicarious learning and modeling, they learned these procedures which they now use with their own children. They frequently are not aware of any alternate means of childrearing. Negative, power-oriented responses have become almost automatic in times of frustration and heightened stress.

School personnel must be aware of the role they play in either reinforcing or restructuring the childrearing practices of parents. School staff are in effect role models for the parent, and in that regard are teachers of child management procedures. Schools must ask such questions as "What lessons do punitive and negatively oriented classroom-management procedures provide?" "What is the message given by a school's policy of using corporal punishment as a response to behavior problems?" "What is implied by the tone of notes sent home with a child regarding that child's disciplinary problems, inappropriate behavior, or failure to achieve?" In general, schools must examine whether adequate attention and reward are given to positive behavior and achievements regardless of how relative the definition of "positive" may be. The child-management practices of a school represent a very important vehicle for the transmission of particular practices to parents. If disciplinary practices in a child's home are already overly negative and punitive, similar practices by the school will serve to reinforce these, inhibit the learning of alternative modes of behavior management, and contribute to the likelihood of abusive behavior.

This section has discussed only a few of the identified characteristics of abusive parents to show how the school, as an institution external to the family unit, directly affects and is affected by these characteristics. Schools must also remember that the abusive parent's sense of distrust, feelings of overall inadequacy, possible past history of failure in schools, and fears of having his difficulties identified by the school all play a part in what will happen when the parent and school meet. Whether a positive parent-school partnership will be developed will depend largely on the school's policies, approach, and attitudes toward parents.

Schools and Abusive Families

Interaction between two people is partly determined by the assumptions and behavioral expectations that they have of each other. This section will examine the effects of these upon the relationship between schools and abusive families. The manner in which schools may inadvertently reinforce negative perceptions and behavior of abusive families will also be discussed.

Assumptions of School about Parents

Into any relationship, people bring with them certain assumptions and attitudes. Even the name a child has, for example, may affect the way people respond to the child. Teachers and other school staff carry with them assumptions and attitudes that certain kinds of parents will be interested in their child's education and participate in the school activities, while others will not.

Just as school staff have developed assumptions about parents, the parents have assumptions about the teacher and the school. Many of these are based upon the parents' experiences with schools when they were pupils. In some cases they will date even beyond that, and will represent attitudes about schools that have been passed down within their family from one generation to another. Another important source of these assumptions is secondhand information that parents have gained from other parents.

As a result, when parent and teacher first meet they each carry with them a set of assumptions about each other, based both upon the individual's membership in a group (parents, teachers, uneducated, poor, and so on), and the individual characteristics of the parent. If there is a question of possible abusive behavior by the parent, and if the child is having difficulty in school in addition, the assumptions of the school staff may be stacked against the parent. The teacher is also likely to have the natural tendency to be angry and indignant about the possible abusive behavior of the parent. In such a situation, parents' assumptions are usually intensified, bringing about added fear and anxiety about meeting with the school personnel.

The existence of such assumptions by school staff is rather natural. Difficulties arise not so much from having such assumptions but rather from acting upon them automatically without recognizing them. If this is done, then what is likely to happen is that actions taken by the school staff will produce the kind of response they had anticipated to begin with. While this may sometimes produce the gratification of having assumptions verified, such a negative self-fulfilling prophecy only creates further barriers between school staff and parents.

Schools have a responsibility to avoid such situations by assisting staff in identifying and examining the assumptions they have about parents as a general group and about special subgroups of parents, such as the potentially abusive parent. Procedures designed to increase self-awareness of teachers and to insure that they have the skills needed to listen accurately and objectively are helpful in this regard.

Behavioral Expectations of Parents and School Staff

An important issue related to the question of assumptions that people have of each other has to do with the behavioral expectations of parents and school staff for each other. These expectations, whether they involve acts of omission or commission, significantly affect the responses people make to each other. There are two major factors of importance with regard to mutual behavioral expectations: (1) Are the expectations each party has for the other appropriate for the situation? (2) Are the expectations clear and understood by each group?

In examining the appropriateness of expectations, it is important to look at the specific situation for which the expectations apply. The general expectation that parents will show an interest in their children's education by attending school activities may lead to disappointment when many parents, who keep individual appointments quite well, fail to show up for large group meetings. The assumption that parents, particularly abusive parents, will automatically fail to come to school activities and are uninterested in their children leads to expectations that they will respond negatively to outreach efforts. These assumptions and expectations may be inappropriate and inaccurate.

Determining the nature of parental expectations concerning the school is more difficult but no less important than examining expectations of school staff about parents. These parental expectations may be inappropriate or unrealistic. For example, parents may expect that teachers will devote more individual time to their child than what they are realistically able to, given the number of children they have. When the teachers fail to live up to the unrealistic expectation of the parent, the parent responds very angrily toward the school. Conversely, parents may expect that because of the large responsibilities of school staff they will perceive attempts by parents to find out how their child is doing or ask questions about the work being assigned as unreasonable, when in fact the teachers would have welcomed or even expected such approaches.

It is important for school personnel to meet with parents early and to seek to identify these expectations. This may take the form of individual and group meetings in which parents are encouraged to share with the school what they expect from the school. When this is done, the school can then try to correct unrealistic expectations in a supportive way, or change some of the school's own practices so as to be able to meet more of the expectations. Expectations must also be clear, and understood by all parties. While all parties will not always be satisfied with what one or the other party is able to do, at least an understanding of this difference at the beginning can prevent conflict later on. For example, while parents may be unhappy that their expectations that the school will provide individual tutoring each day cannot be realized, at least they will receive an explanation of why this is not possible and will not anticipate it happening. Again, in the examination of mutual expectations of parents and school staff the need for great skill in communication by school staff is obvious.

Protectiveness of Child by School

In addition to the questions of mutual assumptions and behavioral expectations between parents and school staff, there are other important factors that particularly affect school relationships with potentially abusive parents. One important issue has to do with the response to suspected acts of abuse by school staff. When confronted with an abusive family, there is a natural tendency to become protective of the child and to see him as the "victim" of the parents. While this is generally quite appropriate, it increases the probability that school staff will perceive parents in an extremely negative way which they then inadvertently convey quite clearly both to the child and the parent.

The communication of these negative feelings only serves to further distance the parent and interferes in the establishment of constructive and positive parent-school relationships. Such a message about the parent by the school also places the child in a difficult situation, caught between his teachers and parents. The child is placed in a position where he must either form a coalition with school personnel against the "common enemy," the parent, or a coalition with parent against school staff. Neither of these situations is constructive. Instead, school staff need to be able to respond to the abused child in a concerned and supportive way, but in a way that is not rejecting or critical of the parents. Children are very sensitive to the kinds of remarks that teachers may inadvertently make which reflect judgments about the parents. Similar negative messages about the parents are sometimes subtly conveyed directly to the parent during teacher-parent contracts. The more negatively oriented the contacts between the school and the parents, the more the abusive parent will be threatened and respond with hostility, denial, or withdrawal from the situation. As this occurs, school personnel become increasingly negative toward the parent, and another reciprocal cycle of negative interactions has begun, with the child being caught in the middle.

This discussion is not meant to undermine the importance of school personnel identifying abuse and taking steps to protect a child. Also, it is recognized that professionals in mental health and social services as well as education have an extremely difficult time dealing with their own feelings about abuse, and preventing these feelings from interfering with their relationship with abusive parents, or abused children. However, in the long run positive parent-school contacts, and the ensuing parental perception of the school as a supportive resource, serve as a form of protection for the child and an assistance to the parent. By providing these, schools serve as important resources to parents and participate in the overall community response to the problem of child abuse.

Strategies for Strengthening the Relationship between Schools and Families

There is no single strategy that would prove adequate to strengthen the relationship between schools and families. This section presents a group of recommendations that taken together or individually may be of value to particular schools and systems. Some of the recommendations would require additional resources while others do not. As long as the primary objective of schools is viewed simply as imparting knowledge to students, there may be objections to "diverting" funds from this purpose by broadening the focus to families. Given, however, the substantial impact of schools upon families, intended or unintended, and the importance of families in affecting the school performance of their children, the allocation of resources to strengthening home-school relationships is quite justified.

1. Greater outreach efforts on the part of school personnel toward home. Many parents are very interested in the education of their children but are reluctant to come to school to ask questions, deal with problems, or work together with school staff toward solutions. As previously mentioned, for many

of the parents the school is a large, impersonal, and somewhat frightening institution. This may particularly be the case with abusive parents who tend to be socially isolated and have extra reason to feel threatened by schools. Invitations to parents to come to school are often impersonal and for group activities, such as meetings and special events; unfortunately, group invitations are more likely to be rejected by apprehensive parents than are individual invitations. When the parents fail to come, this only reinforces the assumption by some of the school staff that such parents are uninterested in their child's education. Greater efforts by school personnel to reach out toward parents with personal, individual invitations would help reverse this trend. This may initially involve a brief phone call and may evolve into nothing more than a hand-written note on a form invitation. It should however, involve setting up individualized appointments, preferably early in the school year before problems have developed. As part of these appointments, the mutual behavior expectations of school and parents for each other should be examined and clarified. Some of these efforts may require additional school resources, or the reallocation of existing resources. However, such a commitment of resources would pay off in student behavior as well as improved parent-school relationships.

2. Involvement of schools as community-based resources. In many communities, the school itself is used for a variety of activities in addition to the daily education program. This puts the expensive school physical plant to wider use. It is also valuable in identifying the school as a neighborhood resource out of which emanates a variety of pleasant and enjoyable functions for different family members. In contrast, the school that sits idle in the middle of a community after the last student has left during the day is viewed more as a distant, impersonal institution intruding on a neighborhood. An additional part of the involvement of schools as community-based resources is the participation of school personnel in the neighborhood activities. This may include professional activities, such as participation on family protection teams, but may also include involvement in general social and civic activities in the community. The relationships developed outside the school building itself can greatly enhance the school's efforts to achieve its educational objectives. To assist in this, incentive should be provided for school staff to become involved in the general community in which the school is based.

3. Increased efforts toward the development of parent-support and education systems. The need for extrafamilial supports for parents grows greater as divorce rates go up and families move from community to community. The parents of students at any particular school immediately have some common interests and possess the capability of providing much-needed support to each other. The school may be able to play an important role in facilitating the development of parent-support systems of both a formal and informal nature through providing the initial mechanisms to bring parents together, and assisting in future efforts to meet. Oftentimes these support groups emerge out of groups

originally meeting for other purposes. Parent-education groups, for example, have the dual potential of providing useful training for parents while also bringing together a group of individuals who are able to be of social and emotional assistance to each other. Such efforts as parent-education and support activities are general in their focus rather than being directed at specific, individual problem children; however, they represent an opportunity for schools to strengthen families while at the same time improving their relationship with the parents they serve.

4. Training of educators. Some educators clearly seem uncomfortable talking with parents while many others operate from a shallow knowledge base regarding the way families function. This is understandable since the focus of training for educators, be they teachers, administrators, counselors, or whatever, is almost exclusively on children. Training directed toward understanding how families function, and the reciprocal influence of schools and families upon each other, is clearly needed. Additional practical, skill-building training which emphasizes techniques for communicating with parents is also much needed for educators. Such training should be provided both in university-based training programs for educators and in in-service training programs. The results of such training are likely to be a greater willingness of educators to interact with parents and involve them in school activities, as well as greater success in parent-school contact.

In particular, educators are lacking in an understanding of the problem of child abuse and the processes and resources that public and private agencies in their community have available for dealing with it. Training of educators needs to go beyond just identification of potential abuse and reporting procedures; it should also include the other steps in the process (such as prevention, treatment, and follow-up services) and a general understanding of the problem.

5. Increased emphasis on positive feedback between school and home. Too often the only time a parent receives individual communication from the school is when there has been a problem. This contributes to a negative relationship between school and home, and a diminished willingness by parents (and students) to cooperate with schools. There are numerous ways in which this pattern, which has the potential to escalate into a serious rift between school staff and parents, can be broken through the use of positive feedback from school to home. This feedback can include brief notes home on a regular basis to simply identify some positive accomplishment of the child, and brief phone calls home with favorable news. Teachers who get into the habit of making positive phone calls frequently find that parents, some of whom they had assumed to be unconcerned about their children, are delighted to receive the calls. This helps to positively reinforce the teachers for making the calls and gets a favorable reciprocal interaction pattern going. Procedures for soliciting written comments from parents to school have been developed (for example, Lordeman, Reese, and Friedman, 1977), and can also reinforce teachers for communicating positive

information to parents. Daily report cards and messages taped on telephone answering devices that parents can hear by calling in (Giannangelo, 1975) have also been used to improve school-to-home communication. One of the benefits of such practices is that parents are more likely to cooperate when problems develop if they have previously received favorable information from the school. Such practices also work against the development of destructive coalitions either between the child and school against the parent, or child and parent against the school.

6. Development of family specialization within education. In view of the impact of schools upon families, and families upon schools, an "Education and Families" specialization within the general field of education is needed. Such a specialization would take a broad ecological perspective toward the educational process and family functioning, and look at educational and social policy issues which have significance for the relationship between schools and home. An additional emphasis should be placed on technology for evaluating the impact of schools and families upon each other, and for translating those impacts into actions. The development of specialists in this area who also receive practical training in dealing with families could provide valuable resource and service people for school systems and individual schools.

7. Evaluation of impact of schools upon families. A continual theme of this chapter has been the need for a comprehensive understanding of the effects of schools upon families, and also of families upon schools. In the same way that educational researchers address issues of improving reading and math performance in schools, and evaluating school effectiveness based on standardized test scores in these areas, so should these researchers be examining the effects of schools upon families. This type of evaluation should be done routinely and on a continuous basis. Procedures for evaluating the effectiveness of schools in this regard should be designed so that they are of maximum practical use to school administrators and to parents. Clearly, any evaluation strategy in this area would need to include a strong consumer-evaluation component, gathered directly from parents. While the primary objective of schools is not to impact upon families, still that impact is sufficiently large to require a sizable evaluation effort in the area.

In conclusion, this chapter has examined the general area of school-family relationships and looked at them particularly as they affect families at risk for child abuse. While school-family relationships appear to be deteriorating in general, strategies for their improvement are available. Before such strategies get implemented on a wide scale, there must be an increased recognition that while schools are primarily in the business of working with children, they are inevitably and inextricably linked to working with families. This linkage can promote or detract from the success of schools in accomplishing their objectives, depending upon how the schools respond to the opportunity.

References

Abbott, J.L. 1973. Community involvement: everybody's talking about it. *National Elementary Principal 52*, 56-59.

Cooke, T.P., and Appolini, T. 1975. Parent involvement in the schools: ten postulates of justification. *Education 96*, 168-169.

Dinkmeyer, D.C. 1973. The parent "C" group. *Personnel and Guidance Journal 52*, 252-256.

Eells, D.R. 1974. Are parents really partners in education? *NAASP Bulletin 58*, 26-31.

Filipczak, J., Lordeman, A., and Friedman, R.M. 1977. *Parental involvement in the schools: toward what end?* Paper presented at the annual meeting of the American Educational Research Association, New York, April.

Friedman, R.M. 1976. Child abuse: a review of the psychosocial research. In *Four perspectives of the status of child abuse and neglect research.* National Technical Information Service, Springfield, Virginia, PB-250-852/AS.

Garbarino, J. 1976. A preliminary study of some ecological correlates of child abuse: the impact of socioeconomic stress on mothers. *Child Development 47*, 178-185.

Giannangelo, D.M. 1975. Make report cards meaningful. *Educational Forum 39*, 409-415.

Gil, D.G. 1970. *Violence against children: physical child abuse in the United States.* Cambridge, Mass.: Harvard University Press.

Giovannoni, J.M., and Billingsley, A. 1970. Child neglect among the poor: a study of parental adequacy in families of three ethnic groups. *Child Welfare 49*, 196-204.

Helfer, R.E., and Kempe, C.H., eds. 1968. *The battered child.* Chicago: University of Chicago Press.

Karnes, M.B., and Zehrbach, R.R. 1975. Parental attitudes and education in the culture of poverty. *Journal of Research and Development in Education 8*, 44-53.

Kempe, C.H. 1973. A practical approach to the protection of the abused child and the rehabilitation of the abusing parent. *Pediatrics 51*, 804-812.

Landsberger, B.H. 1973. Home environment and school performance: the North Carolina experience. *Children Today 2*, 10-14.

Larrick, N. 1976. From "hands off" to "parents we need you." *Childhood Education 52*, 134-137.

Lordeman, A., Reese, S.C., and Friedman, R.M. 1977. *Establishing and assessing two-way communication between parents and school.* Paper presented at annual meeting of the American Educational Research Association, New York.

McIntire, W.G., and Payne, D.C. 1971. The relationship of family functioning to school achievement. *Family Coordinator 18,* 265–268.

Moore, E.M. 1973. Human rights and home-school communication: a critical review. *Educational Review 26,* 56–66.

Parke, R.D., and Collmer, C.W. 1975. Child abuse: an interdisciplinary analysis. In E.M. Hetherington, ed. *Review of child development research, volume 5.* Chicago: University of Chicago Press.

Pellegrino, J. 1973. Parent participation. *Education Canada 13,* 4–9.

Schmuck, R.A. 1974. Bringing parents and students into school management. *Education and Urban Society 6,* 205–220.

Young, L. 1964. *Wednesday's children.* New York: McGraw-Hill.

**Part II
Recognition of
Child Maltreatment**

5

Child Abuse and Neglect: A Medical Priority

Robert P. Bates

Since the beginning of time, children have been maltreated. Various concerned individuals have attempted to uphold the rights of children, but, in spite of this, abuse has persisted. During the Middle Ages, the degree of discipline varied between lenient and savage, but by the end of the eighteenth century in England regulations curbing corporal punishment in schools were established. But even today children are starved, beaten, and in many other ways maltreated, as our society has not yet accepted the fact that the plight of the battered child is one of our major medical-social-legal community problems.

The crying of helpless, abused, and neglected infants and children had been unheeded for a variety of reasons until the last twenty years, when Caffey (1946), Silverman, (1953), and others published their suspicions of child battering. But it was not until Professor Henry Kempe (Kempe, Silverman, Steele, Droegemueller, and Silver, 1962) publicized the "battered-child syndrome" that this problem, which is the tip of the iceberg in the vast spectrum of child abuse and neglect, was recognized. Child abuse can be described as a

physical injury and/or deprivation of nutrition, care or affection in circumstances which indicate that such injury and/or deprivation are nonaccidental. (Fontana, 1973, p. 780)

The major types of abuse are physical, sexual, and emotional. As bruises, fractures, and lacerations are easily detected, physical abuse is the type most often reported. Approximately 10 percent of all injuries in children under five years are presumed to be nonaccidental (Friedman and Morse, 1974). Sexual assault is not rare but is often concealed by the victim and the family. Emotional abuse is extremely difficult to detect and treat, and is often more harmful than physical injury.

The various types of neglect (nutritional, medical, emotional, guardian) are more subtle than abuse, but nevertheless may cause irreparable damage to the helpless child. About 10 to 15 percent of children who fail to thrive are nutritionally deprived, and a high incidence of such deprivation has been found in physically abused children. For religious or other reasons, parents may deliberately deprive their children of essential medical care. Some parents are cold, unloving, and unable to provide the fundamentals for normal emotional development. Occasionally children are not adequately supervised, and therefore suffer major and repeated injuries.

Detection

It is well known that the number of cases of child abuse detected by medical personnel is much lower than the true incidence. In spite of their knowledge of the pathogenesis of child battering, doctors feel handicapped by emotional ties with the family, lack of understanding of their legal, much less moral, obligation, denial of the facts, inability to obtain these facts, and lack of experience. Physicians are often criticized for their "busy attitude" and their inability to work with other professionals as peers. This stems not from a desire to block the team approach, but rather from the very isolated medical-school experience in which they were "reared." Frequently the "baby-snatching" image of the Children's Aid Society clouds the issue of the child's need for protection. But neighbors and relatives, nurses and social workers, and judges, lawyers, and ministers protect in one way or another the abusing parents from help so urgently needed.

The reporting of abused and neglected children to Children's Aid Society or social-welfare agencies varies for many reasons (for example, ignorance, desire for noninvolvement, and definitional ambiguity). Therefore, the true rate will probably never be known.

The marked increase in notification to child abuse registries since the early 1960s attests to the fact that there was a general lack of appreciation of this problem. In 1966, the Province of Ontario established a Central Registry for child abuse; reporting increased from 225 in that year to 769 in 1975, but this is only a fraction of the children in jeopardy in this province of 8,264,465 persons (Ontario Ministry of Community and Social Services, 1975). The reporting practices of each local Children's Aid Society to the Provincial Registry vary so greatly that it is not surprising that some local offices are reporting at the *estimated rate* while others report well below it. The major reporting sources to the Ontario Children's Aid Society in 1975 were as follows: parents, 16 percent; schools, 14 percent; hospitals, 11 percent; police, 9 percent; doctors, 8 percent; public-health nurses, 8 percent; children, 6 percent; relatives, 6 percent (Ontario Ministry of Community and Social Services, 1975). It is of interest that only eight of 2,300 cases of child abuse reported in New York City in 1972 came from physicians (Helfer, 1975). Abuse and neglect are two of the most common ailments of the infant or child. In spite of this, family physicians, neighbors, nurses, pediatricians, social workers, teachers, and so on have generally been uncommitted to the plight of these children. The time has come for us to accept our professional and moral responsibility to the disease. The following sections are designed to alert health-care professionals to the problem of abuse.

An Abusive Pattern

An abusive pattern is a thread that links the perpetrator, victim, and crisis to the inevitable climax. Several pieces of this complex puzzle may fall into place if the following explanatory clues are explored:

1. The profile of the high-risk guardian.
2. The profile of the child at risk.
3. The precipitating factor.

Abusive and neglectful parents may appear as average citizens. Some are hostile, others are pleasant but uncommunicative, and only a few ask directly for the help they are seeking. Interviews with them have elicited a number of critical characteristics that are acquired over many years. Their unhappy lives have often not imprinted them with the quality essential for "nurturing" a small infant. Too often they have come from broken homes or were placed in foster care or institutions. Some of them have experienced some form of abuse in their childhood. These factors may result in a lack of "parenting" ability.

Their *isolation* hinders them from turning to others for help when a crisis arises. These helpless persons, however, often feel that they can successfully solve their problems without intervention from others. Frequently the spouse or common-law partner is similarly needy, insecure, distrustful, and unsupportive. Unfortunately, these people often complement each other's weaknesses. Their low self-esteem is persistent and reflects the lack of confidence established early in their childhood. Many of them expect their children to be little adults and gratify their own unmet needs. These unrealistically high expectations are often linked with a lack of appreciation of the child's needs.

No two abusive parents are exactly the same. Many, however, share some if not all of the above characteristics. For most of these guardians, their immaturity and dependency are central and related directly to the emotional deprivation endured during their childhood. A small but significant number of parents who were abused or neglected in their early life suffer brain damage due either to trauma or malnourishment. Their handicaps (perceptual defects, low IQ, and so on) surface in later life, making them helpless, immature, dependent adults (Martin, 1976).

The diagnosis of abuse or neglect should also be considered when the parents

1. Present a history that cannot or does not explain the injury.
2. Give a contradictory history.
3. Are reluctant to give information.
4. Continue to complain about irrelevant problems unrelated to the injury.
5. Reveal inappropriate awareness of the seriousness of the situation.

6. Physician or hospital "shop."
7. Have delayed unduly in bringing the child in for care.
8. Show evidence of loss of control or fear of losing control.
9. Show lack of love for the child.
10. Appear intoxicated.

According to Brandt Steele (as cited in Helfer and Kempe, 1972) abusing or neglecting parents have about the normal incidence and distribution of neuroses, psychoses, and character disorders. There are, though, a small group, less than 5 percent, who suffer from serious psychiatric disorders such as schizophrenia, post partum, or other types of depression, and neuroses with or without phobias. Also in this group are those parents who suffer from severe alcoholism, abuse of narcotic and nonnarcotic drugs, significant sexual perversion, and those who have been involved repeatedly in serious antisocial, violent, or criminal behavior. Nevertheless, in some surveys, the majority of guardians were married, of average intelligence, and between twenty and thirty-five years of age (Steele and Pollock, 1968). In other studies, a high incidence of premarital pregnancies, illegitimate babies, unstable marriages, and young parents (less than twenty years) has been documented (Spinetta and Rigler, 1972).

What about the child who plays a crucial role in the abusive pattern? Infants often unwittingly and innocently precipitate the violence unleashed upon them. Frequently, for one of the following reasons, the child is considered "special" and receives the brunt of abuse that may also have emotional and physical effects on other siblings. The difficult child may be premature, colicky, mentally retarded, or hyperkinetic. Some researchers have stated that the premature infant is particularly at risk for battering and have interpreted this as failure to bond due to separation of the mother and child during the newborn period (Martin, 1976). Retardation and hyperkinesis appear to increase the possibility of recurrent abuse, and the colicky baby who feeds poorly, sleeps little, and cries a lot imposes a severe stress on the high-risk parent. The "different" child may be a "look-alike reminder" or have congenital anomalies. I often recall a mother who told me that whenever she was angry at her son she would hit him a little harder, as he reminded her of her common-law partner who left, providing no support, just after their baby was born. Many special problems which may culminate in devastating abuse are associated with the unwanted, unplanned, or illegitimate baby.

The triggering factor in an abusive situation is often a crisis. Any stress can make life more difficult, but the most common ones go hand in hand with poverty, unemployment, eviction, and so on. Other crises are marital conflicts, a child's acute illness, intractable crying, death in a family, or overwhelming responsibility for many young children. No matter how necessary and useful it may be to improve the parents' socioeconomic status, these problems should not in any way be confused with the treatment of the more deeply seated character traits involved in abusive behavior.

Approaching the Diagnosis—The Interview

As the majority of abusive parents are appealing for help, the initial interview must be conducted in a sympathetic and supportive manner. These insecure persons, if threatened by an overzealous investigator, may retreat into the maze of the community and not surface again until their child has been reabused, often severely. The development of trust by these parents may be considered the cornerstone of the therapeutic program. Its success or failure may rest with the initial interview.

While interviewing the parents, the interviewer must obtain a detailed medical and social history, keeping in mind the abusive pattern and precise information regarding the injury. The history may be contradictory and often does not explain the injury. The interviewer should not belabor the child's injury but keep the interview parent oriented by expressing an interest in their way of life and problems. Several short discussions are often more rewarding than prolonged interviews. The physician should acquire this information firsthand, as it is the physician who may be subpoenaed to court. A history otherwise obtained will be considered hearsay.

Since the dynamics of each abusive situation are different, the interviewer must assess the parents during the discussion and accordingly determine the direction of the interview. See the parents separately and together, but do not withhold information from one that was given to the other. Be honest, but do not give them more than they want to hear or are able to handle at any one time. With some families it is appropriate to discuss the topic of abuse and neglect in the first interview, but with others this should wait for a subsequent meeting. At these meetings physicians must never point the finger or ask, "Why did you beat your child?" They must, on reviewing the physical examination and X-rays with the parents, make clear why they suspect the child has an unexplained injury not normally incurred accidentally. It is essential to keep the parents informed about everything that is going on and especially about the legal responsibility of the physician to inform the Children's Aid Society or provincial Department of Welfare, in accordance with provincial reporting laws. Physicians should also alert the family that a caseworker will assist them with their family problems and should explain that during subsequent interviews the social worker will further assess the family and assume the major therapeutic role. The physician should remember that the social worker will, nevertheless, depend greatly on the physician's initial assessment of the child and the family.

Clinical Manifestations

1. Physical Abuse ("Battered Child Syndrome")

This may be defined as injuries inflicted by a parent or other caretaker, for example, a babysitter, a boyfriend. The spectrum of injuries is broad, ranging from a few bruises to injuries that cause death.

It is this potential that gives it the highest priority in child-welfare treatment programs. Corporal punishment is generally accepted in our society, but when it leads to an injury it is outside the range of normal and represents child abuse.

Bruising incurred under the guise of acceptable discipline cannot be considered reasonable and safe punishment. Many injuries such as finger and palm prints on the face or buttocks speak for themselves, as do human bite marks. Loop and lash marks on the skin are easily identified and indicative of a doubled-over cord or belt. Most true accidents cause bruising on only one surface, except when a fall down a staircase occurs. In these cases abrasions on the elbows, knees, and shoulders would also be expected. Impersonators, the results of a bleeding disorder or a mongolian spot, must not be mistakenly diagnosed as child abuse.

Approximately 5 percent of physical-abuse cases involve *burns.* Circular areas of similar size on the soles, palms, armpits, or abdomen may be caused by a cigarette. Hot-water burns with a clear water level on the buttocks and perineum are frequently caused by dunking the child as a disciplinary measure for problems in toilet training. Dry contact burns to the palms and soles may be inflicted by holding the child against a hot radiator.

Eye injuries such as a dislocated lens, retinal hemorrhages, or an acute hyphema (blood in the anterior part of the eye) may not be detected unless the examination is thorough.

Fractures of the long bones, ribs, or skull are frequently (15 percent) detected in abused and neglected children. Twisting or torsion forces to the long bones in an infant may produce a chip fracture, often pathognomonic of abuse.

Children with *neurologic* injury may present with coma or convulsions. In a high percentage of these cases a subdural hemorrhage is found. Half of these children have an associated skull fracture and in the rest a whiplash shaking injury probably ruptured the bridging cerebral veins. Half of these patients with subdural hemorrhages had retinal hemorrhages. The physician should remain wary of the diagnosis "chronic subdural hemorrhage secondary to birth trauma."

Intraabdominal *visceral injuries,* for example, tears in the bowel, ruptured spleen or liver, may be caused by a punch or blow and are potentially very serious.

2. Sexual Abuse

Sexual exploitation of children is being increasingly reported to law-enforcement agencies. However, it still remains one of the most undetected types of child abuse. In most cases (90 percent) the victim is a girl, with over one-half under the age of twelve years. One-third of the offenders are under twenty-five years of age, and in most instances (75 percent) are known to the child. Approximately 10 percent are the natural parents. The victim's mother or mother substitute is the person who most frequently reports the situation, with the father or father substitute and the child victim next. As high as possibly 50 percent of all sex crimes are not reported to the police, suggesting that the incidence is much higher than official statistics indicate.

The sexual victim's role varies from totally accidental victimizations to the other extreme of a seductive partner. Many children consent to the offense, thereby shaping the victim's attitude toward the assault, the offender, and her own willingness to testify against him with subsequent guilt feelings. Some researchers have described the young female victim as being "nonobjecting" in 40 percent and "encouraging" in 66 percent to 95 percent of all sex offenses. As a rule, physical force plays a small role in these offenses (Walters, 1975). This may be attributed to the fact that the offender is frequently known to the victim. With most victims, the major sexual activity is exhibition of sexual organs, genital and nongenital petting or fondling, mouth-genital contacts, and attempted penetration without force.

Manual, oral, or genital contact with the genitalia of the victim without the victim's consent is termed *sexual assault*. Noncoital sexual contact is molestation. *Rape* is a form of sexual assault in which the penis is introduced within the genitalia of the victim by fear, force, or fraud. Laceration of the hymen is not a prerequisite for the allegation of rape. *Statutory rape* is a term applied to sexual offenses to individuals who by law are unable to consent to intercourse, that is, adolescents under the age of fourteen in Canada and individuals who are psychotic, retarded, or have an altered state of consciousness due to the effects of drugs, alcohol, and so on.

Abrasions, bite marks, bruises, and lacerations around the thighs may be present, but more frequently no injuries are found. Bladder injuries, rectal and vaginal tears, lacerations of the genitalia, and hemorrhagic shock are very serious findings, but fortunately infrequently found. Recurrent unexplained vulvitis and vaginitis must make the physician suspicious of sexual abuse, and it is most likely if the prepubertal child has venereal disease. A complete evaluation of the allegations should include examination of the siblings. Although sexual abuse greatly incenses the community, it is probably less physically dangerous than physical and drug abuse and medical-care neglect.

The direct effect of sexual assaults upon a child has been greatly exaggerated in the literature. As a rule, they do not have an excessively disturbing effect on either the child's personality or subsequent adult adjustment. The psychosocial adverse effects are in direct relationship to the degree of violence, the extent of the victim-offender relationship, and the family's reaction to the offense. Most victims seek affectionate behavior from the offenders and, in incestuous cases, a meaningful relationship frequently has been present. For this reason the daughter may not place criminal charges against her father for fear of parental separation and his loss. By far the greatest potential damage to the child's personality is caused by society and the parents who feel the need to use the victim to prosecute the offender and to prove to themselves (parents) and society that they were not failures. This shortlived event with usually no permanent sequelae is thus placed out of proportion to its importance and forces the child to reorient toward an adult interpretation of the offense.

3. Drug Abuse

Disturbances within the family play a major role in childhood accidents in general. Specifically, poisoning of children must be viewed not only as an indication of poor safety precautions, but also as a disturbance of interpersonal relationships affecting the whole family. Abuse such as drugging a crying baby with adult sedatives or intoxicating the epileptic with anticonvulsants is rarely intentional, but may be life threatening. Addicted infants must also be regarded as abused from birth. Programs designed to prevent "accidental" poisonings must therefore consider not only measures to reduce the availability and toxicity of dangerous substances, but also treatment-oriented approaches to sort out the underlying pathology of these families.

Maternal psychopathology has been inferred as the prime source of poisoning behavior in children. Frequently a power struggle between mother and child in the crucial two-to-four-year age group, when the drive for autonomy is greatest, culminates in the ingestion as an act of defiance. Once this interpersonal disorder has been diagnosed, the mother's underlying problems (marital dissatisfaction, mental illness, poor ego strength, and sexual dissatisfaction) must be tackled. Too frequently this unifying link in the poisoning cycle is not detected until more serious "accidents" occur.

4. Emotional Abuse and Neglect

Too frequently emotional abuse and neglect are not recognized as an urgent problem until the child's formative years have been destroyed by the terrorizing and rejection that is an integral part of these families' day-to-day existence. This problem, which is easily detected, is far more common than any other type of abuse or neglect. However, because the injuries are more acceptable to our discipline-oriented society than are broken bones, incest, and nutritional deprivation, the treatment program often comes too late.

The misery and deprivation that was so much a part of many neglecting parents' own childhoods are perpetuated in their roles as marital partners and parents. In their indifference toward their children, they rarely wish to hurt them but have little capacity to help them. As a result, their children are more frequently withdrawn than aggressive. They are often denied normal activities and prohibited the usual recreational and educational opportunities open to other children. Normal childhood curiosity and individual interests which are integral parts of their learning experiences are never satisfied.

Abusive language and verbal expressions of hostility are present in a high percentage of severely abusing families. Some parents state bluntly that they hate their children and never wanted them. Others wish their deaths and threaten to kill them. Frequently they are yelled at and called derogatory names such as "idiot" and "monster." They are referred to as objects of ridicule with comments such as "How ugly, clumsy, and hopeless you are." Hopelessness, despair, and defeat are quite obvious in these children's attention-seeking and approval-seeking overtures for love. They trust no one and expect little except rejection. They still have dreams, which are their fantasy substitutes for reality, hidden behind a mask of "frozen watchfulness." Treatment can only come through experiences of love and nurturing, unless the damage is too severe. Normal children develop warmth and confidence through good nurturing relationships.

Emotionally abused children feel unwanted, angry, and bad. Against this intolerable world these severely disturbed children voice their rage in screams, temper tantrums, aggressive behavior, enuresis, and self-inflicted injuries (burns, lacerations) and develop increasingly deep feelings of despair, anger, fear, distrust, and hostility. In helping these multi-problem families, placement may be necessary for the child while the parents receive treatment and the "nurturing" they did not experience with their own parents.

5. Nutritional Neglect

Failure to thrive is a syndrome of infancy and early childhood characterized by growth failure, signs of severe malnutrition, and varying degrees of developmental delay. Of these children, approximately 30 percent have an organic reason (for example, congenital heart, neurological, or gastro-intestinal disease) for the inability to gain weight while the rest are due to underfeeding from maternal deprivation (50 percent) and ignorance or error (20 percent).

Frequently there is no doubt about the fact of neglect, but physicians should not be misled by the feeding history, "He has had a lot of milk, meat, fruit, and vegetables." A review of the social history and a visit to the home by the public-health nurse or social worker may support the clinical impression of failure to thrive. Most mothers involved in maternal deprivation feel deprived and unloved themselves and are often lonely, depressed, overwhelmed, and desperate. Often the infant was unwanted and unplanned and the mother feels detached. On occasion the home is spotless and the siblings healthy. Along with the emaciated appearance, the child may have other signs of neglect (severe cradle-cap, diaper rash, and dirty skin) or abuse (bruises and fractures). Crucial in the diagnosis is the admission of the child to the hospital for a trial period of feeding. If the infant gains weight rapidly and easily, the diagnosis is nutritional neglect (ignorance or maternal deprivation). The potential seriousness of this condition and the parental psychopathology must be carefully weighed in organizing the treatment program, as this child is at high risk for other types of abuse or neglect.

6. Inadequate Medical Care

The provision of adequate medical care is vital to the child's present as well as future well-being. In this respect, abusive and neglectful parents frequently fail to provide adequate medical care. This may be related to indifference or be completely intentional, for example, the child with congenital heart disease not provided with digoxin and diuretics, or the diabetic not given insulin. The refusal of a blood transfusion in a life-threatening emergency might be considered in this category. In one survey it was found that the majority of neglectful and severely abusive parents refused to secure necessary medical care for their children (Young, 1964).

7. Guardian Neglect

All parents have an obligation to provide for the safety of their children who may be severely injured or die from accidental causes if they are not adequately supervised, for example, the child who is injured by a car while playing on a street or dies in a home fire because no babysitter was provided. All too frequently these circumstances are accepted as tragedies without looking more closely at the parents who indirectly were the perpetrators of these acts.

Their Plea for Help

The nurse, more than any other professional, is strategically placed to do case-finding and to listen for the parents' plea for help. She is less threatening than the doctor or social worker. Symptoms and signs of potential abuse may be detected in the prenatal clinic. It is not unusual for the public-health nurse to recognize a mother in extreme distress over her child's behavior. The nurse in a pediatric clinic may detect a mother's frustration with her crying infant. The hospital nurse may be told by the parents how difficult their child is to manage.

One common clue that should be recognized as a plea for help is when a parent brings the child in for "no reason at all." If the child appears well, the underlying reasons for the visit must be sought. The mother may be saying, "There is nothing wrong with my child, take a look at me." The nurse can chat with the mother and obtain valuable information. What are her stresses? How is she holding up? Is the responsibility of wife, home, and newborn infant really overwhelming? She can observe the new mother and her infant to assess the maternal-infant bonding. If the crying infant brings on a great deal of anxiety or the mother does not hold the child closely, this too should be cause for further investigation. If the child is hospitalized, the staff should note the reaction of the child to the mother, father, and other visitors (anger, fear, pleasure, sadness, or withdrawal); toward staff (appropriate, approval or attention seeking, fearful, provocative); and to other children (aggressive, hyperactive, withdrawn). Is the child's general behavior destructive or appropriate? How do the parents react to the child (uninvolved, hostile, frustrated), to the medical staff (demanding, guilty, hostile), and to other parents (talkative, appropriate, little involvement)? This kind of thorough assessment is necessary in diagnosing suspected child-abuse cases.

The nursing profession must assume its role in the detection, prevention, and treatment of the abused and neglected child. No other profession has the opportunity to spend as much meaningful time with these patients and their families. The ability to recognize the problem for what it is, by understanding the history, management, and prognosis of child abuse and neglect, is important in developing a meaningful relationship with these families.

The Impersonators

Physical examination often cannot refute statements such as, "My baby bruises easily" or "He has soft bones." However, laboratory assessment can reveal a different story.

Radiographs may support the diagnosis of child abuse and speak for the infant who is unwilling or unable to tell the tale. All children under three who are suspected of being abused or neglected must have a skeletal survey to check for recent or old fractures. In older children, radiographs may be ordered on an individual basis. The type-II epiphyseal (metaphyseal chip) fracture may be detected, but any type of injury is possible. Multiple fractures in various stages of healing should alert the pediatrician and radiologist to enquire about the social aspects of the case. Osteogenesis imperfecta, Caffey's disease, syphilis, and scurvy, the subtle impersonators, must be ruled out.

In the child who is alleged to bruise easily it may be necessary to do coagulation studies such as a platelet count, prothrombin time, and partial thromboplastin time. However, in my experience it is most unusual to see bleeding tendencies in these children. The physician must ensure that patients with idiopathic thrombocytopenic purpura, leukemia, and other bleeding disorders are not mistakenly diagnosed as abused.

Whenever possible color photographs must be taken for medical documentation of the location, size, and age of the injury; the emaciated appearance of the infant who is failing to thrive or the mongolian spot inadvertently labeled as a bruise. These are, therefore, incontrovertibly recorded for future references.

Management

On occasion it is possible to state beyond all reasonable doubt that a child has been battered or neglected. In other cases, the diagnosis may not be as clear-cut. Provision has been made for this dilemma in the provincial Child Welfare Acts, which state that only a suspicion is necessary for reporting to the Children's Aid Society or provincial welfare departments. In paving the way for the management plan, this opinion must be based on a total assessment and not solely on the history or the physical examination.

A major role for the physician is preparing the family for the involvement of the Children's Aid Society or provincial welfare department. The parents must be informed of the obligation to report suspected child abuse, in accordance with provincial Child Welfare Acts. Frequently this reporting generates anger. Therefore, a firm, but nevertheless sincere and consistent, approach must be maintained. During the initial stages of assessment and treatment, the child's admission to the hospital may be advisable for medical and social reasons. This also ensures the child's safety while the social-agency caseworker investigates the home situation. With both hospitalized and ambulatory patients, a case conference to plan acute and long-term treatment programs must be organized. Both hospitals and social agencies must be oriented with the community to tackle this problem. The management plan will surely fail without a coordinated community approach.

References

Caffey, J. 1946. Multiple fractures in the long bones of infants suffering from chronic subdural hematoma. *American Journal of Roentgenology, Radium Therapy, and Nuclear Medicine 56,* 163–173.

Fontana, V.J. 1973. The diagnosis of the maltreatment syndrome in children. *Pediatrics* (suppl.) *51,* 780–782.

Friedman, S.B., and Morse, C.W. 1974. Child abuse; a five-year follow-up of early case finding in the emergency department. *Pediatrics 54,*404–410.

Helfer, R.E. 1975. Why most physicians don't get involved in child abuse cases. *Children Today 4,* 28–32.

Helfer, R.E., and Kempe, C.H. 1972. *Helping the battered child and his family.* Philadelphia, Pa.: Lippincott.

Kempe, C.H.; Silverman, F.N.; Steele, B.F.; Droegemuller, W.; and Silver, H.K. 1962. The battered child syndrome. *Journal of the American Medical Association 181,* 17–24.

Martin, H. 1976. Which children get abused. high risk factors in the child. In
    H. Martin, ed. *The abused child.* Cambridge, Mass.: Ballinger.
Ontario Ministry of Community and Social Services. 1975. *Statistics from the
    child abuse registry.* Toronto, Ontario.
Silverman, F.N. 1953. The Roentgen manifestations of unrecognized skeletal
    trauma in infants. *American Journal of Roentgenology, Radium Therapy,
    and Nuclear Medicine 69,* 413–426.
Spinetta, J.J., and Rigler, D. 1972. The child abusing parent. A psychological
    review. *Psychological Bulletin 7*(4): 296–304.
Steele, B.F., and Pollock, C. 1968. A psychiatric study of parents who abuse
    their children. In R.E. Helfer and C.H. Kempe, eds. *The battered child.*
    Chicago: University of Chicago Press.
Walters, D.R. 1975. *Physical and sexual abuse of children.* Bloomington: Indiana
    University.
Young, L. 1964. *Wednesday's Children.* New York: McGraw-Hill.

Emotional Child Abuse and Neglect: An Exercise in Definition

Paul G.R. Patterson and
Michael G.G. Thompson

Emotional child abuse and neglect have proved to be most elusive concepts. Despite endless discussions, no workable definition has emerged. Currently the definition issue is either avoided or, at best, the difficulties involved in defining abuse and neglect are acknowledged but no consensus is reached. The following four issues characterize the conceptual problems in this area:

1. Do we include societal, environmental, and institutional abuse as well as personal or parental abuse?
2. The terms emotional abuse and emotional neglect, referring, respectively, to parental acts of commission and parental acts of omission, are sometimes used separately and sometimes used interchangeably. Sometimes neglect is defined very narrowly as ". . . the parent's refusal to recognize and take action to ameliorate a child's identified emotional disturbance" (Whiting, 1978).
3. Should the definition refer to parental behavior only, or how the parent's behavior affects the child, or both? How do we distinguish among the child who is emotionally disturbed, the child who is emotionally abused or neglected because of the behavior of his family, and the invulnerable child who appears to be neither abused nor disturbed despite an equivalent degree of family pathology?
4. How do we define emotional abuse or neglect so that the guilty are clearly identified without imputing the innocent? How does one protect both the best interests of the child and the natural rights of the parents? How do we determine when intervention is desirable and when it is mandatory? Should there be a difference between a psychological and legal definition?

This chapter is an attempt to deal with some of these questions. What is needed is some form of practical resolution to some very difficult and important ethical and moral issues.

Abuse versus Neglect

All discussions of child abuse and neglect are based to some degree upon accept-ance of the principle of *parens patriae*—that is, that the state is the ultimate guardian of the child and that the welfare of the child is paramount to all other considerations. If this principle is accepted, parents' rights are not absolute, but may be forfeited to the state if it is considered that the natural parents are *neglecting the welfare of the child* (Gesmonde, 1972, p. 101). If the principle of *parens patriae* is not accepted, all discussions of child abuse, child-labor laws, children's rights, and compulsory education become academic. If the principle is accepted, however, it is clear that parents are considered to be failing in their duty to the child if they allow the child to be neglected or abused.

In this chapter neglect, or the failure of parents to protect the welfare of the child, is used in a broad sense to include both acts of commission and omis-sion. Thus the concept of neglect is defined in such a way as to incorporate the concept of abuse. This shift of emphasis from abuse to neglect avoids many of the problems outlined above. Neglect is not only a broader concept than abuse, it is also a passive rather than an active term. That is, it does not necessarily imply intent, and, therefore, is less pejorative. Further, it refers to a relative and nonspecific deficiency in parenting that can be manifested in many ways. This is a useful conceptualization because the manifestations of emotional neglect are legion and a broad concept facilitates identification and professional response.

Ideal Definition of Emotional Neglect

One of the difficulties that plagued those attempting to define the concept of emotional abuse was that it implied an act of commission, and, therefore, placed the emphasis inescapably upon parental actions, whereas the real focus of inter-est should have been on the child. Three questions arose from this mistaken emphasis: (1) Are parental actions a necessary part of the definition of emo-tional abuse? (2) If they are how can parental actions that are used by both abusing and nonabusing parents be incorporated into a working definition? (3) How can one diagnose in the child the result of a relative deficit rather than something added by an act of commission, which is much easier to identi-fy? These problems have always been easier to deal with in the area of physical abuse, where the effects can actually be seen, but have posed almost insurmount-able obstacles for the less concrete area of emotional abuse or neglect.

All these problems are obviated by shifting the emphasis to emotional neglect. Neglect is a nonact—even failing to protect a child from one's own irritability—and therefore, by definition, can only be described in terms of its results on the child. This shifts the focus back to the child, where it properly belongs. The effects can thus be diagnosed as deficiencies from a theoretical ideal, rather than as unwanted and hard-to-define attributes superimposed upon that ideal. Furthermore, parental behavior, intent, and culpability become irrelevant issues in the diagnosis of a deficit. The relevance of their behavior only emerges when treatment is considered—that is, whether or not the parents can be counted upon to help restitute an identified deficit.

When the concept is seen this way it becomes possible to provide an operational definition of emotional neglect as any act of omission or commission which results in a "neglected child." A neglected child can further be defined ideally as any child who has failed, for whatever reason, to achieve his maximum potential as a unique human being—that is, any child who appears to be different than he would ordinarily be expected to be at a given age—physically, cognitively, emotionally, socially, or morally. By this definition, it is implied that society or the parents have failed to provide the children concerned with the environment needed to develop to their fullest potential or, alternatively, have failed to protect them from influences which could interfere with their achievement of this goal.

In the older discussions of emotional abuse, with their focus upon parents and their implications of culpability and intent, many struggles were generated in an attempt to provide a definition that did not impute all parents—a task that is so difficult that it is never achieved. With an emphasis upon neglect, however, the removal of intent and culpability as issues makes an ideal definition much more emotionally acceptable. Thus the concept of emotional neglect can be seen as a continuum from nonexistent at one end, to maximal at the other.

Having now defined the neglected child as any child who, for whatever reason, fails to achieve his maximal developmental potential at any given time, the need to differentiate among the invulnerable child, the emotionally disturbed child, and the abused or neglected child is obviated. *All* children are neglected to some extent, and the difference has become only a matter of degree rather than a matter of specific symptoms. The problem now becomes a practical one of defining somewhat arbitrarily the degree of neglect that makes intervention desirable, the degree that makes it mandatory, and the circumstances under which the state should be called upon to step in and exercise its right of *parens patriae*. These issues will be addressed in the following sections.

The Ideal of Development

If we are to define the emotionally neglected child as any child who deviates from an abstract ideal of emotional development, it behooves us to have some idea of what that is. Our knowledge is insufficient at this time to provide any absolute criteria, but we do have some idea of the principles involved which will serve until further knowledge is forthcoming. A workable definition for the moment is "a child who has had sufficient positive genetic, physical, cultural, cognitive, social, and affective input and little enough negative or distorting input to result in a positive and realistic appreciation of him/herself as a person (internal reality) together with sufficient skills to maintain satisfying interpersonal relationships and to otherwise survive comfortably in his/her chosen personal and social role up to a maximum of his/her expected developmental potential" (Sullivan, 1953, p. 309). For the moment we will dismiss the genetic and physical factors as being beyond the scope of this chapter and we will also assume that the parents are providing adequate social, cultural, and cognitive opportunities for the child inasmuch as deficits in these areas, while extremely important, are covered adequately in other literature.

It is in their family that children gain their first impressions about who they are as people, their worth as individuals, the general trustworthiness of significant others in their environment, and what they have to contribute to their relationship with these significant others in order to survive. These basic impressions are very broad and, in combination with the child's basic temperament, form the foundation stones for what is commonly known in later life as the "personality"—that is, the characteristic method or style of coping with both intra- and interpersonal relationships. Although these basic impressions *can* be modified by different experiences in later life, the tendency is more for them to be reinforced if the child remains in the same family, and modification becomes increasingly difficult with increasing age.

These initial impressions are received by the child as if they were "basic messages" sent to him by the people upon whom his very survival depends. The "primary sender" is what Harry Stack Sullivan (1953) used to refer to as "the mothering one"—regardless of the sex or relationship of this person. In our society the primary sender is usually the mother, although this is by no means universally true. It should be noted that, although these messages are described in a cognitive form, in infancy they are always received and registered at a pre-verbal, affective level and are often sent in the same manner—for example, manner of holding, correct or incorrect identification of distress signals with a rapid or slow response, a smile of approval, an irritated gesture. It should also be noted that it is the message received that counts, rather than the message intended, and that many accidental or fortuitous associations and impressions may be formed.

In summary, then, and drawing on the work of Bowlby, Mahler, Erikson, and Sullivan, the idea of emotional development includes an initial strong attachment to one or more significant persons, followed by the development of a good sense of basic trust in the security of the relationship with the primary caretakers. This sense of trust is then used as a secure base from which both physical and psychological separation from the primary caretakers can be explored. The successful carrying out of these explorations, and the subsequent negotiation with the primary caretakers of the conditions for a continued separate relationship, lead ultimately to basic messages that result in an internalized positive self-image and confidence in the ability to sustain positive relationships with others and to survive independently in the world, although with the expectation that others can successfully be called upon for assistance when necessary. These basic internal and external relationships which are so necessary to survival being thus sorted out, children are then free to concentrate upon their interests, both learning from and contributing to the world around them, and thus maximally achieving their fullest potential as human beings.

Patterns of Deviation from the Ideal

The key to achieving the above developmental ideal lies in the concept of respect—respect for the full expression of the child's individual personality, thoughts, feelings, and actions in accordance with his developmental stage; and respect for his limitations and deficiencies, again in accordance with his developmental stage. Such respect will involve knowing the child and his needs and his capacities intimately so that one can supply all his needs as they arise—both his needs for praise, encouragement, and support and also his needs for the provision of necessary limits and protection in those areas where he is not yet able to exercise sufficient mastery or good judgment. Such respect also involves never asking more of the child than he can accomplish, while at the same time never belittling him or expecting less of him than he is capable of; and such respect involves never asking the child to hide, suppress, or distort any part of himself which may be emergent at any given time—from his natural functions to his most intense thoughts or feelings. Finally, it involves making information about the world available to the child at all times, but never imposing it upon him unless it is in the interests of his safety. Any lack of respect in any of the above areas will distort the child's sense of his own internal reality and hence his sense of self-esteem and self-confidence with respect to what he can expect from others; or else it will distort his view of external reality and hence his capacity to cope with the real world. Such a lack of respect would constitute neglect in the full sense as we have defined it above.

Absolute respect for the individual child is absolutely essential for her to achieve her full potential as a human being, and is almost impossible to achieve. Even if one were able to achieve it in a "laboratory specimen," it is not at all certain that it would be desirable, as such an individual would be incapable of living in contact with other individuals without infringing upon *their* rights to maximize their full potential. In a very real sense, therefore, the greatest cause of emotional disrespect or neglect as we have defined it is the necessity for man to effect a compromise with his fellow man in order that they might live together. It might seem impractical to start a discussion of emotional abuse and neglect by pointing the initial finger at society and the institutions of civilization, but many social philosophers and writers down through the ages have argued this same point quite strenuously (cf. Plato, Hobbes, Marx, Freud, Marcuse, Holt, and so on), and it helps us to keep a perspective. While this chapter is not geared to an argument at this degree of abstraction, and certainly is not questioning the benefits of civilization, nonetheless it is important once again to note that when we speak of emotional neglect we are speaking of a continuum that includes all of us, and certainly includes our institutions.

On the more individual level, a child's needs can be neglected by either a deficiency of input (act of omission) or by a distorting of input (act of com-mission) appropriate to his given developmental stage. Deficient input occurs where the parents fail to provide age-appropriate cognitive stimulation, positive regard, and reinforcement or secure boundaries and limits appropriate to the child's developmental stage. Distorted input usually occurs where the needs of one or more of the primary caretakers are greater than, different from, or ir-relevant to the needs of the child. Thus the parent might have a need for the child to be toilet-trained before the child is ready; to stop crying when the child is in legitimate distress; to do well academically when the child is either unable to do so without unrealistic effort or has a greater need to build social relation-ships at that time; to remain dependent when the child needs to be protected and nurtured; and so on. Distorted input can also arise by implications or basic assumptions the child draws from inappropriate parental responses to the child's needs—for example, a parent who fails to provide nurturance when the child is hungry or comfort when the child is distressed can lead the child to believe that adults are untrustworthy or hurtful and uncaring; a parent who fails to provide appropriate feedback or limits to a child's dangerous, irritating, or antisocial behaviors can lead the child to believe that these are acceptable methods of controlling the environment—or even that he is unsafe insofar as it is the child that is in control rather than the parent. It should be noted, however, that while these deficiencies or distortions are often due to psychological inadequacies within the parents, this is by no means always the case. Parental illness or un-avoidable absence, family breakdown, or even the birth of a sibling occurring at crucial developmental periods can be easily misinterpreted by the child and lead him to make assumptions about himself and others that are unwarranted. If uncorrected, these can be equally as damaging as the more direct acts of omis-sion or commission outlined above.

Whatever their origin, such distorted or deficient input to the child at an early age can interfere drastically with the child's self-image, self-esteem, and with his capacity to enter into and sustain subsequent satisfying interpersonal relationships. In serious degree, the resultant patterns of dysfunctionality are very easily recognizable.

Functional Definition of Emotional Neglect

From the above discussion it can readily be seen that emotional neglect occurs on a continuum, and that all human beings to some degree or another suffer from it—whether simply by virtue of the demands of civilization or by the greater or lesser needs of one or both parents which have superceded our own from time to time. We therefore need a definition which refers to the degree of neglect where intervention becomes desirable. The most appropriate criterion would appear to be the degree of dysfunction which the child experiences in coping with himself and the world around him, and this is the criterion which was ultimately used by the Second Annual National Conference on Child Abuse and Neglect in 1977. They defined it as "an injury to the intellectual or psychological capacity of the child, as evidenced by an observable and substantial impairment in his or her ability to function within his or her normal range of performance and behavior with due regard to his or her culture" (Laurie, 1978, p. 203).

Of course this definition is entirely dependent upon the observer's judgment, but since culpability and intent on the part of the parents have been removed from our definition, this really doesn't matter. The observer is not making an accusation, merely an observation, and if this observation is accurate and is offered tactfully enough to the parent, most parents, although certainly not all, will agree to and be grateful for any assistance offered. In the case of the school, the teacher will have a much broader experience with the normal functioning of children than most parents, and any teacher recognizing a child suffering from a sufficient degree of deficient or distorted basic message to render the child dysfunctional certainly has an obligation to make this known to the parents. Some parents will already be aware of it and be grateful for the teacher's expertise in drawing it more clearly to their attention; and others will be strongly defensive about the very suggestion and prove enormously difficult to deal with. In the latter case, the parents are undoubtedly feeling accused, and, unless the case is serious enough to come under the legal definition (below), the initial response should be to back off and be supportive of the parents rather than to insist upon the accuracy of one's impression. Hopefully, such support will eventually allow them to lower their defenses and to listen.

Having identified a significant degree of dysfunctionality and having notified the parents, the next question is, what should one do or advise the parents to do? This is not a chapter on treatment, but the question can be answered very broadly in the following form. All the children who display evidence of faulty basic messages or assumptions due to deficient or distorted input, or early basic messages which have been inappropriately generalized to the current environment, need first to have these basic assumptions clearly identified by a caring adult. They then need to have the reinforcement for these messages selectively eliminated and an alternative replacement message supplied that is more appropriate in the context of their current environment. Note that while a basic corrective reeducational approach is implied in this statement, it can be carried out either directly in the school or home, or within the context of any therapeutic modalities in vogue at the time.

Who should do this? The parents, where possible, with a greater or lesser degree of professional therapeutic support where necessary. Otherwise, any caring and sensitive adults in the child's environment can and should make a contribution up to the limits of their personal ability and role.

Legal Definition of Emotional Abuse

At times a child will appear to be showing such a severe degree of dysfunctionality and distress that the observer will feel that intervention is not only desirable, but mandatory. This is simple when the parents agree and cooperate with a treatment program which is successful. But what happens when either the parents are uncooperative or the treatment program is unsuccessful and the parents do not wish to proceed any further? Under these circumstances it can be considered that the natural parents are neglecting the welfare of the child, and it is time for the state to exercise its right of *parens patriae*. It should be noted that this is the *only* time when parental behavior, intent, or culpability becomes part of the definition of emotional neglect, as discussed by Whiting (1976). We would suggest a modification of the legal definition which she offers as follows: "The legal definition of emotional neglect of a child equals the parent's refusal or inability to recognize and/or take action to ameliorate a child's identified emotional disturbance, intervention in which is considered to be mandatory for the future welfare of that child."

Unfortunately, this leaves unanswered the question as to who determines that the degree of disturbance is such that intervention is mandatory. It has already been pointed out in this chapter that emotional neglect is a matter of degree, as is emotional disturbance, and not something which can be identified as simply present or absent. Clearly, therefore, judgment, training, and experience are all called for in making such a weighty decision, and due respect must be given to the child's need, the parent's potential capacity for fulfilling it with assistance, cultural relevance, and the potential damage that any intervention might do as an inadvertent part of the process. Laurie (1978) has discussed this problem in part and provides an excellent chart for the steps that should be taken once a sufficient degree of emotional neglect has been identified, but leaves unsettled the question as to how this latter is to be accomplished.

Since the decision is clearly an arbitrary one demanding the most expertise available, the authors would make the following arbitrary suggestions. First, the subject is only open to question where the parents refuse to arrange for appropriate treatment on a voluntary basis and it therefore must be involuntarily imposed by the court, with or without removal of the child from the family. The court has neither the experience nor the expertise to determine whether or not the degree of neglect is sufficient to warrant mandatory intervention, and while it must be called upon to authorize such intervention where necessary, the decision of where it is necessary should be left to expert witnesses. In order to allow for particular biases and differences in experience and training among such expert witnesses, the court should insist upon written testimony from a tribunal of at least three independent children's mental-health professionals. At least one of these professionals should be a physician and preferably a child psychiatrist, and if possible one or more of the professionals should be from the patient's ethnic subculture. This testimony should clearly indicate that, in the opinion of the expert involved, the child is significantly dysfunctional to the point of being seriously detrimental to himself or others at the present time; will remain so or will become even more dysfunctional if intervention does not occur; and that such intervention would in all likelihood be of a significantly greater benefit to the child than nonintervention, bearing in mind the potential of intervention itself to do further damage (Whiting, 1978).

Recommendations for treatment, including the necessity for removal for the child's protection, should be included. On the basis of such evidence, the court should than be empowered to order the family to undergo treatment, if the child is not critically at risk in the short term and if there is no evidence that the family has already been unsuccessful in treatment by at least two different agencies, at least one of which was chosen by the parents themselves. In the case where treatment is ordered, the case should be monitored by the local child-protection agency and reviewed, preferably by the same experts as above, within six months. At this time evidence should be given that the treatment has been at least partially successful and is likely to continue to be so, or that treatment has been attempted without sign of significant progress by at least two different agencies, at least one of which has been chosen by the family themselves. Failing any of the above criteria, the court should order the child into the care of the local child-protection agency so that the recommended intervention may be carried out, with provision for review.

Summary

An argument has been presented for the abolition of the pejorative term emotional abuse, which has to be determined as present or absent, in favor of the less opprobrious, omnipresent, and hence more easily definable concept of emotional neglect. Following the suggestion of Laurie (1978), three levels of definition of emotional neglect have been provided—an ideal definition, a functional mental-health definition, and a legal definition. Examples of faulty basic messages or assumptions produced by emotional neglect have been provided, with the point strenuously made that emotional neglect is a continuum phenomenon from which all human beings must necessarily suffer, and that the difference is merely one of degree of dysfunctionality in achieving one's full potential as an individual.

References

Bowlby, J. 1971. *Attachment and loss.* Middlesex, Eng.: Penguin.

Erikson, E.H. 1963. *Childhood and society.* New York: W.H. Norton.

Gesmonde, J. 1972. Emotional neglect in Connecticut. *Connecticut Law Review* 5, 100-116.

Laurie, I.S. 1978. On defining emotional abuse: results of an NIMH/NCCAN workshop. In M.L. Lauderdale, R.N. Anderson, and S.E. Cramer, eds. *Child abuse and neglect: issues on innovation and implementation: proceedings of the Second Annual National Conference on Child Abuse and Neglect.* April 17-20, 1977. Vol. 1, 201-208. Washington, D.C.: U.S. Department of Health, Education, and Welfare.

Mahler, M.S. 1952. On child psychosis and schizophrenia; autistic and symbiotic infantile psychosis. *Psychoanalytic Study of the Child 7*, 286-305.

Sullivan, H.S. 1953. *The interpersonal theory of psychiatry.* New York: W.W. Norton.

Whiting, L. 1976. Defining emotional neglect. *Child Today 5* (1), 2-5.

Whiting, L. 1978. Emotional neglect of children. In M.L. Lauderdale, R.N. Anderson, and S.E. Cramer, eds. *Child abuse and neglect: issues on innovation and implementation: proceedings of the Second Annual National Conference on Child Abuse and Neglect.* April 17-20, 1977. Vol. 1, 209-213. Washington, D.C.: U.S. Department of Health, Education, and Welfare.

7

Is Physical Punishment of an Adolescent Abuse?

Patricia Libbey

The purpose of this chapter is to suggest that many professionals are uncertain whether the physical punishment received by some adolescents is a form of abuse inflicted by their parents or guardians. Moreover, they may also be uncertain about what kind of treatment or intervention should be recommended. This uncertainty, more likely to occur in cases where the injury is minor, seems to exist because professionals working with adolescents understand that often parents who physically hurt a misbehaving adolescent do so for disciplinary purposes. They themselves may believe that minor physical punishment is a proper and effective means of discipline or, if they don't believe it is a good method of control, they may believe it a parental right to choose this method of discipline.

Child-abuse-reporting laws are not written to help professionals decide whether to report an injury due to physical punishment as abuse. Rather, these laws are phrased to distinguish an intentional injury from an accidental injury. As a consequence, child-abuse-reporting laws do not help professionals who are *uncertain* whether to classify as abuse injuries inflicted by parents whose intent was to discipline. An attempt will be made here to demonstrate why this uncertainty persists and some suggestions will be offered as to why it is an important attitude to have, at least at this time.

Uncertainty over whether to report an injury and what to do about the case if we decide to classify it as abuse is influenced by what we learn about the incident itself. Moreover, our notions of what we or the community define as an acceptable or unacceptable form of physical punishment influences our decision to report. Most researchers in adolescent abuse have indicated that this is an important issue especially with adolescents since they may be misbehaving and the injury is usually minor. Other researchers are certain, however, that physical punishment of any kind is abuse.

Beliefs about severity, the behavior of the adolescent, and the acceptability of parental style of discipline may influence decisions regarding reporting. Researchers (Berdie, Baizerman, and Lourie, 1977; Fisher and Berdie, 1978; Libbey and Bybee, 1979) have indicated that uncertainty about whether a case is discipline or abuse and what to do if it is abuse may occur more frequently with adolescents than with small children. These researchers suggest that in contrast to the perceived helplessness of a young victim, the adolescent's behavior is often provoking or perceived as being provoking, and that the adults involved may believe that physical punishment was deserved as a corrective measure.

That uncertainty may exist in the minds of some should be evident from three sources: (1) from a review of adolescent-abuse cases reported to county welfare agencies, (2) from the various meanings researchers ascribe to physical punishment, and (3) from contrasting meanings of physical punishment found within the law and between the law and opinion surveys.

The Existence of Uncertainty When Reviewing Cases of Reported Adolescent Abuse

Researchers in adolescent abuse observe that because of the developments that characterize adolescence it may be difficult to decide if the injury is a result of abuse or acceptable discipline (Libbey and Bybee, 1979; Fisher and Berdie, 1978; Lourie, 1977). They assert that the behavior of the adolescent is probably contributing to the abuse, because the adolescent's behavior either *is* or is *perceived as* acting out (Lourie, 1978), provoking (Berdie, Baizerman, and Lourie, 1977), delinquent, a problem, or disruptive (Garbarino, 1978). In short, he may be behaving in ways that most parents or guardians are likely to see as in need of control by some kind of acceptable disciplinary action. In addition to pointing to the likelihood of adolescent misbehavior and the possibility that abuse may also be perceived as acceptable discipline, Lourie (1977) and Libbey and Bybee (1979) suggest that the minor nature of the injuries may influence our decision to classify it as discipline.

Two articles have reviewed cases of adolescent abuse reported to welfare agencies. Lourie (1978) describes three patterns of adolescent behavior and parental response in relation to the frequency and severity of physical punishment. Libbey and Bybee (1979) describe four patterns of adolescent abuse. Lourie's patterns are based on the perceptions of a social worker and a psychiatrist. He reviewed seventy cases, but only summarized them for the reader. Libbey and Bybee's patterns are based on a systematized report filled out by the social worker. The social worker handled all twenty-five cases in consultation with school personnel and other professionals (for example, probation officers, therapists) who had been or were working with the adolescent and parents.

Lourie's three patterns of adolescent abuse are summarized as follows:

Adolescent Only

The adolescent is described as an "angel" by the parents prior to adolescence, but is seen as "overindulged" by the observer. This adolescent's attempt to grow up is "fraught with provocative testing behavior and labile emotions." The parents are described as "very different" from other abusive parents. They are scared by the adolescent's attempt to break away. They never hit their children until adolescence, and the abuse is likely to be an accidental injury resulting "from a slap or a shove or as the result of a carelessly thrown object" (Lourie, 1978, p. 3). Lourie (1978, p. 4) also distinguishes these parents from others by reporting that they appear to have a "lower level of pathology." This abuse is described as sporadic.

Quality Change

Lourie says of adolescents in this pattern that "when they reach adolescence, they go 'wild' because their parents are so over controlling" that they do not "give their children opportunity to learn control for themselves." The parents were characterized as having used corporal punishment "deemed appropriate by community standards" when the adolescent was younger, but this became "blows delivered with closed fists and greater force" in adolescence. Parents are "frustrated with the child's inability to respond to discipline" (1978, p. 3). Their loss of control over the adolescent leads to their own loss of control which leads to abuse. Conversely, Lourie believes that this very rigidity may lead to abuse "in a very controlled situation." The severity of the punishment becomes worse as the child grows older. .

Chronic

This adolescent's behavior, which is probably the result of earlier child abuse, is so problematic that it usually hides the abuse. He is "lost in our school systems, the mental health systems, and the juvenile justice systems, where abuse is rarely noticed." The parents are overwhelmed and disorganized either because of their own inadequacies or by the child's behavior.

The parents and adolescents described by Lourie present an interesting variety. Though, of course, already labeled and reported as abuse, we can speculate on whether we would have reported the incident. In the first pattern, what are we to make of an accidental injury which results from a shove? The parents appear to care a great deal, but sporadically lose control. In the second pattern, how would we respond to parents who are rigid disciplinarians and who apparently believe in corporal punishment for their children who are wild? Further, is loss of control an intentional act? In the third pattern, how would we perceive overwhelmed, disorganized, and socially isolated parents, and delinquent, failing, or disturbed adolescents?

Libbey and Bybee (1979) were interested in the questions about frequency and severity of abuse, adolescent behavior, and parental styles of discipline that professionals working with youth might have in deciding whether to report an injury. In their review of twenty-five cases, they found four patterns which fit on a continuum of severity and frequency. The patterns were similar to Lourie's, with a few differences. They, too, characterized the first group of onetime minor injuries as having been inflicted by parents who "showed warmth and concern" for adolescents who never misbehaved in childhood, but were having "over-heated arguments" with their parents. Incidents were described by participants as accidental or a temporary loss of control. Only one of five mothers in this group of intact families was described by the caseworker as overindulging. In the second group the adolescents and the injuries were similar to the first except that abuse had been occasional, one or both parents were characterized by the caseworker as rigid and punitive disciplinarians, and a stressful event, such as illness, had occurred recently. The third group also included sporadic incidents which had occurred only in adolescence, but injuries were all relatively more severe since they were to the head and the adolescent and/or the parents showed severe behavior difficulties or emotional disturbances. This assessment by the social worker was based on the parents' involvement with other agencies in the past for these problems. The fourth group was like Lourie's third group of chronic abuse. They, too, appeared to be lost in other institutions. Their abuse had been discovered by perceptive workers only after a therapeutic relationship had been established. Most parents also appeared ineffective and overwhelmed. The adolescents had repeatedly run away, attempted suicide, or had been diagnosed by other agencies as mentally or emotionally retarded. Similar to Lourie's chronic pattern, this fourth group was a small percentage of the adolescents the agency handled over a nine-month period of time.

As with Lourie's cases, we should ask ourselves if we would have labeled these cases as acceptable discipline or abuse. Clearly most adolescents were misbehaving, a large proportion of parents believed they were using acceptable discipline, and most cases were not serious injuries. We should also ask ourselves what we imagine might be the outcome of our decision to report or not report an injury. The descriptive patterns of adolescent abuse also suggest that the cases are so different that we may be uncertain about what to do about a case we suspect as abuse until we learn more about the situation. In the cases reviewed by Libbey and Bybee (1979) the social worker made a variety of decisions, ranging from no further contact to removal from the home. If the abuse is minor or has only occurred once, if the parents appear very concerned and caring, and the adolescent seems mature and wishes to handle the situation on his own, we may decide it likely that it won't happen again. If, on the other hand, there are other family problems, for example, alcoholism or social failure, we may wish to contact other agencies who can help serve the family. It may be that if abuse appears chronic, the parents are uncooperative, and the adolescent is in danger we may wish to use the force of the courts in handling the case.

Uncertainty on Reviewing the Meanings Researchers
Ascribe to Physical Punishment

The meaning of what kinds of parental acts constitute abuse differs among researchers in child abuse. When viewed together they represent a great range of opinions. This variety can contribute to our uncertainty unless one particular expert convinces us that he is right. Below is a summary of several prominent notions of what constitutes abuse.

Garbarino (1977, 1978), who prefers to use the term mistreatment instead of abuse, is one of the few researchers to date who has concentrated largely on adolescents. He is particularly concerned about those adolescents who find their way into the juvenile justice system. He believes that most of these adolescents were mistreated and that mistreatment is the reason they are delinquent. However, Garbarino does not include the delinquent behavior of the adolescent as part of his explanation for the parents' mistreatment. Instead, he believes that the parents have made a "pathological adaption" in response to the ecology of the social and economic environment they live in. His model is linear. Conditions in the environment (for example, poverty, social isolation) lead to frustration and anger in the parents, which leads to mistreatment, which in turn leads to delinquency. In his view, the parents who mistreat adolescents, however, are not qualitatively different from normal parents. He says that they are on a continuum of violence with normal caregivers—only *quantitatively* different. These normal caregivers may use physical punishments. Although it may be less severe, he characterizes it as normal violence. He says that on the continuum of violence the mistreatment of adolescents "lies somewhere between child 'abuse' and wife 'battering.'" His implication seems quite clear. Physical punishment is abuse, and abuse is violence. We must do all we can to prevent this violence, and help people who are its victims.

Garbarino does not stand alone in equating physical punishment with abuse and violence. He cites Gil as expressing the same belief. Gil (1973) says that spanking by parents, which leaves no visible injury, is an "ancient, cruel ritual" and is detrimental to growth. He also believes that corporal punishment should be outlawed in the schools as an "unambiguous sign to all parents . . . to use more constructive measures to bring up and discipline children" (Gil, 1973).

Gelles and Straus (1979) included spanking in their definition of violence in their national survey of family violence. They explain that in their view any "act carried out with the intention or perceived intention of physically hurting another person" is violence (Gelles and Straus, 1979, p. 20). They point out that since spanking is "an act intended to cause physical pain" it is therefore violent (1979, p. 20). Although Gelles and Straus in this study say spanking is a form of violence, they do not say that spanking is like abuse. Abuse to them is a different form of violence. "Abusive violence" (1979, p. 25) is a more severe violent act. Their "child-abuse index" includes "kicks, bites, punches, beatings, threats with a gun or knife, use of a gun or knife" (p. 24). Although abuse is not the same as spanking in their view, they recognize that "there has been a tendency to *broaden* legal definitions of 'child abuse'" (1979, p. 22; italics in original). Their own definition of violence was developed for the purposes of research. They do not speak, as Gil does, of outlawing corporal punishment. They are careful to write about violence as a "topic of interest" or as a "social issue" which needs more research to explore "the extent of family violence and attempt[s] to identify which families [are] more likely to be violent" (1979, p. 16).

We might wonder why they believe it is necessary to know the extent and nature of violence. Do they regard violence as a problem requiring social and political action? There is not a clear answer to this question in their article, but some statements have strong implications. They find their estimates of family violence "startling," and say that if these rates showed up in a "deadly communicable disease" or "violence outside of the home," many people would think they indicate an "epidemic" (p. 28). The implication of this statement is that perhaps it is time to act to reduce the rates. But how could we reduce rates? They review many factors which researchers have suggested are the roots of violence. Their conclusion is that stress (for example, from unemployment, troubles related to a low socioeconomic status), and the family (which is by nature a focus of high conflict and stress, yet isolated from outside aid), in combination with implicit cultural norms favoring violence, "sets the stage for a high level of violence that is *endemic* to American families" (1979, p. 36; italics added). In summary, they appear to regard violence which includes the physical punishment of children as a problem needing our attention, but they do not give specific recommendations about the child-abuse-reporting law.

Wald is critical of those "who advocate extending the reach of neglect laws" (1975, p. 987). He includes physical abuse in the term neglect and believes intervention cannot be justified "simply because a neighbor, relative, social worker, or judge disapproves of a given parent's disciplinary measures" (1975, p. 985). He feels, therefore, that intervention should be limited to cases "where there has been or is likely to be serious physical injury" causing "substantial risk of death, disfigurement, or impairment of bodily functioning" (1975, pp. 1011–1012). He states that this definition forces the intervener to focus on the consequences of the act to the child and not on the act itself, or, as he says, "not simply on the fact that a parent has physically punished his child" (1975, p. 1012). He has three reasons for his concern about overintervention. First, parental autonomy in childrearing has been a "basic tenet of our laws" (1975, p. 989). Second, we have limited knowledge and lack agreement about child development and proper parenting to justify more extensive state supervision (1975, p. 992). Third, he asserts that "there is substantial evidence that, except in cases involving very seriously harmed children, we are unable to improve a child's situation through coercive state intervention" (1975, p. 993).

Research in child abuse has been instrumental in passing laws in every state and province establishing reporting procedures in identifying abuse cases (Pfohl, 1977). Some legal schools (McCatheren, 1977; Wald, 1975) are now advocating that these laws be sharply restricted.

The Existence of Uncertainty in Society as Reflected in Contrasts between Public Opinion and the Law and Conflicts within the Law

Abuse-reporting laws were written with the intent of reducing uncertainty. Laws aspire to order and guide human conduct (Fuller, 1973; Pound, 1959). Abuse-reporting laws are an attempt to reduce uncertainty in three ways. First, they tell us *what kind* of injury to report. Accidental injuries should *not* be reported. Intentional injuries should be reported. Second, the laws stipulate *whom* to report to, usually the police *or* a welfare agency. And, third, the laws are written to reduce uncertainty over *whether* to report by attaching a penalty for failure to report.

Although the laws are written to bring order and clarity about what to do or not to do, they may not always accomplish this end. Laws may be at variance with public opinion, desires, and practices, as was clearly demonstrated in the repeal of Prohibition. Furthermore, laws are sometimes contradictory (Fuller, 1973, p. 11).

If we look at surveys as an expression of popular belief and practice, we find that around 90 percent of all parents use physical punishment at some time when their children are growing up (Erlanger, 1974; Stark and McEvoy, 1970). Yet the abuse laws in thirty states simply say that an injury that results from parental intent should be reported as abuse. Physical punishment for disciplinary reasons is not excluded from these laws. The potential for conflict exists. Laws in twenty states require reports of any serious injury. Perhaps this distinction could separate abuse from discipline in the minds of some people. But it also seems conceivable that a black eye from a slap on the face is serious to one person, and not serious to another. Furthermore, if we look into the tort laws on physical punishment for disciplinary purposes, we find that they state that parents or guardians can use "severe punishment for a serious offense . . . [as long as] . . . a less severe method appears likely to be ineffective" (American Law Institute, 1965).

Conflict between laws pertaining to physical punishment occurs in another context for school officials and teachers. The abuse law requires teachers or other school personnel to report an injury they suspect was inflicted by the parent, yet it is conceivable that the same student who was hit at home could be legally paddled at school. Most states and provinces allow corporal punishment in schools for disciplinary reasons (see Wood and Larkin, 1978, for a thorough review).

Concluding Remarks

This chapter has endeavored to show that uncertainty over whether to report physical punishment in adolescents and what to do about abuse is likely to exist. For centuries, many parents have used some form of physical punishment as a way to discipline their children. Researchers, particularly in child abuse, have seriously challenged the belief that parents should be able to choose this method. The abuse-reporting laws can be used as a way for the state to intervene in the family when physical punishment is used. Professionals working with young people may experience some ambivalence about reporting physical punishment if they are sensitive to varying community norms, if they are aware of other laws permitting the use of physical punishment, or if they believe themselves that some degree of physical punishment may be necessary.

The likelihood of the existence of this uncertainty has been discussed in this chapter not only because it is there but, even more importantly, an argument has been made for its existence in the belief that uncertainty should exist.

What are the benefits of uncertainty? Two come to mind.

1. Uncertainty can create an attitude of open inquiry—an openness that leaves room for alternative explanations—a readiness to suspend judgment until both, or many, sides have been heard. If as professionals, we desire to provide even informal due process before evoking our authority under the law, we must cultivate our ability to see both sides. If as researchers we hope to contribute in some way to understanding the human condition we should first cultivate our uncertainty. Robert Coles (1979) in an address to social-science students at Harvard expressed this approach very nicely. He said, "[Students] should expose themselves to the kind of tentativeness, the capacity for ambiguity, irony, and inconsistency that will protect them from this relentless urge to resolve everything, to categorize everything, to trace everything back to antecedents before beginning advanced study of a topic."

2. Uncertainty that creates an attitude of open inquiry can also increase our capacity for empathy. Empathy toward the parents or guardians as well as the adolescents can perhaps lessen the feelings of shame and fear on the part of the parents that, Wald (1975) believes, can in the long run do more harm than good. We don't often hear the word love used in discussions of the law or even discussions of intervention procedures. But empathy is what Walter Kaufmann terms love, one of his four cardinal virtues. In his book *Without Guilt and Justice* (1973) he argues persuasively that we should move beyond punishment and guilt in childrearing and in our treatment of those we claim have done wrong. He believes that love, along with honesty, courage, and humbition (high aspirations accompanied by humility) should take their place. It seems fitting therefore to conclude with his explanation of love.

. . . Love, as a cardinal virtue, is the habit of trying to imagine how others feel and what they think; to share grief and hurts at least in some small measure; and to help. (1973, p. 118)

References

American Law Institute. 1965. *Restatement of the law, Second, Torts.* Vol. 2. St. Paul: American Law Institute Publishers.

Berdie, J., Baizerman, M:, and Lourie, I. 1977. Violence towards youth: themes from a workshop. *Children Today 6,* 7-10, 33.

Coles, R. 1979. *Seminar for social science students.* Cambridge, Mass.: Harvard University Press.

Erlanger, H.B. 1974. Social class and corporal punishment: a reassessment. *American Sociological Review 39,* 68-85.

Fisher, B., and Berdie, J. 1978. *Adolescent abuse and neglect.* San Francisco: Urban and Rural Systems Associates.

Fuller, L. 1973. *The morality of law.* New Haven: Yale University Press.

Garbarino, J. 1977. The human ecology of child maltreatment: a conceptual model for research. *Journal of Marriage and the Family 39,* 721-736.

Garbarino, J. 1978. *Meeting the needs of mistreated youth.* Paper presented at the Third Kansas Government's Conference on Child Abuse and Neglect. September 29.

Gelles, R.J., and Straus, M.A. 1979. Violence in the American family. *Journal of Social Issues 35*(2): 15-39.

Gil, D. 1973. *Violence against children.* Cambridge, Mass.: Harvard University Press.

Kaufmann, W. 1973. *Without guilt and justice.* New York: Dell Publishing.

Libbey, P., and Bybee, R. 1979. The physical abuse of adolescents. *Journal of Social Issues 35,* 101-126.

Lourie, I.S. 1977a. The phenomenon of the abused adolescent: a clinical study. *Victimology 2,* 268-276.

Lourie, I.S. 1977b. The abuse of adolescents. In A. Thomas, ed. *Children alone.* Reston, Va.: The Council for Exceptional Children.

Lourie, I.S. 1978. *Family dynamics and the abuse of adolescents: a case for a developmental phase specific model of child abuse.* Paper delivered at the Second International Congress on Child Abuse and Neglect, London, England, September.

McCatheren, R. 1977. Accountability and the child protection system: a difference in a proposed standard relating to abuse and neglect. *Boston University Law Review 57,* 707-731.

Pfohl, S. 1977. The discovery of child abuse. *Social Problems 24*(3): 310–323.

Pound, R. 1959. *An introduction to the philosophy of law.* New Haven: Yale University Press.

Stark, R., and McEvoy, J. 1970. Middle-class violence. *Psychology Today 4,* 52–65.

Wald, M. 1975. State intervention on behalf of neglected children: a search for realistic standards. *Stanford Law Review 27,* 985–1112.

Wood, F., and Lakin, C. 1978. *Punishment, aversive stimulation in special education.* Minneapolis: University of Minneapolis.

Sexual Victimization of Children

Ann Wolbert Burgess and
Nicholas Groth

A person may achieve sexual contact with another person in three basic ways: (1) through *consent,* which involves negotiation and mutual agreement, (2) through *exploitation,* which involves a person's capitalizing on his position of dominance (economic, social, vocational, and so on) to take sexual advantage of a person in a subordinate position, and (3) through *assault,* which involves threat of personal injury and/or the use of physical force. The latter two methods constitute sexual victimization since a person is intimidated due to the individual's vulnerable status and, therefore, is not in a position to freely decide and determine his own sexual behavior. Only through negotiation and consent can sexual relations properly be achieved. However, such consent is precluded in sexual encounters between a child and an adult since the adult, by virtue of being mature, occupies a position of biopsychosocial authority and dominance in regard to the child. A child by definition is an immature person and most children have not developed sufficient knowledge or wisdom or social skills to be able to negotiate such an encounter on an equal basis with an adult. Even a physically mature child is not matured enough emotionally to cope with sexual demands from an adult. The child can easily be taken advantage of by an adult and although the child may agree to and cooperate with the sexual activity, the child does so without awareness or appreciation of the impact such activity may have on his or her subsequent psychosocial development, that is, his personality formation, attitudes and values, identity issues, and the like. In general children are not well informed about human sexuality or adequately prepared to deal with this important area of human behavior, and the offender can exploit their innocence in self-serving ways to the physical, social, psychological, and emotional detriment of the children.

Gaining Access to the Child

The child molester may gain sexual access to his victim through deception or by directly approaching the child. In the majority of cases the offender will use some type of psychological pressure, such as enticement or encouragement, to persuade the child to enter into sexual activity, but in some cases the offender may resort to force, either in the form of threats and intimidation or through brute physical strength.

Pressure Situations

The most common approach used by a child molester is to initially establish a nonsexual relationship with the victim which has meaning to the child. The offender becomes a familiar and trusted figure in the child's life. Over time sexual intimacy is introduced into the context of this involvement. The offender may deceive the child by misrepresenting social standards ("All boys and girls do this—it's okay.") or misidentifying the activity ("We're going to wrestle.") or tricking the child ("I'm going to give you a bath.") or presenting the activity in the context of a game ("I've hidden some money in my clothes and if you find it you can have it."), and then the offender rewards the child's cooperation with money, candy, toys, or other gifts. Children will exchange the sexual activity for these other, nonsexual rewards, and one of the most prized rewards is attention. The child molester will capitalize on the child's need for attention to lure the child into the sexual activity by making the victim feel special or important.

In sex-pressure situations the offenders appear to strongly identify with the child, to be highly invested in the child emotionally, and to use the child to gratify their own needs for recognition, affection, approval, and validation. The offender feels more competent in regard to children and looks to them to gratify unmet life needs. Sex is seen as the proof and measure of the child's acceptance and love.

When this is the dominant motive the offense is characterized by a relative lack of physical force in the commission of the assault; in fact the offender generally behaves in counteraggressive ways. This offender makes efforts to persuade the victim to cooperate and to acquiesce or consent to the sexual relationship, oftentimes by bribing or rewarding the child with attention, affection, approval, money-gifts, treats, and good times. But he is usually dissuaded if the child actively refuses or resists, and he does not resort to physical force. His aim is to gain sexual control of the child by developing a willing or consenting sexual relationship. At some level, he cares for the child and is emotionally involved with him. The pedophilic interest can be understood as the result of a projected identification on the part of the offender with the child. In sex-pressure situations, sexuality appears to be in service of needs for physical contact and affection, loving, open, affectionate, attractive, and undemanding. They feel safer and more comfortable with children. Very often victim and offender know each other prior to their sexual involvement and sometimes they are related.

This involvement can be continuing and fairly consistent over time. The following case illustrates a pressured sex offense:

> Fred is a fifty-one-year-old married man convicted of eight charges of indecent assault of a child under fourteen. Over a six-year period, Fred engaged several of the neighborhood male children ages ten to twelve in sexual activity involving fondling and fellatio. He owned a swimming pool, and the children would come over to swim and would change into bathing suits in the basement of his home. At times Fred would suggest they not wear swimming suits, and horseplay would lead to sexual contact.

The sex-pressure offenders comprise the vast majority of child molesters.

Forced Situations

In a lesser number of cases the offender may directly confront the child with sexual demands in the content of verbal threats (for example, "Do what I say and you won't get hurt."), intimidation with a weapon (for example, brandishing a knife), or direct physical assault (for example, grabbing the child). These tactics are directed at overcoming any resistance on the part of the victim even though the intent is not to hurt the child. Such sexual assaults constitute child rape, in which sexuality becomes the means of expressing power and anger. The offender's modus operandi is either one of intimidation, in which he exploits the child's helplessness, naivete, and awe of adults, or one of physical aggression, in which he attacks and overpowers his victim.

The exploitive offender essentially forces himself upon the victim. He typically employs verbal threat, restraint, manipulation, intimidation, and physical strength to overcome any resistance on the part of his victim. He may strike the child, but whatever aggression exists is always directed toward accomplishing the sexual act. It is not the intent of the offender to hurt his victim, and he will usually only use whatever force is necessary to overpower the child. The physical risk to the victim is inadvertent rather than deliberate injury. He makes no attempt to engage the child in any emotional way. Instead he sees the child as an outlet solely for self-gratification. The child is regarded as a disposable object, one to be used and then discarded. The sex act constitutes the extent and duration of the relationship, and thus typically it is a temporary and unstable involvement.

This offender relates to his victim in an opportunistic, exploitive, and manipulative way. Self-entitlement characterizes his orientation toward the child and sexuality appears to be in the service of a need for power. Such offenders describe the victim as weak, helpless, unable to resist, easily controlled and manipulated. They feel stronger and more in charge with children.

The majority of child offenders intend no actual injury to their victims, submission being their objective, but at the same time there are also no strong defenses against hurting the child, if necessary. This type of offender exhibits a lack of concern for the consequences or cost to others of his sexual activity; he experiences his motivation to be strong sexual needs which he is incapable of delaying or redirecting. Children are objects of prey: they are stalked and hunted, and any resistance on their part can quickly release anger and hostility in this offender. He will not take "no" for an answer and will enforce his sexual demands through coercion.

The following case illustrates a forced sex offender:

> Roger is a thirty-year-old white male convicted of sexual contact in the first degree and given a sentence of three to ten years. He is divorced and has a son eight years old. Since adolescence Roger has been attracted to prepubescent girls between the ages of eight and twelve. In his last offense Roger was driving home from work when he saw an eight-year-old girl get off the school bus. "As she proceeded down the road I approached her and told her I would walk her home because there was 'a man in the area with a gun. She was not facing me and so I dropped my trousers to expose myself and began masturbating. She turned around and screamed and I pushed her to the ground and fell on top of her. In the excitement I ejaculated. Although I never had intercourse with any of the victims, I would fantasize about it."

There is an extremely small group of children offenders who derive pleasure in actually hurting the victim. Sexuality and aggression become components of a single psychological experience: sadism. The sadistic child offender inflicts sexual abuse on his victim, who serves as a target for his rage and cruelty. Physical aggression is eroticized. Consequently the physical and psychological abuse and/ or degradation of the child is necessary for the experience of sexual excitement and gratification in the offender. The youngster is attacked or assaulted. He or she is generally beaten, choked, tortured, and sexually abused. It is the intention of the offender to hurt or punish the child in some way. More force is used in the assault than would be necessary simply to overpower the victim. Instead the victim is brutalized. The offender finds pleasure in hurting the child and typically the assault has been planned out, thought about, and fantasized for some time prior to its actual commission. In this respect it is not an impulsive act; it is premeditated. Sexuality becomes an expression of domination and anger. At some level the child symbolizes everything the offender hates about himself and thereby becomes an object of punishment. The victim's fear, torment, distress, and suffering are important and exciting to the sadistic pedophile, since only in this context is sexual gratification experienced. The complete domination, subjugation, and humiliation of the victim are desired and typically a weapon such as a gun, knife, rope, chain, pipe, or belt is used for this purpose in the commission of this offense. The offender relates to the victim in a brutal, violent, and sadistic fashion. His intention is to hurt, deprecate, defile, or destroy the child. The extreme of this condition results in the "lust murder" of the victim.

There is a wide variety of sexual acts performed or demanded by offenders in their offenses. In some cases, such as in exhibitionism, there is no actual physical contact between the offender and his victim. Such offenders confine their activity to simply exposing their genitals in full view of the child. In other cases there is physical contact with the external surface of the victim's body. This would include hugging, kissing, fondling, sucking, and masturbating against the child. In still other sexual contacts the offender sexually penetrates the body of the victim in some fashion: orally, anally, or vaginally. And, in still other cases, some offenders progress over time from fondling to intercourse. The child's reaction to such contact is often dependent on the type of acts the offender performs.

Children usually describe the experience in terms of whether or not it hurt. It is important to realize that not all sexual contact between adults and children is considered negative or painful by the child. It may be pleasurable, especially in hand-genital contact.

As aggression and violence increases, there is an inverse relationship between the amount of violence exhibited in the offense and the incidence of such offenses. The most common sexual encounter between adult and child is one in which the adult exposes himself to the child; the rarest type of sexual offense, where the child is murdered.

Impact on Victim

There are several issues that need to be assessed in terms of long-term effects on young victims. Research is just beginning to provide data on this area of investigation. Our work with sexual-assault victims from the Boston City Hospital has helped to identify the following issues that appear to impact on the young person.

1. Relationship of secrecy and sexual activity. Sexual activity that occurs over a period of time usually means that the child has been pressured into secrecy.

If the offender is successful with his victim, he tries to conceal the deviant behavior from others. In his attempt to achieve sexual control of the child, he will try to pledge the child to secrecy in several ways. The child may not be aware of the existence of the secret. The offender may say it is something secret between them, or in the entrapment cases he may threaten to harm the child if the child does tell.

In most situations the burden to keep the secret is psychologically experienced as fear. Victims have spontaneously described the following fears which bound them to the secret: fear of punishment, fear of repercussions from telling, fear of abandonment or rejection, and a communication barrier in knowing what words to use. The enforced silence may have some relationship with later behavior in which the child seeks nonverbal ways of dealing with stress. Addictions to alcohol and drugs have been noted in adults with a history of early sexual trauma.

2. Conflict in feelings if the offender is a family member. Psychologically, to face the decision of having to side with one of two family members is experienced as a sense of divided loyalty. When the assailant is a family member, familes are caught between two conflicting expectations. Should they be loyal to the child victim and treat the offender as they would treat any assailant—thinking of their duty as citizens to bring such an offender before the law? Or should they be loyal to the offender and make an exception for him because he is a family member and let their duty to him as a particular individual prevail? Clearly they cannot honor both expectations. They must choose, and the choice may be a difficult one. Careful attention to the feelings of the child is important for conflict resolution when the offender is known.

3. Vulnerability to physical and psychological symptoms. Young victims are more prone to express their distress through physical and psychological means. The issue of school problems and the potential for a school phobia is important to bear in mind.

4. Surveillance issue. Children who have been pressured into secrecy over sexual activity often have been kept under surveillance by the adult authority figure. This enforced surveillance may have some relationship to the victims' feelings about themselves.

5. Sexuality. There are several components to the issue of sexuality and how it relates to the young victim. The issues may include (1) premature introduction into adult sexuality; (2) learning to use sex in the service of nonsexual needs such as in the service of reward and approval.

Role of School Personnel

Identification

There are two important considerations for school professionals. First, offenders seek out children in the school environment. Second, potential offenders may exist within the school environment (the school yard as well as in areas that provide access to children such as school transportation vehicles).

Teachers are in key positions to detect sexual victimization because they see the child in day-to-day activities and can note any change in behavior from the daily activities. Especially in incest situations, the teacher may be a primary ally to the child since, by the nature of incest, the parent will not be protective of the victim. If there are special classes or education modules that deal with personal safety and human sexuality or family-life issues, the children may more easily be able to turn to the teacher to discuss concerns they feel discouraged from discussing at home.

Signs of Suspected Sexual Victimization. The following signs should raise the question of possible sexual victimization for teachers in suspecting sexual victimization.

1. Changes in the child's school behavior. For example, truancy, inattention in class, or progressively failing grades. Although such symptoms may be due to many factors, it is important to rule out sexual victimization. Social withdrawal from classmates is another important sign.

2. Sexually explicit behavior. Stylized sexual behavior that includes either physical, written, or verbal behavior, sexualizing pictures or making sexual drawings, using sexual language that is not usual for the child's peer group, or wearing clothes that appear extreme and out of proportion to the child's peer group may be signs. These signs come to the teacher's attention through notes sent by the student, papers left in view, or comments heard. Teachers also may note that a student is developing a reputation for indiscriminate sexual activity.

3. Biopsychosocial changes. Symptoms of enuresis (urinary incontinence) or encopresis (soiling) that are noted during school hours. Other students may complain that the child smells. Other symptoms include the child's complaining of stomachaches, headaches, or urinary symptoms. A high index of suspicion should be maintained on children in whom there is a *sudden* change in behavior.

Investigating Suspected Sexual Victimization

There are several essential points to remember in investigating any suspected sexual victimization of a child. Physician Suzanne M. Sgroi identifies these key areas in terms of

1. Overall approach involves keeping an open mind, keeping cool, and staying alert to the situation as a potentially dangerous one.
2. The investigation should include medical examination by a physician who is knowledgeable regarding sexual victimization, a credible witness in court, and unafraid to participate in this area.
3. The medical examination should follow specific guidelines.
4. The interviewing should be for facts and be within therapeutic parameters. The child should be interviewed alone and the language and techniques should be appropriate to the developmental age of the child.

The investigation of suspected sexual victimization should include an approach toward child protection. Dr. Sgroi's guidelines regarding this component of the total investigation are as follows:

Approach toward Child Protection

A. *Reporting.* Be prepared to report *all* cases of child sexual assault to
   1. Child protective services.
   2. The Sex Crimes Analysis Unit (even if the facts of the case do not warrant or permit prosecution, a report should be made for statistical purposes if such an investigative and research unit exists).

B. *Avoiding Confrontation.* Avoid confrontation between the child victim and the alleged perpetrator whenever the alleged perpetrator is a family member. *Never* confront the alleged perpetrator with the child's own accusation against him or her in an intrafamily situation *unless* you are certain that the child or alleged perpetrator *can* and *will* be removed from the home. To permit or initiate this type of confrontation in the absence of an effective plan to protect the child from possible retribution by the perpetrator is to risk serious bodily injury or even death of the victim.

C. *Offender-Child Relationship.* Don't presuppose that the relationship between the child and perpetrator following the alleged incident will be negative if sexual assault actually occurred. On the contrary, a warm, affectionate, and loving relationship may exist and continue between the child and an incestuous parent. Observable evidence of spontaneous, fearless, and affectionate behavior between the child and alleged perpetrator neither supports nor disproves the allegation of sexual assault and should not be cited or treated as such.

D. *Sex Bias Concerning Targets.* Because females are traditionally regarded as the most common targets of sexual assault, it is easy to harbor a built-in bias that the only *child* victims of sexual assault are little girls. Do not overlook the very real possibility that little boys may be targets of sexual assault as well in both intrafamily and extrafamily situations. All too often attention is focused on female children in a situation where male children are equally or perhaps at greater risk, depending on the circumstances. Whenever child sexual assault is being investigated, both male and female children should be considered possible targets and interviewed and examined accordingly.

E. *Continuum of Exposure.* In general, the incident of intrafamily child sexual assault that comes to community or professional attention is rarely the first incident that has occurred within the family. Be aware that the incest phenomenon usually proves to be a continuum of exposure to sexual contact experienced by the child victim over a long period of time. A continuum of exposure should therefore be presupposed by the investigator unless specifically proved otherwise and examinations should proceed

accordingly, regardless of how long ago the alleged incident is said to
have occurred.

F. *Irresolution.* Every professional who is called upon to assist child victims
of sexual assault must learn to live with irresolution of many cases.
Frequently the total facts elicited by investigation will neither support nor
disprove the allegation. Do not automatically regard all *unproved* cases as
unfounded. Child victims of unproved cases are often more needy of
professional support and assistance than are proved victims of child sexual
assault. (1978, pp. 153-156)

Implications for School Personnel

The public-health concepts of primary, secondary, and tertiary intervention are
key to any program planning. In order for school personnel to be prepared to
deal with suspected as well as detected sexual victimization of children we
suggest the following:

School Protocol. School administrators should have a procedure for dealing
with sexual victimization, both when detected as well as if suspected. Resource
people within the school can help to provide a team approach to plan a protocol.
School personnel need to be familiar with the sexual abuse laws of their community. The community resources for providing psychosocial intervention and
treatment should be available to school personnel.

Teacher Response to Sexual Victimization. In those situations where a sexual
offense has been committed on the school grounds in full view of the children,
not only should the needs of the direct victim be addressed but attention should
also be given to the impact that witnessing such an assault has on the other
children. When the incident has been confined to one of exhibitionism, it will
be important for the teacher to discuss the event with the class using a
vocabulary or language that would be appropriate to the age level of the children
(for example, describing such behavior as silly and wrong and pointing out the
proper ways of behaving, such as, "We don't undress in public"). Children need
to be encouraged to report to their teachers any sexual approaches made to
them by adults. Teachers need to be alerted also to the fact that a child who has
been victimized and perhaps has missed school because of the incident may
find it very hard to return and face his classmates because of the embarrassment
he is facing over what has happened.

Prevention of Rape: Education and Community Coordination

A word needs to be said about the prevention of sexual assault. Families are concerned about this problem and very often will ask, "How can we teach our children about sexual assault before it happens?" Two suggestions can be made. First, parents and schools can help, and second, interagency program planning is important. The need for everyone to work together on this issue of prevention is essential. We emphasize that we do not have good data on how people successfully avoid sexual assault but we realize we must raise issues regarding prevention and thus offer the following issues for discussion.

Parents and Schools

Parents often ask, "What can I tell my child about rape? How can it be prevented? If it happens, what should I do?" In answer to these questions, we suggest some ideas that have been tried with children, offering them for discussion.

1. Parents should be encouraged to talk with their children before anything happens. In these talks: (a) Assess how much the child already knows about the subject. Some junior high and high schools are beginning to implement rape-education programs in their curricula. (b) Talk about encountering dangerous situations in general. What do children identify as dangerous; what dangerous situations have they already encountered, and how have they handled them? (c) Role-play some dangerous scenes with the children. Ask children what they would do if a stranger approached them to get in his car or if a man told them he would give them money if they did something for him. Also ask the children what they would do if confronted with a gun or knife, or it they were grabbed and pushed into a car. Talking it over and suggesting tactics they might think of provides an opportunity for parents to assess their children's reaction and point out alternatives in their thinking.

2. Parents can discuss with their children issues concerned with sexual assault. Parents can also reinforce previously taught general safety rules. (a) Protection in the home. Rules such as reporting all strange telephone calls to parents; not to let any strangers in the house; telephoning the police if they suspect any emergency and a parent is not available. (b) Protection of the self. Always travel with a friend or adult; avoid dark, deserted areas when outdoors; ask for directions only from authorized persons, such as a police officer. (c) Psychological self. Keep your mind alert and watch where you are going; rehearse in your mind what you would say if a stranger asked you a question or stopped you. (d) High-risk areas. Talk with school officials and police officers about dangerous areas known in the community; be knowledgeable regarding teenagers who hurt or pick on children.

3. Parents can discuss with their children what to do if they are threatened or actually assaulted. (a) If threatened, keep calm and try to talk your way

out of the situation. Try to get out of the situation in as safe a way as possible. (b) If attacked, try to keep a clear head. Observe the perpetrator for any identifying features. Focus your mind on survival and remember everything you can that will enable you to identify the person afterwards. Memorize the make of the car or license number, what he says to you, and any scars or distinguishing marks. (c) After the attack, escape safely and report to parents, police, or the hospital. Many agencies have victim services that can help the child and the family. Be sure to get follow-up care to decrease any chance of long-term symptoms.

4. The schools have a part to play in educating children to the laws of the society. History or social-studies classes are excellent for having children study state laws that are designed to protect them. Such study would help children to know the legal terminology as well as the reporting laws. Schools can teach the legal definitions of rape, incest, and more general child abuse so that children will know when someone is breaking the law. (a) If schools do teach the laws in class and children are aware that they can report parents, school nurses and police officers need to be prepared to work with children when they do report. Also, services, both immediate and follow-up, should be available.

In summary, the sexual victimization of children is an issue of increasing concern. Teachers are in key positions both to identify and to assist the child who is the target of such abuse. Interagency cooperation is necessary in such situations and teachers can take a leadership role in this enterprise.

References

Burgess, S.W., Holmstrom, L.L., and McCausland, M.P. 1978. Counseling young victims of their families. In A.Q. Burgess, A.N. Groth, L.L. Holmstrom, and S.M. Sgroi, eds. *Sexual assault of children and adolescents.* Lexington, Mass.: LexingtonBooks, D.C. Heath and Co.

Groth, A.N., and Birnbaum, H.J. 1979. *Men who rape: the psychology of the offender.* New York: Plenum.

Groth, A.N., and Burgess, A.W. 1977. Motivational intent in the sexual assault of children. *Criminal Justice and Behavior 4*(3): 253-264.

Groth, A.N., Burgess, A.W., and Holstrom, L.L. 1977. Rape: power, anger, and sexuality. *American Journal of Psychiatry 134*(11): 1239-1243.

Sgroi, S.M. 1978. Comprehensive examination of child sexual assault: diagnostic, therapeutic, and child protection issues. In A.W. Burgess, A.N. Groth, L.L. Holmstrom, and S.M. Sgroi, eds. *Sexual assault of children and adolescents.* Lexington, Mass.: LexingtonBooks, D.C. Heath and Co.

9

Outraged: What It Feels Like to Be an Abused Child

J. Zemdegs

I had a dream last night.[a] I thought these dreams had ended. But yesterday my mother phoned and the reminder was planted for when I would fall asleep. After all, I am twenty-nine years old, it has been eleven years since I experienced that same terror, frustration, rage—as does a caged animal knowing that danger is near. I guess it never really leaves. It's always there, just below the surface, waiting to spring to life.

I should explain the dream. It is based on a real-life happening. My father was in another quiet rage. My mother screaming at me in the background. I knew that if I didn't get out my father's rage would, and I risked mental and physical damage. Something inside me would eventually snap. I would realize that I couldn't—wouldn't—stay for the unfounded and useless cruelty. Like a terrified animal, seeing the one chance to escape, I would run, run, run, all the while fearing the large hands would snatch me back, just as I was reaching the point of freedom. My stomach felt sick, every limb tingled. I had to get free. The feeling of tremendous joy and enormous relief when I was safe would quickly be overriden by the feeling of helplessness, knowing I had nowhere to go but back home. The dream would change and I remember that my father somehow was catching up to me. I ran, but he followed, and that desperate terror increased as I felt him get closer and closer . . . I woke up.

It is hard to awaken from a dream that is so life-like. It takes a few minutes to realize it is just a dream. Those days *are* over. The fear is no longer needed, but it seems to taint my day. I remember how it *really* was.

Being abused becomes a part of every moment. It doesn't happen just once per week or once per day. One eats, drinks, and sleeps abuse. It's all-consuming.

There is a close similarity between being an abused child and a soldier who has been captured. Both are prisoners of war. As such, much can be learned about what it feels like to be an abused child, if one recalls all that has been written about the life of a prisoner of war (POW) in Vietnam.

What are the Problems?

As was the case of the Vietnam POW, survival (emotional and physical) is the

---

[a]The "I" in the text belongs to the young woman whose experiences comprise this chapter. The identity has been changed to preserve the privacy of the people involved. Every experience recorded has happened.

greatest problem for the abused child. This involves two important subdivisions; survival within the home (inside world) and in the world outside the home (outside world). One must understand how an abused child learns to survive a typical day.

The average school-aged child gets up thinking about the events that may take place that day; what to wear; what to eat for breakfast. Perhaps he is looking forward to chatting with his parents.

For the abused child, waking up is pleasant for about five seconds. A sick feeling in the pit of his stomach takes over as he remembers where he is and who he is. The one thought on his mind is how to get through the next hour until he has to leave for school. Subconsciously, he replays over and over in his mind maneuvers or "guerrilla war tactics" to outmaneuver the enemy and to protect himself from abuse.

For example: "What would happen if I say 'Hi' this way or that; if I wear my hair this way or that; if my facial expression shows this or that; if I eat or don't eat at all?" All of these would have certain effects on his parents. The effect he strives for is neutrality. All he desires is to escape from the house with the minimum of abuse and contact. If this proves successful he is out the door. Once outside, slight relaxation occurs. Now he begins again.

"How do I explain these marks on my face? If I say this, they will think that. How do I explain that my homework has not been done? If I tell them about the beating they may think this or that." This reasoning is more pleasant because his thinking is not based on fear, but rather on acceptance from the outside world and for his own pride. In the home there exists a no-win situation. "If you do you're damned and if you don't you're damned." The outside world is more lenient, more understanding. *You have a chance with them.*

For most children home is their security, their source of information about the world around them and about themselves. It is a place to go for comfort, trust, and friendship. It is the nucleus of their existence. For the abused child the exact opposite is true. The outside world becomes the place of comfort, approval, love, trust, friendship, security, attention, and guidance. It also becomes his source of information about himself and his surrounding environment. It eventually becomes the nucleus of his existence. The derelict on the street, teachers, friends, families of friends, janitor—all become his "substitute family." His guard is down. However, he does not trust blindly, for each person is tested. If people show they like or approve of him, he gives them his "all."

One might well imagine the many pitfalls which could arise from this:

1. *Dangers of trusting a stranger.* I could relate many close calls I had because anyone who was nice to me or looked as lost as I did was trustingly made a friend.

2. *Many painful letdowns.* The outside world does not realize just how much one needs them to care, to love, to guide. The smallest promise or word of kindness is treasured by the abused child. Normal forgetfulness or thoughtlessness by the outsider is interpreted as rejection by the abused child.

Survival—Inside World

In the home environment the abused child is constantly on the alert for danger. The enemy has proven to be erratic. What happened the day before and how he handled it doesn't hold true the next. He learns to expect the unexpected and to take nothing for granted. New maneuvers are constantly replacing old ones. He becomes an expert in observation, like a blind person who acquires fantastic hearing ability. Every sense becomes acutely tuned, especially sight and hearing.

He watches every movement of the eyes, every expression on his parents' faces, looking for some thread of a pattern to warn him of impending danger. He listens for the sound of their footsteps, light or heavy, where exactly they are in the house. He listens for voices—soft, loud, angry, frustrated, and for the sound of each word, straining to hear if his name is being mentioned.

When a soldier faces battle, the emotions commonly experienced are

1. pounding of the heart;
2. sickly feeling in the pit of the stomach;
3. cold sweat;
4. nausea;
5. shaking.

These are considered as normal battle reactions (Jones and Johnson, 1975).

I felt all of the above feelings every time I heard my name in my parents' whispered conversations or when I heard the sound of their footsteps, knowing full well the battle was to begin.

Avoiding isolation with my parents in the home was one way that I coped. I never stayed home from school, no matter how sick I felt.

Maintaining One's Sanity (Inside World)

From an early age an abused child senses that the outside world is different from the inside world, but trying to keep his sanity is extremely difficult. At home he is isolated. There are no witnesses. It's basically his word against his parents'. "Sick but slick" is an appropriate term for abusive parents. They look like human beings; they walk and talk like any other human being. They even manage to act fairly normal in front of other people (Wright, 1976). Thus it is very difficult for an eight-year-old to believe that "he's not crazy, the rest of the world is!" After all, parents to a child of early age are naturally considered to be "godlike" and can do no wrong. The following will explain this a little further.

One evening at the supper table, while my father was in another white rage (I say white because I could always tell by the white color of his face that he would soon explode) I was about to pick up my knife and fork to begin eating when all of a sudden he grabbed my wrist, squeezed it painfully, and screamed that I was going to stab him. To say I was shocked is putting it mildly. In fact, I was terribly hurt and frustrated because despite my honest protest, he refused to believe me. Later, I replayed this incident over in my mind in an attempt to make some sense of it (in my ten-year-old way). The more I did this the more absurd it became. Worst of all, the only witness was my mother and from past experience I knew her answer would not depend on the truth. As a result I could not distinguish what was real and what was not.

For the abused child there is no truth to explain the lies; no hero; no happy ending to restore his sanity.

Preoccupation with replaying the scene takes up an enormous amount of energy and most of all, time. From this alone, one can understand that the ability of an abused child to concentrate on anything else becomes severely limited. However, this mechanism is vital for the emotional survival of the abused child. One discrepancy is enough for the child to realize that the truth has been distorted.

Another way in which I maintained sanity was to look in the mirror. This simple procedure reassured me that in fact I was not the monster my parents insisted I was. "Mirrors never lie," and all that I could see staring back were the wide eyes of a little girl.

Maintaining Sanity (Outside World)

Keeping one's sanity in the outside world isn't a problem except in two situations:

1. If the child tells of the abuse and no one believes him. This hurts. He expects his parents not to believe him, but he doesn't expect his "family" (outsiders) to.
2. If someone has misunderstood what he has said or done this sets up a strong need to justify himself. The abused child cannot tolerate a strong need to justify himself. The abused child cannot tolerate unjustified rejection.

Thus, unknowingly, he becomes very defensive. Every point must be set straight and proven to his "family" because loss of their approval or affection could be emotionally fatal.

Coping with Pain (Inside World)

There are two kinds of pain that the abused child has to cope with, physical and emotional—this can be further subdivided: verbal and nonverbal.

Our society pays much attention to physical pain with damage. It's funny, but one can take the physical abuse much more than the emotional. Somehow, physical pain is more tangible. One has some control over it, but the emotional is more abstract, more painful. The attack is pointed directly at the soul—how one looks, walks, talks, feels, and thinks—all that holds a human being together. Nothing is left untorn.

One can have emotional pain without the physical pain, but cannot have physical pain without the emotional pain and scarring.

When a child cuts himself he goes to his parents for them to "kiss it better" and bandage the wound, but what does the child do when the physical pain (cut, bruise, and so on) is inflicted by the parents? Who puts the bandage on and "kisses it better"? In most cases, the abused child wouldn't dare to ask for a bandage. The parents would interpret this as the child pointing to the wound and saying, "Look at what you have done."

How does a child cope with the pain he is not able to acknowledge? In two possible ways: (1) he learns to control the pain. (2) he learns to administer his own original first aid and to do it discreetly. Controlling pain comes with practice.

I remember regularly coming home from skating, inevitably a few minutes late. My hands, due to the lack of proper clothing, were painful and swollen from the cold. My father had a knack of zeroing in on the most vulnerable spots (that is, as soon as I got home he sent me downstairs and strapped my hands, sometimes it seemed for an eternity). I cannot describe to you how painful this was, but I coped with it in two ways:

1. I knew what was coming, so psychologically I prepared for it on the way home. I would force myself to remember how it felt the last time and that the pain only lasted a limited time.
2. While being strapped I would concentrate on anything but the pain. In agony I would go up to my room, stand by the radiator and look at myself in the mirror. Telling myself that the pain would soon leave helped. What helped a little more was the self-reminder that I was not a monster.

The POWs in Vietnam coped with their imprisonment by using a mechanism termed "passive resistance." An abused child uses this to its fullest extent. An example of this mechanism: during a beating he observes that if he shows too much fear then he gives the enemy pleasure. He must also show enough fear in order not to incur any additional unnecessary beating. The abused child learns to become a fine actor. The cues bring forth a "happy medium" of fear, crying, and so on.

As stated earlier, emotional pain is much harder to control and comfort. After being physically abused, the emotional pain far outweighs the physical pain. The torment lies deep in his soul. Normally when a child is hurt by something that was said, the parent comforts this intangible hurt by hugging and talking to the child. When there is no one to comfort the abused child, the child learns to comfort himself in the same way. He hugs and talks to himself. This usually is accomplished by assuming the fetal position. In my research I noted that many POWs, after being abused, did exactly the same thing.

The most painful memory I have stems from an episode of physical abuse. I was ten or eleven years old. My mother held me down across my bed while my father strapped me, and not being too selective, managed to strap me all over my body. Yes, the physical pain was bad, but the emotional torture and scar that it left was unbeatable. Pain is a funny thing. I always found that it helped to have my hands free to try to protect my body (no matter how futile).

What was important was the act itself, the ability to do something, to have some control over an uncontrollable situation, no matter how little. This time that minute comfort was denied me. It was being tied down that tore me apart. That outraged me. Not the pain from the belt. Not the senselessness of the vicious beating, but being tied down. Being forced to openly accept their abuse.

The child, while being abused, cannot ignore the nonverbal communication. His parents' eyes are full of hatred. Their faces are contorted in rage. No words are necessary to imprint forever in his memory the full fury of their hatred and rage. And all directed at "him." A child is no fool and no matter what the parent, teacher, or social worker may tell him later, the imprint is burned in his memory and nags at his conscience.

The saying "Sticks and stones may break my bones, but words will never hurt me" is opposite to what the abused child feels.The "sticks-and-stones" part of the pain is controllable, but the abusive words always hurt. I remember repeatedly trying to block out what my mother was saying. Inevitably a word would get through and the hurt, frustration, and anger would swell to a breaking point. I would break my self-imposed silence. This only added fuel to the raging fire.

There were three residual effects: (1) pain from the abusive words; (2) anger at my parents for saying these things; (3) the confusion and burning pain of self-doubt—that nagging, sick feeling that what they said might be true. Considering how fragile self-confidence and self-esteem are to any normal school-aged child this additional load of self-doubt was often unbearable.

Fear

The fear of the known and of the unknown plagues an abused child almost twenty-four hours a day. Yes, even while he sleeps. The sources of fear include fear his parents will embarrass him; fear of being scarred for life, especially about the face; fear of not being able to cope with the next day; fear that the outside world will get to know the *real* him, the one his parents keep referring to as "the monster"; and there is always the fear of emotional and physical abuse.

Fear is also present when the child is outside the home environment. It is a different kind of fear. It lacks the terror aspect felt in the home. In the outside world the abused child fears rejection.

The Problem of Being "Different"

An abused child feels that he doesn't "fit" into either the inside world or the outside world. The inside world has shown him this, not only by the abusive treatment but by being left out of the family unit and being told that he's different than the rest of the family.

Also, the abused child senses that he doesn't totally fit in with the outside world. He knows that he is different but does not understand why. His problems are not the problems of most school-aged children. His worries are not theirs. His concept of happiness, his priorities in life, and his needs are different and are based on different reasons. Happiness to an abused child is a very elusive feeling, that is, not being beaten. My mother used to play "cruel" games on me. Happiness to me was not giving her pleasure while she played them.

Worrying about what kind of clothing to wear was never a problem for me. I was never given a choice. My mother would buy me a pair of shoes from the "bargain basement" of a department store. If I said they didn't fit, she would get very insulted and would threaten to return them. I would then have to do without. Now I had a choice. If the shoes were not too hideous-looking I would suffer the pain. If they were, I would keep my old pair of shoes despite the holes.

This feeling of "being different" is accentuated by looking different. I remember when I was in grade seven my mother insisted I wear her winter coat. Needless to say, it was very big and hung to the ground. I coped with this every day by going into an old garage that was just up the street where I would painstakingly pin the coat up. God knows what it looked like, but to me I felt it looked like everyone else's. Unfortunately, I had to go home for lunch, which meant that I had to undo all the pins before reaching home. This process had to be repeated four times a day.

An abused child also feels that he looks different because he bears the marks of a beating. He sees that he is the only one with the swollen nose, black eyes, and scratches. To match my face, my mother would "hack off" my hair with a razor blade (my father would hold me in the chair until I stopped struggling). I was then forced to sit down and have a normal breakfast with the whole family. My heart would burst after these episodes because she had left my hair only an eighth of an inch long. My hope for outside approval, with most of my scalp showing, was slim. There is nowhere one can hide one's head.

The fear of outside rejection and my pride prevented me from giving up. I would secretly pick up two fallen strands of hair and hide them. Then, on my way to school (I was a busy girl before school), I would tape them to the sides of my head. In class I would worry whether the curls were lopsided or if one of them would fall off. Inevitably one did. My classmates were always very kind to me. They refrained from making any comments about how atrocious it looked, until a month or two later. One can appreciate how time-consuming just these two processes were to a ten-year-old child. Again, this process was vital to my emotional survival. It held off the pain of degradation until I could cope with it.

Friendships

As discussed earlier, an abused child's outlook on life is different from those of his peers. Because of these differences it is difficult for him to develop and maintain "normal" friendships. Frequently, an abused child is not allowed to have friends either because (1) his parents refuse to allow him to visit friends' homes or have his friends visit his, or (2) an abused child is too embarrassed to have his friends visit his home for fear of the way his parents will act in their presence.

An abused child's need to give love and be loved is as great as any other child's, but he is denied love by his parents, and, therefore, looks for love in "friendships" in the outside world. However, the "needs" that he is trying to fulfill require that his friends replace the love of a mother, father, sister, and so on. This is an impossible need to fulfill outside of a family. Therefore, the friend fails to live up to this unrealistic concept of friendship. The abused child feels let down, hurt, and may terminate the friendship feeling rejected.

These feelings of hurt are made even more painful if the abused child is taught that only two extremes exist in life (that is, right or wrong, love or hate, black or white). The abused child has not learned of that "gray area" wherein it is possible to dislike something about someone and still like them; that it is possible to forgive and forget; that people are forgetful, make mistakes, and are sometimes even thoughtless. The abused child knows little of "forgiving and forgetting." His parents never afforded him that luxury. Therefore, a mistake is equated with being "bad."

So much is denied an abused child that when a friendship is made and it gives him a positive feeling about himself, he becomes very possessive. Overcoming jealousy, learning to share, and learning to "forgive and forget" are the hardest concepts an abused child has to learn. Again, he has great difficulty maintaining friendships when he is not allowed to accept his friends' invitations to do things and eventually the invitations cease.

Concentration

An abused child's ability to concentrate on his responsibilities and the world around him may be severely reduced. He may be too preoccupied with "survival." This may be especially noted with respect to school grades, that is, a gradual decline. I was an A student until grade six. This fell to a B by the time I finished grade seven and I was passed on trial and subsequently made to repeat the grade. My marks remained borderline until I went to nursing school, where they sharply rose (I was not living at home).

Failing in school presents complicating problems. Shame of failing, loss of group belonging (since the rest of his classmates proceed to the next grade and he is left behind), and the loss of affection from his teacher, who expected more from him. To the abused child this means another blow at emotional survival. Now he has to start all over again—trying to fit in.

Communication

The family is a resource of information for the average school-aged child, a place where the child can try out his ideas about himself and the outside world. For the abused child, this resource is often cut off. Where then does he get his information from? Who does he tell his troubles to in order to put them into perspective? Who answers all the inquisitive questions children have about the outside world? For me there was no one.

I learned through trial and error that I could not ask my parents even the most simplest of questions. Why?

1. If I was hurt by what another child said my parents would agree—I was bad, ugly, and so on.
2. If my mother asked, "What was wrong?" and I told her, all of a sudden an emotional storm would break out. Suddenly she would turn the most simple problem into a major crisis. She would be at the center of it all. Somehow she managed to turn the whole situation around, so that she was the one being slighted. Everything I ever did would be raked up. I was always left wondering what the original problem was.

Questions I had about the outside world, that is, geography, and so on, were also impossible to ask for a number of reasons.

1. How does one talk to someone who usually doesn't acknowledge your presence and on many previous occasions has totally ignored your questions?
2. Even saying "Hi" begins to stick in one's throat. One feels two-faced—on one hand trying to pretend that nothing is wrong and on the other hand knowing full well they hate you.

As a result, an abused child uses all his powers of observation and perception in order to find the answers and makes extensive use of the outside world, that is, teachers, friends, strangers, and so on. Many problems arise from this. Outsiders do not realize just how dependent the abused child is on their answers being complete and correct. The abused child often takes their every word verbatim.

In addition, the abusive parents make it very clear that the child has very little to say that is worthwhile. The abused child may find it difficult to believe that the outside world thinks any different. Therefore, the abused child tends to be a better listener than talker.

Feelings of Guilt

Guilt feelings are often present in the mind of an abused child. The basic source is from the "inside world," but what is worse, it spills over into the outside world. What does an abused child feel guilty about? Everything!

The abused child has learned that he is the cause of most unpleasant events that happen in his immediate world. For example, if someone looks at him in the wrong way he is plagued with trying to figure out what he has done to offend them. Thank God someone pounded into my head, at the age of twenty-three, that something or someone else could cause another's displeasure.

In the abusive environment where I spent the "best years of my life," there were no moments to treasure (at least none that I care to). We existed from one crisis to another. And guess who was the cause of it all? Yours truly. For example, the dog running away from home (the environment was so bad even he wouldn't stay), the loss of one of my mother's friends because she was caught lying, ruining Christmas because a dress my mother bought me didn't fit, but mostly for the unpleasant atmosphere that existed because I was being physically and emotionally abused.

That much guilt is very hard to shrug off the shoulders of a ten-year-old child. It just gets too heavy. As one can imagine, this weight of guilt has a knack of retarding one's growth emotionally.

Degradation

The dictionary defines "degrade" as "to reduce from a higher to a lower rank of degree; to deprive of office of dignity; to lower the physical, moral, or intellectual character of" (*Webster's*, 1959).

This form of torture was extensively used on the POW to "break his spirit."

To use this form of torture on any child is monstrous. Abusive parents are thus accused. They deprive a child of dignity by holding him down to beat him, by forcing him to smile and pretend nothing was done after they marred his face, and so on. By forcing him to face all the ridicule the world has to offer, *alone*. And by verbally tearing at a child's soul.

An abused child uses whatever coping mechanisms the human mind has to offer. Unfortunately, they are not always successful, but somehow he gathers just enough strength to try one more time.

Outrage

To give the inexperienced a better understanding of the word "outrage," I again return to the dictionary: "to subject to violent injury; implies exceeding one's power to bear or endure; excites hatred" (*Webster's*, 1959).

The well-known saying "swallow one's pride" applied to the abused child, but it's not only pride that he must swallow. It is also his love—for there is no one around who wants to receive it in a healthy way. It is also his pain, his yearning for love, his frustrations, his desperate need to belong. And there are, of course, his feelings of hatred and anger.

In our society we bury the garbage and waste that cannot be disposed of in any other way. So it is for human beings. We all have a reservoir for emotional garbage to be buried, those emotions or feelings that cannot be disposed of. For the abused child, his reservoir fills at an unusually fast rate. Every minute of abuse excites "hatred" and "outrage." A normal reaction is an abnormal happening.

This in itself starts a new war internally, a very private war that even the child is unaware of. No one is there to tell him that he has a right to his feelings. The only cry of outrage that the child hears is his own. There is no one else to lend support. There is no cry of outrage from his parents, sisters, brothers, neighbors, and especially from the outside world. Our society states very clearly, "Thou shalt love and honor thy parents." To hate one's parents? No. Never! That would be wrong. So tightens the lid on the now very volatile pressure cooker of emotions.

What prevents a pressure cooker from exploding? A safety-release valve. When the pressure inside exceeds that which the cooker can bear, it lets off some of the steam. This excess steam can be called "overflow." Make no mistake. The volatile contents are still intact.

The feelings of an abused child are very similar to the steam of a pressure cooker. The overflow can be compared to hostile behaviors in the form of delinquency, disruptive behavior in the classroom, and so on. Sometimes the pressure, for whatever reason, builds up faster than the safety valve can let steam blow off. In the case of a pressure cooker, it explodes or self-destructs. For the abused child? Self-destructive behavior, or abusive behavior in the fullest sense of the word.

Intervention by "Society"

I remember the outside world being very kind to me. Some of my friends' parents must have sensed that I was a lost soul. They talked to me, gave me treats after school, and just generally seemed to take me superficially under their wing. This meant so much to me and gave me a little relief from my suffering, what I call "battle fatigue." However, this also presented problems. My life began to be placed in jeopardy by well-meaning parents and society.

My first episode of society "wisely interfering" was when my mother had the school psychologist interview me. I think she was hoping that the psychologist would say I was mentally ill. Apparently I passed with flying colors, but to my horror the abuse took a sudden turn for the worse. It was a few years ago I learned why. The kindly psychologist told my mother gently that if she stopped beating me I would fair a lot better and would even stop hating her.

One can see the term "sick but slick" is perfect. The psychologist saw a very concerned, well-dressed parent only wanting to help her daughter. Little did she know my mother. It is very interesting to note that I would have told her what my mother was like and what dangers lay before me if she told my mother, but she never asked!

My next experience of "society" interceding was my own doing. When I was in grade seven, I had a classmate who was a ward of the Catholic Children's Aid Society. She described to me what sounded like heaven, that is, no beating. Armed with a donated streetcar ticket, I followed some ambiguous directions, feeling that at long last I would be safe. After all, my friend swore that they would help me. I got lost and went to a police station. When I mentioned I was looking for the Children's Aid Society I could see that raised too many questions, so I told them I was going to visit a friend. The policeman, still skeptical, gave me very vague directions. It was dark when I finally, and quite by accident, reached my destination. I remember walking in, going over to the front desk, and telling them I wanted to stay. I gave them an example of abuse regarding my mother beating me when I misspelled a word while she helped me with my homework. The next thing I remember they said they had talked to my father and were sending me home in a taxi. They told me everything would be just fine.

When I arrived home my parents were on their way out. They wouldn't look at me or talk to me, but my father turned to my sister and brother and asked if they were afraid to be in the same house with me. I didn't get beaten that night. Perhaps the society helped, but the next week the abuse again was stepped up to an even fiercer level because now I had shamed my parents (and they, of course, maintained innocence in the matter).

Another episode began with a telephone call. I had no idea who was on the phone or what was being said. The next thing I knew, my mother was running down the stairs screaming and began punching me. I was cornered by her blows between the kitchen counter and the table. I thought I was going to throw up from the full force of her fist hitting my ten-year-old stomach. My father finally dragged her off me. I thought he might help with a word or a look, but instead he proceeded to drag me to the cellar stairs and throw me down them. During the battle I pieced together that my girl friend's mother had called. Apparently she implied that from her observations, my mother's treatment of me left something to be desired. In her own way, she too thought she had helped. Little did she know what agony I was going through while she had her cup of tea and contemplated what she had said.

One day, after a night of beating, I arrived at school looking like I had been in a terrible street fight. My face was swollen. I had bruises around my eyes and scratches. By this time I had realized that telling society anything was not the smart thing to do, that is if I wanted to avoid being hurt. Since I looked the part, I thought an acceptable excuse would be to say I had been in a street fight. My friends didn't seem too skeptical, so I got through most of the day without much trouble. At the end of the day my teacher, who I really liked, cornered me. I finally broke down and reluctantly poured my story out. I shall never forget the look on his face. He was shocked. All he could say was, "I can't believe it. I know your father. He taught me when I was in high school." Nothing further was said. In fact, the teacher avoided any further individual contact with me.

Yes. You see, my father was a high-school teacher. Very well respected. He was even head of a department. Amazing, isn't it? A child abuser teaching your children, day in, day out. He even sang in the church choir. Both my parents never missed Sunday Mass. Never drank or smoked and were considered to be law-abiding citizens.

Who Will Listen to the Children?

Much has been written about the many undetected cases of child abuse. No wonder. Who listens to the children? Society is often "hung up" on theories that adults are being manipulated by children and perhaps feels that information gathered from a child is not worth listening to.

Often, society never bothers to ask children about their feelings or whether they want society to intervene. After all, who knows better how his parents are going to react than the child himself? He has had to make it his business to know for the sake of survival. Ultimately, the decision of society's intervention should rest with the person who has to live with the consequences. The abused child.

Listen to the abused children. They have much to tell. And tell they will. No, don't ask them to tell on their parents. They will refuse to do that out of fear of reprisal, out of a sense of pity for the parent, and what it would do to them. And out of the love/hate emotion they truly feel for their parents.

I remember I made a decision not to go to the police. I had proof, the marks on my face, and so on, and despite the urging of a friend's father, I could not bring myself to do it, mostly because I felt I wouldn't win (because I knew I wouldn't be believed—much like the rape victim in our courts; the victim becomes the accused) and because I could envision what it would do to my father's career as a teacher. The price seemed to be too high to pay. I would only be returned to the abusive environment anyway.

Listen to the children. They will tell you how they feel—indirectly. They will tell you of the pain and what is important to them. One must be careful not to ask them out of pity.

They just need someone who asks because they care and who will not look away from the view they see.

What Happens to the Abused Child When Released from His Home Environment?

I remember when I finally left home to attend nursing school. I somehow felt that everything would be much better once free from abuse. I couldn't have been further from the truth. I had learned through trial and error how to cope well in the abusive environment. I knew who the enemy was and how to survive. My main purpose in life was to be released from the war mentally and physically intact. I accomplished my mission.

What I never realized was I didn't know how to cope in a normal environment. I knew nothing of a world without pain, torment, and fear. And freedom? Suddenly I was without purpose. Worst of all, I didn't know what was happening. It was so gradual. There were two major stresses going on at the same time, that of outrage (the new inner war) and now the pressures of being in a new environment I was not prepared for.

To get a better understanding of what happens to the now-released child we must return to our original concept. That of the POW and Vietnam veteran. Most of us are familiar with stories told of the Vietnam vet who, after returning to the United States, goes on a shooting spree ending in his own death. The POW who survives years of captivity only to fall apart when returned home. Why?

The term for this recent and growing phenomena is *major (delayed) stress response syndrome*. Basically it is a delayed normal reaction to an abnormal situation. It occurs after a latency period of apparent relief (usually about a year later).

In the case of the soldier, in his training and his tour of duty in Vietnam he is exposed to a climate of fear of the known and the unknown. Fear of unexpected violence and danger. The soldier's main purpose for that time is to survive.

This is much like our abused child, is it not? The soldier also uses specialized coping mechanisms for war. Examples of these are "passive resistance," denial, and numbing. Like the abused child, the soldier believed he too would be fine once he was sent back home intact. What actually happened, in a significant number of cases, was the opposite. For the first few months the Vietnam vet coped well because he was still using the same coping mechanisms, but to a lessening degree, as he realized danger was no longer present. Once these coping mechanisms were fully relaxed the delayed stress reaction took over.

The abused child also experiences a slow relaxing of his warlike coping mechanisms. The fear is no longer needed. These coping mechanisms like the POW's, help keep the lid on the pressure cooker of emotional inner war and outrage.

Some of the symptoms of this syndrome include

1. severe depression and anxiety;
2. emotional depression and anxiety;
3. guilt feelings;
4. persistent abdominal complaints without evidence of gastrointestinal disease;
5. nightmares;
6. reaction rage;
7. frustration at not being able to make any sense out of their past and not being able to talk about it;
8. secondary effects of self-destructive behavior and antisocial behavior (Horowitz and Solomon, 1975).

The Vietnam veteran has difficulty in being successfully helped by individual therapy sessions. This is attributed to

1. the therapist's not being familiar with the symptoms of the stress syndome;
2. the therapist's not understanding how the veteran felt and not knowing how to help. That is, many vets were told: "Why are you dwelling on the past?" or "It's over. Forget it."

I, too, ran into this type of statement. I also concur with the feeling that it takes another vet to understand the problems of a vet. In my case another abused child.

The vets started rap sessions with other vets in the presence of a therapist. This has now proven quite successful. What they found most helpful was being told, "It's a normal reaction to an abnormal situation."

It is interesting to note that I experienced all of the above, starting approximately eight months after I had left home and lasting for six years. Why so long? Because there was no one to tell me what it was, why it was, and how it got to be. There was no one to tell me that it was a normal reaction to an abnormal situation. And most of all, there was no one who could or would listen to what I had to say. No one to understand.

I was fortunate because, simultaneously, I was being educated about people and their relationships, both formally and informally, with other people. Formally, by taking sociology and psychology courses at school. Informally, by observing all the people around me such as other nursing students, teachers, and patients.

During that time I could be likened to a mad scientist. Watching, questioning, and absolutely fascinated by how my friends' parents talked, thought, and acted. Oh yes, I saw the bickering, the "my parents don't understand me" syndrome, but they all had what I never dreamed of. A softness within the interaction, no matter what problems there were.

Through this mechanism, I realized that there was a huge puzzle I was beginning to solve, step by step. I began to understand why the puzzle was there and during the next six years I laboriously fit the pieces together.

The largest and most important piece slammed into place quite by accident when I was twenty-six. A patient happened to mention that she was a psychologist on the abuse team at a well-known hospital. Without mentioning any reason for my inquisitiveness, I asked her the definition of abuse, a description of abusive parents, and if it was possible for only one child to be beaten where there was more than one in a family, and if so, why? Her answers brought a sudden gust of fresh air, and with it a tremendous feeling of relief. The last piece was in place.

I could then make sense out of my past. I finally gave up hope of ever receiving love from my parents (in any kind of normal way).

Like the POW, I feel that the twenty-two years I spent in fear, agony, outrage—years spent yearning for something I was never to have (parental love and acceptance) were wasted years.

No, the *outrage* never leaves, but we have learned to live together and to respect each other.

Recommendations to Help the Abused Child

1. *Educate "society" about the problems of child abuse.* Child abuse is an illness much like alcoholism. Information about it should be made available to all, to help identify cases of child abuse and understand the causes and effects of child abuse.

2. *Educate the primary-health-care workers* on how to detect child abuse. Questions about his treatment by parents should be a standard question asked on routine histories. This could identify potential child abusers, and education could be started for them.
3. *Start "rap" sessions for abused children* similar in concept to those of the vets.
4. *Set up drop-in centers for abused children* located in the school system, in a church, and so on.
5. *Start a hot line for abused children* for them to talk to someone after abuse or when they need relief from "combat."
6. *Educate the abused children about why they are being abused:* their reactions to the abuse are normal; their potential to abuse their own children. To stop the abusive cycle that exists, we need
   a. education about abuse;
   b. self-discipline;
   c. a will to succeed;
   d. support groups similar to AA for alcoholics.
7. *Organize a network of teachers and nurses to help and support the abused child.* This is his vital link with the outside world and can provide him with much-needed comfort.
8. *Listen to the children.* In cases of suspected abuse listen to the child. He knows the circumstances and problems that affect him more than anyone else. His opinions must be heard and respected.
9. *Study the needs of abused children after they leave the abusive environment by*
   a. studying the POWs and Vietnam vets;
   b. studying the relationship between suicide rates and abused children;
   c. setting up a program to ease these home—war—veterans back into a normal environment.

References

Horowitz, M.J., and Solomon, G. 1975. Predictions of delayed stress response in Vietvets. *Journal of Social Issues 31,* 67–80.

Jones, F.D., and Johnson, A.W., Jr. 1975. Medical and psychological treatment policy and practice in Vietnam. *Journal of Social Issues 31,* 49–65.

Webster's New Dictionary. 1959. Springfield, Mass.: G.&G. Merriam Co.

Wright, L. 1976. The sick but slick syndrome. *Journal of Clinical Psychology 32,* 41–45.

**Part III
Professional and
Interprofessional Response**

10 The School's Role in the Coordination of Child-Protection Efforts

Margot Breton

In the literature on child abuse and neglect there is a growing recognition of the need for school-based child-protection efforts (Breton, 1979; Lee, 1980; ten Bensel and Berdie, 1976; Murdock, 1970; Gil, 1964). There is also a burgeoning awareness of the necessity for schools to link up with neighborhood-based natural helping networks (Garbarino, 1980). Child-protection teams are seen as the most effective mechanism through which school staff can be helped to detect, report, and participate in the treatment of child abuse and neglect, whereas linking up with neighborhood networks is seen as a method of primary prevention of child maltreatment.

To advocate these two types of efforts on behalf of children is to demand that schools, already expected to meet many different needs of children, apart from their needs to learn, take on yet additional functions. If we make this demand, we must be ready to prevent problems of system overload. Therefore, ways must be found to facilitate the incorporation of these child-protection functions into the traditional educational system.

One effective way is to assign to an individual the responsibility of coordinating these functions. Without such coordination, functions will be unnecessarily duplicated and may even operate at cross purposes. For instance, an in-school child-protection team may spend hours trying to figure out who, in the community, could best serve as a parent aide to an abusive mother while a neighborhood group connected to the school could propose a number of such persons within a matter of minutes.

To further facilitate the incorporation of new functions into a system, it is important that their coordination be done without unduly upsetting the system— in other words, it must be done at minimum cost. In the present context, this implies finding someone, within the school staff, who will most naturally step into the role of coordinator, and whose appointment as such will be accepted by the staff. But as this person will be coordinating the effects of a school-based inter- professional team *and* neighborhood-based natural helping networks, she[1] will need to be accepted not only by the school staff but also by various groups and natural helpers[2] in the community. This means she must be capable of moving freely from school to community, be as familiar with and knowledgeable about one milieu as the other, and especially have as much credibility in one environment as in the other.

School social workers, public health nurses, counselors, teachers, and psychologists increasingly operate at the interface of schools and their communities. (Davis and McEwen, 1977; Easton, 1978; Forrer, 1975; Griggs and Gale, 1977; Meares, 1977; Tagg, 1976; Volpe, 1976). According to a recent survey,

> school social work today is in transition from a predominantly clinical-casework approach to solving students' problems to that of home-school-community liaison and educational counselling with the child and his parents. (Meares, 1977, p. 200)

Depending on circumstances, any of these professionals could take on the coordinating function just described. To do so, however, they must expand their perception of their role to include this specific function.

This chapter attempts to define what this expanded role involves. First, a brief look is cast at the coordinator's role on the child-protection team. Second, a description is given of the role in relation to neighborhood helping networks. Third, some of the principal tasks involved in coordinating the efforts of child-protection teams and those of natural helping networks are specified. In conclusion, an indication is given of the measures the coordinator can take to minimize the problems which may develop from closer collaboration between school and community.

The Coordinator's Role on the Child-Protection Team

The role of the coordinator on the school child-protection team should be formulated so as to maximize her effectiveness both within the school and within the community. Because schools are still, to a great extent, systems based on authority, the effectiveness of anyone assuming the role of coordinator will depend on the kind of official backing received and on the kind of authority granted within the system. For in authority-conscious systems, people who carry no authority are often unable to get others to take them or their endeavors seriously. Therefore, to ensure that both school staff and people in the community recognize the importance of the link-up between them, and actively support it, the person responsible for the link-up should also assume the leadership of the school child-protection team.

By becoming team leader and assuming a formal position of authority within the school system, the coordinator would also increase the probability of receiving the backing of the school principal, without which her efforts, and the efforts of team and community groups, would all be in vain. School principals are *the* supreme authority in the schools and they tend to recognize and support people who occupy positions of authority. For this reason the coordinator of the school child-protection team and the neighborhood-based natural helping networks should also be the protection-team leader. In other circumstances, anyone on the team who would be skilled in facilitating the group process could assume the position of leader (Brill, 1976; Kane, 1975; Lee, 1980; Wise, Beckhard, Rubin, and Kyte, 1974).

The Coordinator's Role in Relation to Neighborhood Natural Helping Networks

To play an effective role in relation to the natural helping networks that exist in the school's neighborhood, the coordinator must recognize their potential as a means of preventing child abuse and neglect. Furthermore, she must be prepared to perceive and relate to natural helpers as peers, without which her interaction will come to naught, as Collins and Pancoast point out in their study of the "Day Care Neighbor Service": "The welfare worker remarked that . . . she did not become cognizant of the helping potential of Mrs. C., and Mrs. Y., until she began to work with them as colleagues" (1972, p. 93).

Convinced of the preventive potential of natural helping networks and ready to treat natural helpers as equals, the coordinator can then take on a number of tasks which will result in productive interactions with these networks. These tasks should include consulting with groups and individuals in the neighborhood, supporting the development of, and leading community groups, enabling community participation in school programs, working on behalf of existing groups for the use of school space, and reaching out in the community to detect natural helpers and natural helping networks.

Consultation

The coordinator will want to offer her services as a consultant to groups and individuals in the community, either on an intermittent or on a regular basis, in a manner similar to that of professionals acting as consultants to Parents' Anonymous groups (Holmes, 1978). The key here is role flexibility; the coordinator must be prepared to interact with natural helping networks in the way both she and they judge appropriate, remembering that mutual-help groups can act "as self-sufficient programs, concurrent treatment programs, [or] as sources of information and users of consultation" (Powell, 1975, p. 756). This consultative role will be instrumental in fostering a climate of goodwill between school and community, for people do welcome expert help and advice when it is not imposed on them. The coordinator can share her expertise in such areas as the use of small-group processes, helping networks to iron out interactional problems, resource information and referral, helping groups and individuals to get connected with various welfare and social institutions, and personal and family counseling.

Group Leadership

There often exists, in neighborhoods, potential mutual-help groups which never get established for want of proper encouragement and leadership in the initial stages of group development. We know, indeed, that most successful self-help groups had some professional input at their origin (Caplan and Killilea, 1976). The coordinator who is community oriented, and who is already connected to some neighborhood networks, is in a position to detect this unmet demand for leadership and to act upon it. This does not mean that she will personally take on the leadership of all these potential groups. She may, and should in terms of her credibility as a community member, lead some groups, but she should also enlist the support of as many other leaders as possible, for this is vital in assuring the recognition of the importance of such group services. She should recruit and supervise leaders from both the school and the community: teachers may be interested in leading particular groups; nursing, social-work, education, or psychology students can be enlisted as part of their practicum training in the school, and natural helpers from the community can be supported in their wish to be of service.

Community Participation in School Programs

Recognizing the helper-therapy principle, which states that those who help are helped most (Riessman, 1965), the coordinator will endeavor to find ways of introducing people from the neighborhood into appropriate school programs. This could mean asking women to serve as lunch ladies, working in the cafeteria and overseeing the lunch period, or inviting talented individuals, unemployed young people, or isolated mothers, for instance, to help out with arts-and-crafts classes, or getting the known nurturers or mothering types to act as aides in day-care programs or to participate in classes on child management.

In any given community, there are many capable individuals who would be willing to help the local school fulfill its purpose. It is usually the neighborhood natural helping networks who know about these individuals and who are able to reach them. Therefore, the coordinator should use the networks as sources of information and enlist their help in planning and organizing the participation of members of the community in various school programs. For such joint community-school efforts to be successful, the idea of community participation must be accepted by both parties. Promoting such an idea will be a major task of the coordinator.

Advocacy

Furthering the idea of community participation in school programs is one aspect of the public-relations function the coordinator must assume. The other is advocating the use of school space by community groups. The school principal may have to be convinced that these groups will act responsibly and not damage school property: this is a common concern on the part of principals. On the other hand, some groups may have negative feelings toward an institution they perceive as powerful and authoritarian and be reluctant to meet in a school.

But self-help groups often have difficulty finding an appropriate meeting place, and the neighborhood school certainly appears more normal and less threatening an institution than, for example, a social-work agency or a mental-health center. Therefore, if it is possible for a school to provide space for groups, the coordinator should make the necessary arrangements to ensure that the possibility becomes a reality.

Reaching Out

As she becomes familiar with the neighborhood and its inhabitants, the coordinator should be on the alert to detect unknown natural helpers and emerging natural helping networks and to offer them the school's support. It is a real tragedy when people who are eager to do something for themselves, and for others, remain ignored, while at the same time there are children in the neighborhood school desperately in need of the kind of individual attention no teacher can be expected to provide. The integration of these two groups should be one of the main priorities of the coordinator.

Coordinating the Efforts of Child-Protection Teams and Neighborhood Natural Helping Networks

Bringing together people who want to help the children who need help can be a preventive or a rehabilitative endeavor. In either case, it is a task suited for the person who coordinates the efforts of school and community on behalf of maltreated children. Such a coordinator will obviously be concerned with questions of prevention, detection, reporting, and treatment of child abuse and neglect. To determine more precisely what is involved in this coordinating role, it will be useful to look at these questions separately.

Prevention

In order to capitalize on the preventive potential of neighborhood natural helping networks, the coordinator must first help the school staff to become aware of this potential. This she can do most effectively through her participation on the protection team. It is from that base, so to speak, that she can disseminate the idea of cooperating with the networks.

This cooperation can then take a variety of forms. One is to support existing groups through consultation, leadership, or the provision of space, as indicated earlier. Another is to develop programs for high-risk families, such as a school-based center manned by neighborhood volunteers. A different type of prevention program involves expanding school curricula to inform students about normal human development, child abuse, and ways to prepare for parenthood (Broadhurst, 1975). This program, in turn, can be expanded to offer information on child development and child management to members of the community, who would first be contacted by natural helpers.

Many schools presently sponsor a variety of informal adult-education programs, such as seminars and evening workshops on parental discipline, changing sexual mores, or teenaged drug problems. However, these programs often do not reach the parents who need them most. The coordinator should involve neighborhood natural helpers in a reaching-out effort aimed at ensuring that school-based programs are accessible to the most needy families in the community. Thus the potential of natural helping networks to prevent child maltreatment would be effectively tapped.

Detection

Professional attention in the area of child abuse and neglect has been focused mainly on the very young child. Almost half of the maltreated children, however, are of school age (Drews, 1972; Gil, 1964; Thomas, 1977). Therefore, teachers must become aware that they are strategically located for detecting abuse and neglect and must be trained to recognize the indicators of the problem.

In-school child-protection teams can facilitate the development of staff awareness and of appropriate training programs (Breton, 1979). The coordinator, concerned with extending this awareness and this capacity to detect to the neighboring community, should encourage the team to devise training programs applicable both to school and to community groups. There is no reason why seminars on child abuse and neglect indicators, for instance, should not be offered jointly to teachers and neighborhood natural helpers. It would be the coordinator's task to see that the programs were flexible enough to accommodate different concerns; for example, after viewing films or slides on indicators and after a large group discussion, the seminar members could break up into specific interest groups. All parts of the program need not be conjoined if that does not suit the participants.

Reporting

The coordinator should promote the same kind of educational programs as those just mentioned to inform school staff and community groups of abuse and neglect reporting laws. For it has been observed that when schools facilitate the reporting of child abuse, the rate of actual identifications increases significantly (Martin, 1976; Murdock, 1970), as do the services to children and their families (Nicholson, 1977). However, it also has been pointed out that, in some instances, school reporting and referral efforts become productive only if school personnel are first assured that the community supports their involvement in the detection and prevention of abuse (Broadhurst, 1977). Conjoint programs would be an effective way to assure and strengthen this support while it would also help the community to take a more active role in reporting the maltreatment of children.

Treatment

The school environment is a significant yet largely untapped resource for the treatment of child abuse and neglect. Children have to spend a large amount of their time in school; they are also willing to stay even longer to participate in all sorts of extracurricular activities. When a child has been identified as abused or neglected, the child-protection team should come up with an in-school treatment plan which capitalizes on these internal resources. However, abusive parents, whether because they are distrustful or because they resent attention given to their children, will often forbid the use of such resources. The coordinator should enlist the cooperation of neighborhood natural helpers to persuade abusive parents to let their children participate in after-school groups, for instance. This persuasive work can be time-consuming, and natural helpers are often in a position to do it most economically.

Neighborhood natural helpers may also be in the best position to help school child-protection teams find people who would be available to take care of children in crisis situations. As Lauderdale (1977) has pointed out, there are such individuals in most neighborhoods; the problem is to locate them. The teachers, the school public-health nurses, social workers, counselors, and psychologists, as well as the neighborhood natural helpers, all know of some such individuals: it would be the coordinator's responsibility to combine their knowledge in order to locate and expand this network of nurturers.

Finally, it may well be that one of the most important of the coordinator's tasks in terms of the treatment of abuse and neglect of school-aged children lies in being receptive to treatment ideas from the natural helpers in the community and to relay these ideas accurately to the protection team, and vice versa.

Conclusion

The kind of liaison between school and community described in this chapter poses a number of problems which the coordinator must tackle. It is obvious, for instance, that there will be divergences of opinions on the use of discipline and corporal punishment among team members and neighborhood natural helpers; moreover, opinions will probably vary within the team as well as within the community. The coordinator will need to be tolerant of differences and unafraid of conflict, interpreting the ideas of one group to the other and helping each to understand the basis of the other's opinions.

Furthermore, closer cooperation between school and community always presents the danger that some professionals will look down on nonprofessionals, either discounting their input outright or adopting a paternalistic and patronizing attitude. The coordinator will have to be sensitive to this kind of discrimination and try to weed it out when possible. In this respect it will be profitable to help the school staff minimize the use of professional jargon, which will have the added benefit of facilitating the work of the child-protection team.

Discrimination is often the result of perceived threat, and this applies to school personnel who may feel jealous or insecure about others invading their turf. The coordinator's role will be to clarify the boundaries among the different functions of the professionals and the natural helpers, and reassure everyone by reinforcing the particular expertise of each team member as well as that of each natural helper.

Close collaboration between school and community is demanding, and school staff do not have much extra time to devote to causes, even though they may feel very strongly about some. The coordinator will need to protect their time by filtering and processing the information that will be exchanged between the school and community.

It is evident also that this coordinating role will be very demanding on the person who assumes it. To fulfill it effectively the complete support of the school principal is essential. This means that the principal must accept the concept of the school as a community resource, as being "part of a larger system that contributes to the development of social health and as an institution participating in community life" (Anderson, 1974, p. 526).

One of the problems facing community life is the abuse and neglect of children. To participate in new efforts aimed at alleviating this problem is a challenge that the school must be ready to assume.

Reference Notes

1. To lighten the style, and in deference to the rightful canon of the age, only the feminine will be used.

2. The term "natural helpers" is used in the same sense as employed by Collins and Pancoast, who define it as "certain central figures who saw themselves and were seen by others as willing to invest themselves in helping to make arrangements, in giving advice, and in providing direct help" (1972, p. 7).

References

Anderson, R.J. 1974 School social work: the promise of a team model. *Child Welfare 53*, 524-530.

ten Bensel, R.W., and Berdie, J. 1976. The neglect and abuse of children and youth: the scope of problem and the school's role. *Journal of School Health 46*, 453-461.

Breton, M. 1979. The use of child protection teams in schools. *Social Worker 47*(1): 21-24.

Brill, N.L. 1976. *Teamwork: working together in the human services.* Philadelphia: Lippincott.

Broadhurst, D. 1975. Project protection: a school program to detect and prevent child abuse and neglect. *Children Today 4*(3): 22-25.

Broadhurst, D. 1977. When I see an abused or neglected child what do I do about it. In M. Thomas, ed. *Children alone: what can be done about abuse and neglect.* Reston, Va.: CEC.

Caplan, J., and Killilea, M., eds. 1976. *Support systems and mutual help: multidisciplinary explorations.* New York: Grune and Stratton.

Collins, A.H., and Pancoast, D.L. 1972. *Natural helping networks: a strategy for prevention.* Washington, D.C.: N.A.S.W.

Davis, L.G., and McEwen, M.K. 1977. Child abuse and the role of the school counselor. *School Counselor 22*(2): 92-96.

Drews, K. 1972. The child and his school. In C.H. Kempe and R.E. Helfer, eds. *Helping the battered child and his family.* Philadelphia: J.B. Lippincott.

Easton, F. 1978. The school social worker as an internal consultant for renewal in public schools. *Social Work with Groups 1*(2): 161-172.

Forrer, S.E. 1975. Battered children and counselor responsibility. *School Counselor 22*(3): 161-165.

Garbarino, J. 1980. Using natural helping networks to meet the problem of child maltreatment. In R. Volpe, M. Breton, and J. Mitton, eds. *The maltreatment of the school-aged child.* Lexington, Mass.: LexingtonBooks, D.C. Heath and Co.

Gil, D.G. 1964. What schools can do about child abuse. *American Education 5*, 2-4.

Griggs, S.A., and Gale, P. 1977. The abused child: focus on counselors. *Elementary School Guidance and Counseling 2*(3): 187-194.

Holmes, S. 1978. Parents' Anonymous: a treatment method for child abuse. *Social Work 23*, 245-247.

Kane, R.A. 1975. *Interprofessional teamwork.* Syracuse: Syracuse University School of Social Work. Manpower Monograph #8.

Lauderdale, M. 1977. Family structure and professional roles. In M. Thomas, ed. *Children alone: what can be done about abuse and neglect.* Reston, Va.: C.E.D.

Lee, B. 1980. The use of interdisciplinary problem-solving groups in educational settings. In R. Volpe and M. Breton, J. Mitton, eds. *The maltreatment of the school-aged child.* Lexington, Mass.: LexingtonBooks, D.C. Heath and Co.

Martin, H. 1976. *The abused child: a multidisciplinary approach to developmental issues and treatment.* Cambridge, Mass.: Ballinger.

Meares, P.A. 1977. Analysis of tasks in school social work. *Social Work 22*(3): 196–201.

Murdock, C.J. 1970. The abused child and the school system. *American Journal of Public Health 60*(1): 105–109.

Nicholson, M. 1977. Policies and procedures for reporting. In M. Thomas, ed. *Children alone: what can be done about abuse and neglect.* Reston, Va.: CEC.

Powell, T.J. 1975. The uses of self-help groups in supportive reference communities. *American Journal of Orthopsychiatry 45*(5): 756–764.

Riessman, F. 1965. The helper-therapy principle. *Social Work 10,* 27–32.

Tagg, P. 1976. Nursing intervention for the abused child and his family. *Pediatric Nursing 2,* 36–39.

Thomas, M., ed. 1977. *Children alone: what can be done about abuse and neglect.* Reston, Va.: CED.

Volpe, R. 1976. The role of the educator in the provision of adolescent health services. *School Guidance Worker 32*(2): 48–54.

Wise, H., Beckhard, R., Rubin, L., and Kyte, A. 1974. *Making health teams work.* Cambridge, Mass.: Ballinger.

11 The Use of Interdisciplinary Problem-Solving Groups in Educational Settings

Bill Lee

Child abuse and deprivation are complex and difficult phenomena (Helfer and Kempe, 1968) for all professionals in the human services (Sayre, Foley, Zingarella, and Kristal, 1973).[a] However, they carry particular difficulties for those who work in the school system. First, in regard to the teacher, there exist heavy demands on time and energy. In the normal course of events of a school day, a teacher is called upon to expend large amounts of physical, emotional, and intellectual energy in relating to a large number of individual children. Thus the teacher may have little energy left over to deal with problems as emotionally charged and complex as child abuse and deprivation.

Second, these problems carry with them a particularly heavy emotional charge. A number of writers have demonstrated how feelings of frustration, fear, and anger are commonly aroused when individuals are confronted with situations of deprivation or abuse (Bakan, 1971; Elmer, 1963).

Third, issues of child welfare and safety often carry with them legal ramifications that arouse uncertainty and apprehension, particularly for those who are not familiar with the actual responsibilities and safeguards built into the relevant laws and regulations. Further, an individual may feel unclear in relation to reporting; for example, does one report suspicion, or is hard proof necessary? To whom should the report be directed? To the principal? To police? To the local child-welfare authority?

Finally, the professionals who practice within the school system tend to do so on an individual basis, that is, the nature of the professional task focuses the practitioner's attention on specific aspects of the child: the teacher on the intellectual, the nurse on the physical, and the social worker on the interactional and environmental aspects of the behavior of the children seen. This situation has two important ramifications: (1) it reduces the likelihood of information and perspective being shared and thus reduces the opportunities for identification of abuse and deprivation; and (2) subsequent to identification, it reduces the ability of the various individual practitioners to offer each other

---

[a]The model presented here comes out of the author's experience with four multi-disciplinary teams, one based in a hospital, one in an elementary school, and two in a children's aid society.

the support and challenge necessary to deal effectively with these emotionally loaded and complex situations (Bakan, 1971).

The Problem-Solving Group

One viable means of dealing with these difficulties is the formation, within the school, of an interdisciplinary problem-solving group that would focus on child abuse and deprivation. The two main objectives of such groups would be the enhancement of identification skills and the development of effective intervention strategies. A third objective would be the provision of a supportive structure for people dealing with abuse and deprivation cases. Issues of child welfare are taxing. It is important that practitioners be provided with a medium for the recognition of their emotional needs as well as for direction regarding intervention.

The consensus grew out of the realization that professionals who deal with child abuse must be provided with a support system for making what can be, and often are, life-and-death decisions. Moreover, this support system should be easily accessible so that proper action is taken as soon as needed (Breton, 1979).

Furthermore, the interdisciplinary composition of the group would assist members in recognizing that simplistic attitudes are insufficient to deal with the problem of abuse and deprivation. A team is composed of members chosen because of their own specific expertise, on the understanding that to accomplish the identification tasks it is necessary that each member contribute this specific expertise (Brill, 1976).

In that a number of experts are brought together to try to find solutions to a problem, then surely the complexity of the problem is highlighted and members begin to come to grips with the necessity of rethinking personal values and attitudes (Breton, 1979).

To attain these ends a group should be organized around the following principles:

1. The group must be interdisciplinary to ensure that information, perspective, and skill are shared purposefully. Membership should thus include teachers, the school or public-health nurse, and the school social worker. If social work is not represented within the school a social worker from the local child-welfare agency should be sought. While these are the basic three disciplines that must be represented, it may be advisable to invite other practitioners as the needs of particular cases dictate. It was in the capacity of a children's-aid social worker that the author was a member of one such school-based group. The other members on that team were from the school: the vice-principal, guidance counselor, two teachers, and the local public-health nurse.

2. Meetings must be task focused. To attain the first two objectives mentioned earlier, meetings must be oriented to the development of specific recommendations for realistic actions.

3. Meetings must take place at regular intervals and be time limited. As indicated above this is a task-focused endeavor and, as such, timing and duration should be predictable. This will assist participants in planning their own time and allows for reasonable and realistic expectations about the effort involved. It is also important for the members to meet often enough to maintain the immediacy of the work. It is the author's experience that once per week is a maximum and once per month an absolute minimum, perhaps too little.

4. There must be a high degree of accountability within the group. This is one of the most difficult as well as most important aspects of the problem-solving group.

What is referred to by accountability is that each member must recognize that the group as a whole has the right to direct and question aspects of intervention in particular cases of child abuse and deprivation; in other words, group members become answerable to each other. This accountability is twofold: first, any member bringing a problem to the group must be able to expect an attentive hearing and reasonable suggestions for action; second, if a suggested strategy or task is agreed upon by the group, the member responsible must be prepared to carry it out to the best of his or her ability. Further, the participant must be prepared to report to the group on the degree of effort made and the degree of success attained.

The purpose for insisting on this is simply that without it a group cannot hope to achieve the degree of commitment and interest necessary for its maintenance. Individuals cannot long be expected to give of themselves in a demanding and creative manner if their input is treated in a casual way (Gordon and Howe, 1979).

5. The emotional tenor of the group must combine support with challenge. Effective problem-solving demands critical, analytical thought. Thus participants who bring a problem situation before the group must be assisted or challenged to analyze and think through the issues involved and the way they have been handling them so far. A person will not continue to lay problems before the group if he is not seriously listened to and the issues are not considered. And members will not continue to listen and offer criticism and suggestions if these are not seriously considered. Thus feedback, from the group to the individual and the individual to the group, is the key to successful functioning.

At the same time, as we have noted above, situations of child abuse and deprivation are emotionally charged and at times become quite draining on the professionals involved in them. Thus the participants must be prepared to demonstrate a caring attitude toward those seeking assistance. This is not to suggest that members be allowed to effect bad practice, but that the difficulties involved in the effecting of good practice be recognized and discussed in an open and understanding manner.

6. Leadership has always been recognized as a crucial element for the attainment of productive group processes (Napier and Gershenfeld, 1973). Leadership,

of course, is a complex matter. However, there are four responsibilities that must be highlighted in this context: (1) guiding the discussion and helping members to stay on track; (2) watching the time and not letting discussions run on too long. While watching the clock may appear to be a minor responsibility it is nevertheless important. Letting discussion run down as well as cutting it off too soon can lead to frustration among the members and can keep the group off balance; (3) monitoring the process of the group: this involves making sure that all perspectives have been heard and that the group does not get caught in destructive patterns. Clearly other members should be prepared to take such responsibilities, too, but the leader has the major responsibility in this regard; (4) summing up the discussion and making sure that whatever action has been decided on is clear to all members. This is a particularly important function in . that accountability can only be expected from members when activities and responsibilities are clearly understood.

The Tasks of the Group

To facilitate the presentations and discussion of the tasks facing a problem-solving group, it is useful to think of the process of the meetings in terms of five phases.

1. Problem presentation. In this phase the member who is bringing a question before the group outlines the case situation and asks for assistance around specific issues. Information presented here should be basic: names, ages, grades of children, family constellation, agencies involved, and the length of time the situation has been identified. Subsequent to this presentation the presenter should indicate to the group the difficulties he or she is having and in what areas direction from the group is required; that is, what is the problem to be solved?

2. Clarification. In this phase the group members do two things: obtain factual information from the presenter that will assist them in understanding the nature of the case and difficulties faced, and check out with the presenter the nature of his feelings about the case and about the individuals involved. What is aimed at here is a common understanding of what the situation is and how the individual is relating to it.

3. Discussion. This phase is the most significant one. The basic information is now present, and while some questioning may still be required, the emphasis is now on information exchange and strategy development.

Information exchange can take place in two areas. The first area involves knowledge about the case itself. Individuals who are working with the child or the family have an opportunity to put forward what they know. This may clarify a situation: for example, a teacher who is concerned about the change in the level of activity of a child in class may be informed by the school nurse that a medication has recently been prescribed, or the social worker may inform the teacher that there has been a recent change in the family's situation. The second area of information exchange is in the sharing of skills. For example, a social worker who is involved with a child in an after-school group may be able to offer the teacher helpful suggestions in handling the child's dysfunctional classroom behavior.

Strategy development is the other important process which occurs during the group discussion phase. "How is the presenter going to structure the intervention?" is the focal question here. The question may eventually broaden to, "How are we, as a group of professionals, going to intervene with this family?"

It is very important to have a format for the discussion of these questions. The purpose of a format is not to rigidify the discussion but to facilitate it, so that school-based intervention will not only be the most useful possible to the family and child, but also be coherent with interventions of the other institutions—hospitals, CAS, Family Court—that may be involved. In his previously mentioned experience with interdisciplinary groups, the author has identified four basic questions (see the first column of table 11-1) that invariably have to be covered to obtain productive results. This, of course, does not preclude the discussion of other issues that in various circumstances may be equally important: feelings of frustration, anger, or discouragement, for example, may be evident in the presenter and must be addressed by the group. In fact, this one task of the group should be seen as assisting the members to identify and deal

Table 11-1
Format for Group Discussion

Topics	Service Objective	Possible Tasks
Child safety	Ensure safety of child	Decision regarding what is necessary to obtain the least possible risk situation
Information and assessment	Clear picture of strengths and weaknesses of the family and its environment	1. Share information regarding family environment 2. Fit it together in a coherent, logical manner 3. Locate areas where important information is missing
What other agencies are or should be involved	Coordinated, efficient, and humane problem solving	1. Share information regarding practitioners known to be involved 2. Appointment of liaison
Who should maintain primary responsibility for intervention (that is, action)	Clarification of roles	Assigning of personnel to carry main contact 1. with family 2. with child

with feelings that are affecting practice. While clearly the orientation is not one of therapy, it is human, and thus we can expect to face feeling issues from time to time.

In any event, no matter what other issues are present, the issues of safety, information, and assessment, the degree and quality of agency involvement, and case responsibility cannot be left uncovered. These questions lead to discussions of service objectives and ultimately to assignment of tasks (see table 11-1). It is the assignment of tasks that are the fruit of the problem-solving process.

4. Recommendation. In this phase the leader must sum up the major statements of the group and formulate them as recommendations for the presenter and any other member whom the group may have decided should participate in the intervention (again, see table 11-1). It is important to emphasize that these are group recommendations transmitted through the leader. If members sense that the leader is going beyond this or that he is missing something they have a responsibility to enunciate their concern. Clarity, accountability, and a sense of consensus are crucial to successful group process for problem solving and must be operative in this phase.

Part of any recommendation should relate to a time frame, that is, to how long it should take to put the recommended strategy into action. This time frame is important in terms of accountability, and also in terms of the last phase of the group process, that of the "Report on Action."

5. Report on action. This should be taken during the last part of the meeting to obtain feedback from members who sought direction from the group during a previous meeting. The members should report on how the agreed-upon strategy was carried out and with what results. This is an important mechanism whereby accountability is actualized. First, knowing that they will have to report back to the group induces members to insist on clarity from the group when it gives direction for action, for they know that their professional practice will be evaluated by their peers and they will want to be able to account for their success, or the lack of it. Second, reporting forces the group itself to evaluate the quality of its analysis and advice. A strategy may have failed because the advice given was unrealistic; or the advice may have been given in an ill-defined or confusing manner. In either event, the feedback received is valuable and can be used to alter practice, whether at the individual or group level.

Training Needs

While most of us belong to many groups, both formal and informal, and while most of us are involved in some sort of group interaction every day, the initiation of and development in an interdisciplinary problem-solving group requires specific skill development. The two areas in which skills must be developed are member participation in the group process and group leadership. The initial formation period can be used advantageously for training purposes. The group may not be ready to solve problems very effectively at that point, but the members can learn to work with each other and use the group processes: this investment in learning will yield long-term benefits.

The group-formation phase is important because, as was stated at the beginning of the chapter, group problem solving, particularly of an interdisciplinary nature, is not common in schools. Furthermore, groups usually take some time to form, time during which members test each other, and eventually get to know and trust one another. Very often participants need assistance in learning such skills as presenting cases in a logical and coherent manner, initiating discussion, tuning in to underlying feelings, confronting, etc.

Leadership demands similar training. Its importance as a major factor in effective group functioning has been noted, and some leadership functions have been identified. However, very few of us are born with the skills necessary to carry out these functions and we must, therefore, learn them.

But, given the responsibilities that a group dealing with child abuse and deprivation will have, training both in the areas of member participation in the group process and in group leadership should be seen as an integral part of such a group's development.

Dealing within the school context with the problem of child abuse and deprivation should be seen as dealing with demanding and complex phenomena within a demanding and complex system. An appropriate response to the schools' responsibilities in dealing with the problem of abuse and deprivation must take into consideration this dynamic. The formation of an interdisciplinary problem-solving group, while by no means a total answer, provides one meaningful response. It recognizes the systemic nature of the problem and provides a wide range of professional input, thus fostering an organized, coherent, and supportive planning and intervention structure. In a real sense it allows professionals to act rather than react. In any endeavor in which people deal with the lives of children this is a significant advantage. It is one that should be utilized to the fullest.

References

Bakan, D. 1971. *Slaughter of the innocents.* Toronto: CBC Learning Systems.

Breton, M. 1979. The use of child protection teams in schools. *Social Work* 47(1): 21–23.

Brill, N.L. 1976. *Teamwork: working together in the human services.* Philadelphia: Lippincott.

Elmer, E. 1963. Identification of abused children. *Children 10,* 180–186.

Gordon, W.I., and Howe, R.J. 1979. *Team dynamics in developing organizations.* LaJolla, Calif.: NTL/Learning Resources Corporation.

Helfer, R.E., and Kempe, C.H. 1968. *The battered child.* Chicago: University of Chicago Press.

Napier, R.W., and Gershenfeld, M. 1973. *Groups theory and experience.* LaJolla, Calif.: NTL/Learning Resources Corporation.

Sayre, J.W., Foley, F.W., Zingarella, E.S., and Kristal, H.I. 1973. Community committee of child abuse. *New York State Journal of Medicine 73,* 2071-2075.

Using Natural-Helping Networks to Meet the Problem of Child Maltreatment

James Garbarino

Who helps? How one answers this question sheds light on how one sees the world. The last half-century has seen a massive increase in professional and bureaucratized human services. The proliferation of social work and mental-health agencies and services has obscured the fact that our society relies on the private sector for most of its helping transactions. Most of the helping that is done is done within the context of informal relationships—friends, neighbors, and relatives. Whether it be economic assistance (Boulding, 1976), childcare (Collins and Pancoast, 1976), or mental health (Gourash, 1978), informal helping networks provide the bulk of the services. Professionals are generally "the last resort" (Gottlieb, 1978; Gourash, 1978; Tannenbaum, 1974).

A rich person is one who is enmeshed in a network of people who have the resources and motive to help. A poor person is isolated. The principal determinant of a person's subjective sense of well-being and quality of life is to be found in the richness of his enduring interpersonal relationships (Campbell, 1975). The stresses and strains of life are mediated by these relationships: a socially rich person can afford a high level of stress, and a socially poor person cannot afford much stress at all. Likewise, a socially rich environment is one characterized by social diversity and extensive, interlocking social networks. This is doubly true when it comes to children (Cochran and Brassard, in press; Garbarino and Jacobson, 1978; Garbarino and Sherman, in press). This concept of social riches underlies the writer's view of how the schools can meet the problem of child maltreatment (Garbarino, 1979a). "If the vital importance of social networks in establishing and maintaining a healthy social environment is accepted, then it follows that neighborhoods must become the focus of attention when the quality of life of families is in question. In dealing with cases of child abuse the school must not lose sight of family support systems."

Having established the role of social networks in a healthy social environment, the dual concepts of social impoverishment and freedom from drain will be introduced to explain the characteristics of an unhealthy social environment. These concepts provide a basis for looking at the quality of life for families with a neighborhood orientation, an ecological approach to child maltreatment emphasizing the role of geographic concentrations of high-risk families in high-risk neighborhood settings (Garbarino, 1980). This discussion of the role of family-support systems in child abuse will provide the basis for a more specific discussion of the school.

129

The school has a natural place in the life of children and it functions as a prosocial support system for families when it capitalizes upon this natural role. The issue facing educators is this: "Can the school link up with natural helping networks to support families and protect children?" There are three areas in which this process of linking up can be accomplished. First, schools can take the lead in supporting parent self-help groups. Second, schools can do their part in supporting and encouraging children who are placed in foster care. Third, schools can take the initiative in linking adolescent peer networks to helpful adults. All three of these roles are important, and I believe examining each of them will shed light on both the wisdom and the feasibility of schools using natural helping networks to meet the problem of child maltreatment.

The Role of Family Support Systems in Child Abuse

No single theoretical perspective or technique is sufficient to solve the problem of child maltreatment (Friedman, 1976). Part of any comprehensive and unified approach to the problem should include strengthening family-support systems and social networks. While there are many personal and cultural problems that can produce child maltreatment, none of these problems must inevitably produce abuse and neglect. All of them can be overcome *if* the social environment of the family is sufficiently supportive, *if* it provides adequate reinforcements for childcare, and *if* it embeds the parent and the child in a network of people willing and able to provide protective behaviors when the situation calls for it. In the absence of such a socially rich environment even the smallest disruptions of family life can be damaging to the child.

The concept of support systems derives in part from the work of Gerald Caplan, who describes support systems as

> continuing social aggregates that provide individuals with opportunities for feedback about themselves, and for validations for their expectations about others, which may offset deficiencies in these communications within the larger community context. . . . People have a variety of specific needs that demand satisfaction through enduring interpersonal relationships, such as for love and affection, for intimacy that provides freedom to express feelings easily and unself-consciously, for validation of personal identity and worth, for satisfaction of nurturance and dependency, for help with tasks, and for support in handling emotion and controlling impulses. (1974, pp. 5–6)

> They tell him (the individual) what is expected of him and guide him in what to do. They watch what he does and they judge his performance. (1974, pp. 5–6)

In a society where independence and autonomy are the unchallenged criteria for mental health, it is easy to forget how much each of us depends upon these support systems for our psychic well-being and for adequate performance in the various roles we are called upon to fulfill, such as parent, worker, and citizen (Garbarino, 1978).

Our preoccupation with independence and autonomy makes it difficult to see the role of support systems in preventing child maltreatment. When stripped of the nonessentials, it is clear that child maltreatment is permitted, and even stimulated, by isolation from potent prosocial family-support systems (Garbarino, 1977). This isolation both undermines the mental health of the individual family member and deprives the family of the protection and nurturance of the outside community. Whether the individual be isolated from his peers or a network of peers be isolated from the social resources of the community the outcome is the same: children are placed in danger. Schools can play a major role in reducing this dangerous social isolation and in replacing it with social integration. A socially integrated educational estalbishment becomes a family center. Its staff develops enduring and effective relationships with the social networks of its students and their families.

Investigators have documented a pervasive pattern of social isolation in the lives of abusing and neglecting parents (Friedman, 1976). Evidence based on research with animals reinforces this conclusion (Rock, 1978). Support systems and social networks are particularly important in understanding child abuse and neglect because these problems center on the inadequacy of social control, on the adverse consequences of narrow repertoires of behavior, and on the importance of constructive, precise feedback to parents in encouraging adequate childcare and discouraging mistreatment (Garbarino, 1977). At the simplest level, the isolated child is the unprotected child. Even for the simple act of identification and reporting to occur the child must be exposed to adults outside the home. For the warning signs of mistreatment to be detected a more intimate and enduring relationship is required. When such relationships exist, even when they are based on professional roles, constructive action can be taken (Garbarino and Stocking, 1978; Gray, Cutler, Dean, and Kempe, 1977).

But these lower-level protective behaviors are not the whole story. If the victims are to escape the developmental damage associated with abuse and neglect they need access to developmentally enhancing relationships outside the home. The evidence suggests that by and large abuse does not cure itself, either for the perpetrator or the victim (Helfer and Kempe, 1976; Martin, 1976). As Harold Martin has recognized, in publishing the first single volume on ways to help the abused child, our interest in dealing with parents has not been matched by an interest in helping the children of these parents (Martin, 1976), Recently investigators studying the relationship between early experience and later life have found that children can survive and even thrive in difficult stressful situations if they have allies (Benjamin, 1980). Thus the child from an abusive or neglecting home may be able to overcome the damage that that mistreatment inflicts if he has enduring relationships with helpful adults outside the home, relationships that can help compensate for the developmental damaged inflicted by the abuse and neglect. Educators don't need to be told that they often fill this role for children.

Thus far social networks and support systems have been talked about as if they were only characteristics of individuals. Quite to the contrary, they are best understood as social concepts, as characteristics of environments in which children and families live. This notion leads inevitably to consideration of social impoverishment in the environments in which children and families live. By social impoverishment is meant the denuding of resources upon which parents and children can call to cope with stress and demands for social readjustment. A socially impoverished environment is one in which these resources are not available in adequate quantity and quality to meet the needs of children and families. A socially rich environment, on the other hand, is one in which these resources are in more than ample supply so that individual deficiencies and family difficulties needs not result in developmental damage (Garbarino and Sherman, in press). The key concept in understanding what it means for an environment to be socially rich is suggested by what Alice Collins and Diane Pancoast (1976) call freedom of drain. A socially rich environment is one in which there are individuals and families characterized by a low level of demand and a high level of resources. These individuals are capable of giving of themselves because their own needs are well met. Thus they are free from the drains that stress and day-to-day demands produce. Such a person may be the grandparent figure, the person whose own children are grown, whose resources are not strained by the day-to-day demands of childcare, who is in a position to give without the expectation of direct reciprocal return of time, energy, and even material resources. Clearly, professional helpers can be such people who are free from drain, particularly if they define their role in this way.

The foregoing discussion implies a neighborhood orientation to child abuse and neglect (Garbarino, 1980; Garbarino and Crouter, 1978). It suggests an ecological approach to child maltreatment because it emphasizes the role of geographic concentrations of high-risk families located in high-risk neighborhood settings as a principal factor in understanding the quality of care for children. It is in these neighborhood settings that social networks and support systems exist and it is to these neighborhoods that schools must look if they are to understand the social resources of their students and those students' families. There is every reason to believe that these neighborhood settings are most important for families with the least material resources (Lewis, 1978). Thus they are particularly important for low-income families and for professionals in understanding their responsibilities for dealing with the problem of child abuse and neglect among low-income populations. Schools can first look at the populations they serve and the settings in which those populations live. This orientation provides the rationale for efforts to develop parent-helping-parent groups among adults and peer-help groups among young people.

The Role of the School

The school has a natural place in the lives of children (Garbarino, 1976). It is intrinsically intended to be a prosocial support system for those children and their families. Can the school link up with natural helping networks where they exist and stimulate them where they do not exist? The answer to this question will decide in large part how effective schools can be in helping to prevent and cope with child abuse and neglect (Garbarino, 1977). There are three applied areas in which the school can answer this question on a day-to-day basis.

The school can take the lead in supporting parent self-help groups, with special emphasis on such groups with a neighborhood focus. Despite the fact that modern transportation policies and desegregation efforts have tended to erode and weaken their neighborhood focus, most schools, particularly elementary schools, do retain a neighborhood affiliation. In general, but particularly in high-risk areas, schools can take the lead in sponsoring parents-anonymous groups. The effectiveness of these groups in helping abusive parents control their behavior has been repeatedly demonstrated (Lieber and Baker, 1977). The cost is low and can often be incorporated into existing school functions such as those provided by school psychologists, a guidance counselor, or a social worker. Schools can take the initiative in assisting neighborhood-based parent groups. Such groups can consider basic child-development issues, parent education, and problems of child management. Finally, schools can take the lead in identifying and establishing relationships with natural neighbors, people in neighborhoods who are free from drain and may be able to offer assistance to families in need of help of both a preventive and rehabilitative nature. In all three of these areas the school must act in concert with the broader range of human-service agencies, particularly visiting nurses, child-protective-service workers, and community organizers. If the school becomes a focal point for neighborhood activity in support of families it is making a positive contribution to preventing child abuse and neglect. Models for such a neighborhood orientation exist in the broad field of community mental health (Saunders, 1979; Scheinfeld, Bowles, Tuck, and Gold, 1970).

A second area in which schools can be active is in supporting children in foster care (Garbarino, 1979b). Foster care, as it is presently organized, represents a threat to the very children it seeks to help. Researchers in a variety of settings have concluded that the single most important determinant of the impact of foster care on the child is how well the biological parent is integrated into the child's life while the child is in foster care (Fanshel, 1975). Often an attempt is made to keep the biological parent out of the child's life while the child is in placement. By all accounts this undermines efforts to successfully reunite the family. Schools can play an active role in making foster care work by arranging teacher-parent conferences that include both foster and biological parents, by arranging support groups for students in foster care, and by making every effort to ensure that foster-care placement does not disrupt the child's educational experience. Wherever possible schools should seek to keep children in the same school if foster-care placement becomes necessary. My own research shows that most children have at least one adult outside their families to whom they feel close (Garbarino, Burston, Raber, Russell, and Crouter, 1978). Particularly when this person is a teacher it is imperative to hold the child's social network intact when he is placed by maintaining attendance in the same school. Where this is impossible, liaison with the other school should be established and maintained with the expectation that when the child returns home the school will be able to smooth the process of adjustment.

A third area in which schools can take the lead in linking up with natural helping networks involves working with adolescent peer groups to better connect them to helpful adults (Garbarino and Jacobson, 1978). While this is true with children of all ages, it seems particularly important when dealing with older children and adolescents. Youth-helping-youth programs can and should include peer counseling and referral projects in which teenagers work with school-based protective service agencies. In the United States adolescents account for a third of the total number of reported cases of abuse, a fact which places the school in a central spot for dealing with this aspect of maltreatment. The fact that schools account for a major share of the reports involving adolescents highlights this role.

Schools can do a number of things to help use peer networks on behalf of teenagers who may be victimized (Garbarino and Jacobson, 1978). First, they can work to provide a liaison between the school and child-protective services. Where there is an adolescent-abuse specialist within a child-protective-service unit there should be a one-to-one correspondence of that specialist to a liaison person within the school. The school's representative, in turn, should make every effort to identify existing networks of peers among the students and to recognize leaders within those groups. These peer-group leaders can then become part of referral networks by which students can refer themselves or their peers through the peer networks to the school adults and ultimately on to protective services when the need arises. Second, schools can distribute materials on abuse to students and encourage staff to act as a confidential intermediary for victims and their peers. Such materials are available and have been distributed in school districts with a generally positive reaction from both staff and students (contact the author for further information).

Finally, schools can support self-help groups for students at risk or who have already been victimized. These support groups allow the natural healing processes of peer interaction to work on behalf of the young person who may have experienced abuse and neglect at home. What is more, these groups get youngsters at every stage of the process, from the teenager who is not yet willing to acknowledge that he or she is being abused, to the youngster experiencing the difficult trial of case investigation and disposition, to the child who has been placed in foster care and needs assistance in resolving the feelings that placement engenders, to the teenager who has run away from home.

This discussion began with the question, "Who helps?" The schools can help. They do help, albeit imperfectly. The power of the schools as helpers, like the power of all professional institutions, can be magnified by working with the private sector that offers the bulk of day-to-day helping. Such a community-oriented school promises to improve the quality of life of its children.

References

Benjamin, M., 1980. Abused as a child, abusive as a parent: Practitioners beware. In R. Volpe, M. Breton, J. Mitton, eds. *The maltreatment of the school-aged child.* Lexington, Mass.: Lexington Books, D.C. Heath and Co.

Boulding, K.E. 1976. Publicly supported, universally available education and equality. *Phi Delta Kappan,* 58(1): 36–41.

Campbell, D.T. 1975. On the conflict between biological and social evolution and between psychology and moral tradition. *American Psychologist 30,* 1103–1126.

Caplan, G. 1974. *Support systems and community mental health.* New York: Behavioral Publications.

Cochran, M., and Brassard, J. Social networks and child development. *Child Development* in press.

Collins, A., and Pancoast, D. 1976. *Natural helping networks.* Washington, D.C.: National Association of Social Workers.

Fanshel, D. 1975. Parental visiting of children in foster care: key to discharge? *Social Service Review 49,* 493–514.

Friedman, R. 1976. Child abuse: a review of the psychosocial research. In Herner and Company, Eds. *Four perspectives on the status of child abuse and neglect research.* Washington, D.C.: National Center on Child Abuse and Neglect.

Garbarino, J. 1980. An ecological perspective on child maltreatment. In L. Pelton, ed. *The social context of child abuse and neglect,* New York: Human Sciences Press.

Garbarino, J. 1979a. The role of schools in the human ecology of child maltreatment. *School Review 87,* 190–213.

Garbarino, J. 1979b. *Making foster care work: a note on using social networks and natural helping systems.* Unpublished paper, Center for the Study of Youth Development, Boys Town, Nebraska.

Garbarino, J. 1977. The human ecology of child maltreatment: a conceptual model for research. *Journal of Marriage and the Family, 39,* 721–736.

Garbarino, J. 1976. The family: a school for living. *National Elementary Principal 55,* 66–70.

Garbarino, J., Burston, N., Raber, S., Russel, R., and Crouter, A. 1978. The social maps of children approaching the transition from elementary to secondary school. *Journal of Youth and Adolescence 7*, 417–428.

Garbarino, J., and Crouter, A. 1978. Defining the community context of parent-child relations: the correlates of child maltreatment. *Child Development 49*, 604–616.

Garbarino, J., and Jacobson, N. 1978. Youth helping youth as a resource in meeting the problem of adolescent maltreatment. *Child Welfare 57*, 505–512.

Garbarino, J., and Sherman, D. High-risk neighborhoods and high-risk families: the human ecology of child maltreatment. *Child development* in press.

Garbarino, J., and Stocking, S.H., eds. 1978. *Supporting families and protecting children.* Boys Town, Nebraska: Center for the Study of Youth Development.

Gottlieb, B. 1978. Social networks, social support and child maltreatment. In J. Garbarino and S.H. Stocking, eds. *Supporting families and protecting children.* Boys Town, Nebraska: Center for the Study of Youth Development.

Gourash, N. 1978. Help-seeking: a review of the literature. *American Journal of Community Psychology 6*, 413–423.

Gray, J., Cutler, C., Dean, J., and Kempe, C.H. 1977. Prediction and prevention of child abuse and neglect. *Child Abuse and Neglect 1*, 45–58.

Helfer, R., and Kempe, C.H. 1976. *Child abuse and neglect: the family and the community.* Cambridge, Mass.: Ballinger.

Lewis, M. 1978. Nearest neighbor analysis of epidemiological and community variables. *Psychological Bulletin, 85*, 1302–1308.

Lieber, L.L., and Baker, J.M. 1977. Parents anonymous—self-help treatment for child abusing parents: a review and an evaluation. *Child Abuse and Neglect 1*, 133–148.

Martin, H.P., ed. 1976. *The abused child: a multidiciplinary approach to developmental issues and treatment.* Cambridge, Mass.: Ballinger.

Rock, M. 1978. Gorilla mothers need some help from their friends. *Smithsonian 9*(4): 58–63.

Saunders, S. 1979. Primary prevention from a neighborhood base: a working model. *American Journal of Orthopsychiatry 49*, 69–80.

Scheinfeld, D., Bowles, D., Tuck, S., and Gold, R. 1970. Parents' values, family networks and family development: working with disadvantaged families. *American Journal of Orthopsychiatry 40*, 413–425.

Tannenbaum, D. 1974. *People with problems: seeking help in an urban community.* Research Paper No. 64, Center for Urban and Community Studies, University of Toronto.

Abuse in School-Aged Children: The Role of the Community-Health Nurse

Judith Mitton

In recent years the problem of child abuse has been acknowledged as an important health problem demanding the attention of a wide variety of professionals. Initial concern focused on those children who seemed to have few defenses against abuse, namely, infants, toddlers, and preschoolers. The problem of abuse, however, affects children of all ages. This chapter focuses on the school-aged child and the role of the community-health nurse in combating abuse.

Because school-aged children are relatively healthy, they do not come to the attention of doctors as often as other age groups. The community-health nurse is the health-care professional who has the most frequent contact with school-aged children and their families. One of her major responsibilities is community-health promotion. Such a mandate dictates that she meet people in a variety of settings including their homes, or in the case of children, in schools. One writer described this nursing role as follows:

> ... Public health nurses are concerned with three levels of preventing illness: primary, secondary, and tertiary. Primary prevention includes health promotion and specific illness prevention; secondary prevention refers to early detection and prompt treatment of the illness, resulting in limitation of disability; tertiary prevention includes rehabilitation. (Leavell and Clark, 1979, p. 1)

> In terms of the specific health hazard in child abuse, these levels would be to prevent the maltreatment of children, to detect it early enough to limit disability, to assist in the rehabilitation of the child and the family if maltreatment has occurred. (Cunningham, 1979, p. 1)

Such a broad focus justifies and supports the community-health nurse's involvement with the problem of child abuse at all stages of prevention. Moreover, she has the background necessary for such involvement:

> ... familiarity with existing community resources within the community and the inter- and intra-agency systems designed to deliver those services; experience and expertise in problem-solving and advocacy for and with the family in their own milieu; ability to assess and plan for meeting family needs as a whole. (Friedman, Juntti, and Scoblic, 1976, p. 106)

Role Responsibilities

The emphasis in primary prevention has long been focused on parents of young children, but the stresses parents experience as their children enter the school-aged and adolescent periods can trigger patterns of abuse as well (Martin, 1976). The nurse needs to recognize this possibility and continue to work with families, exploring with them their concerns for their children and their approaches to the handling of problems.

The community-health nurse can assist in the development of mothers' self-help groups to discuss family life, childrearing, and child development. Through such groups mothers see that they are not alone with their problems and that there are people they can turn to when they need help. Such groups also foster the development of more positive self-images and boost the confidence levels of mothers. This is important, because the negative aspects of these characteristics are often found in abusive parents (Pollock and Steele, 1972).

Abuse is not limited to physical assault, but also includes the grayer areas of physical and emotional neglect. Neglect is sometimes the result of lack of knowledge, rather than a conscious plan. The community-health nurse has opportunities to visit homes and assess a family's level of functioning and to detect areas where teaching could be beneficial. Explaining proper nutrition and promotion of environmental stimulation for young children are examples of health teaching that can decrease the possibility of neglect.

Because of her community and school focus, the community-health nurse can assess both settings and detect problem areas that may lead to abuse. Moreover, the nurse may assist schoolteachers in evaluating situations where children are having problems, such as learning difficulties, changes in behavior, or a continuous low level of health. She can then contact the parents and observe how these situations are perceived and handled by them. She may also identify situations within the home setting that could create difficulties for the child in school and alert the teacher regarding any required special assistance. Abuse may not be occurring, but, by intervening early, parents and children can be helped so that abuse will not become a reality.

There has been a sharp rise in the incidence of teenaged pregnancy and a similar increase in the number of young mothers keeping their babies. Abuse appears to be more likely in situations where the pregnancy is unplanned, the mother is in her teens, and there are marital difficulties or a single-parent situation (Ayoub and Pfeifer, 1977). As a part of primary prevention, schools should be instituting classes for school-aged children and adolescents relating to family life and parenting. The community-health nurse can play an integral part in such a program and work with schoolteachers to create and present classes which will prepare these young people for the realities and responsibilities of childrearing. Such classes may be part of the regular curriculum or developed as extracurricular programs, depending on the assessed needs of the students.

Secondary prevention relates to early detection of abuse and intervention to prevent lasting complications. The community-health nurse routinely sees schoolchildren for health-screening programs and treatment of illness that occurs while the children are at school. These encounters are ideal opportunities to assess children for the possibility of abuse. Naturally, all children seen by the nurse are not automatically suspected of being abused, but because of her health-care background the nurse should be alerted by indicators that do become apparent during these interactions. A suspicion should lead to further investigation. This could include discussions with the child's teacher, or the school social worker, or a home visit. The teacher may have noticed, over a period of time, a pattern of behavior or physical appearance that lends itself to being labeled abuse. The social worker may have had contact with the child and his family and have information that could contribute to the findings. When the nurse makes a home visit to discuss the health problems she has identified in the child, she can assess the home situation for indicators which do or do not support a suspicion of abuse.

When abuse is suspected, the nurse has a legal and professional responsibility to report her suspicions to the appropriate reporting agency, be it a children's-aid society, police department, or local child-abuse team. Mandatory-reporting laws usually bring with them legal protection for the nurse against claims that may be laid by parents suspected of being abusers. The accurate and factual data the nurse provides can be very helpful in the investigation of suspected child abuse.

The nurse can also act as a resource person for schoolteachers. Often teachers have a limited understanding of the problem of abuse and its various manifestations. By discussing the types of indicators of abuse the nurse can help the teacher become sensitive to the problem. Since teachers see children every day they are actually the front-line professionals for identification of abuse in the schools. In most jurisdictions, however, the nurse is the only professional routinely in the school who has the legal right to physically examine a child. Consequently, the nurse can assist in checking out the suspicion of abuse.

The third and final level of prevention involves rehabilitation once the problem has been identified and treatment initiated. Because a nurse can often make more frequent home visits than other professionals on the abuse team, she may be designated as the person to do family follow-ups. This can involve working with the abusing parent(s) and child at home, or with the parents themselves if the child has been removed from the home setting. If the child has been placed in protective care, the nurse may also work with the foster family to assist them in their interactions with the child. Children who have been abused often develop behaviors that seem to provoke anger from adults (Martin, 1972). Adults working with these children often need guidance to create a beneficial environment.

Since the school-aged child spends a large proportion of his time in school, it is necessary for school personnel to take some responsibility for the support of the abused child. The teacher should be informed of the treatment plans instituted for the child and his family. She should be aware of the support she can provide for the child while he is in her classroom. If the community-health nurse has good communication with the teacher, she can often be of assistance in this area. She can help teachers utilize healthy parenting behaviors for children. "If inadequate parenting exists at home, the adequate parenting behavior of teachers could enable the child to broaden his scope of coping responses without fear of harsh punishment or criticism of failures" (Bridges, 1978, p. 73).

The teacher's observations about the child, his school performance, peer interaction, and so on should also be shared with others involved in his treatment as they help evaluate its effectiveness. This sharing of information by professionals, for the benefit of the child and family, is the ideal. In many situations there is no feedback about the outcome of an investigation to the professionals who initially identified the abuse. The concerns about human rights and invasion of privacy that have spawned many restrictions on release of information are justified in many circumstances. However, professionals cannot use such restrictions as an excuse not to communicate and thus deprive the abused child and his family of assistance that could be available to them if other professionals only knew it was warranted.

Role Perception

In the preceding section, discussion focused on the responsibilities of the nurse concerning the problem of abuse of school-aged children. A person has responsibilities because of the position he holds, but the success he has in carrying them out is often tied strongly to the perceptions held of him by those with whom he interacts. This is very much the case with the community-health nurse and her handling of the problem of abuse. The way in which the nurse is perceived by children, parents, and school personnel can have a direct influence on her effectiveness.

The community-health nurse may take on a special role in the eyes of the schoolchild. In Wold and Dagg's words:

> She is genuinely viewed as a helping person who, unlike the teachers and the administrative personnel in the school, has no direct control or authority over the students' lives, the school nurse can be a trusted adult to assist the child with his problems without fear of reprisal. (1978, p. 113)

Young school-aged children are usually not afraid of telling the nurse about an injury but will often try to protect their parents. In many instances, children feel they have deserved the treatment they received. The nurse in conjunction with the teacher may help deal with this distortion.

Older children and adolescents may tell the nurse details about their family life that they do not want others to know. This puts the nurse in an awkward position. She does not want to lose the trust of the child but she has a legal and professional responsibility to report all cases of suspected abuse. The child must be made aware of the necessity of reporting and, at the same time, be assured of continued support from the nurse and other professionals in the handling of the problem.

The community-health nurse is generally viewed by families as a helpful and nonthreatening individual. In many instances, abusing families are initially more receptive to a nurse entering their home than they are to visits by other qualified professionals (Cross, 1978). Recognizing how she is perceived by abusing families, the nurse must set out to establish a trusting relationship with parents. This may be a time-consuming endeavor since "many abusive parents have had childhood experiences which taught them to mistrust people" (Josten, 1978, p. 111). But such a relationship is vital to successful assessment and intervention. Honesty, dependability, and helpfulness on the part of the nurse are basic to gaining the trust of parents (Josten, 1978). The nurse must be open with the families about her role in their situation and be clear as to what she can and cannot do. The life experiences of many abusive parents lead them to feel that professional helpers are unreliable. Therefore it is essential for the nurse to follow through on what she promises to do. In part, being helpful means determining where people perceive they need assistance. By helping to meet parents' assessed needs the nurse is proving her credibility as a professional worthy of trust.

Most abusive parents are lacking in good parenting skills and require assistance to develop appropriate behaviors. Within the relationship the nurse establishes with parents, she can act as a role model in the development of positive parenting skills. Constructive handling of feelings is often a problem for abusive parents, therefore, by observing how the nurse handles embarrassment over making a mistake, and how she accepts their right to be angry when they dislike something she does, parents can learn new techniques that will help to channel their feelings more appropriately (Josten, 1978).

Because school personnel often perceive community-health nurses as knowledgeable about child abuse, nurses are usually one of the first professionals brought in when abuse is suspected. As previously mentioned, teachers in many localities are prevented by law from examining a child to the point where removal of clothing is required. The school nurse can perform such an examination and thus becomes a necessary resource for the teacher. School social workers may also perceive the community-health nurse as a valuable resource person and often rely on input from her to help them in their assessment of the family situation.

Using the perception that others have of her as a useful resource person, the nurse should work to strengthen the links among all school personnel involved with the problem of abuse. By drawing from both her experience in schools and in the community, she can contribute data which will be useful to both teachers and social workers as they approach the problem of abuse. In this way the community-health nurse can foster the development and strengthen the effectiveness of a team of school-based professionals dealing with the problem of abuse.

A discussion of the community-health nurse's responsibilities related to child abuse must include some reference to the nurse as an individual with private thoughts and feelings. Child abuse is a very emotion-laden topic and nurses often respond with anger and disgust toward parents who have abused a child. Anger toward parents can lead to a wish to punish them, and intervention efforts may take on this goal. Child abuse is a manifestation of family dysfunction. As such, it affects each member of the family, and each member needs help in order for the family to regain stability. All parents have positive and negative feelings toward their children. In most cases they can control the negative feelings and work them through in ways that do not involve abuse. Some parents, however, lack these coping behaviors and child abuse is the end product. Putting abuse into this type of perspective can assist nurses, and other professionals, in reducing the anger and recognizing that abusing parents are worthy of help.

Related to the idea of parents as villains and children as victims is the concept of rescue fantasy.

> Rescue fantasy usually means a form of behavior observed when the nurse or any other helping person appears to feel that she can save or in some way rescue a person for whom she is caring. (Scharer, 1978, p. 1483)

The feeling that she must save the child from the terrible situation she has discovered may actually prevent the nurse from recognizing the real needs of the child and his family and from instituting supportive interventions that will have long-term benefits. A conscious recognition of this need to help others should help the nurse keep her intervention in perspective.

Another type of behavior that can relate to the rescue fantasy is the need of some nurses to be all things to all people. Some nurses become very depressed and angry when they are not able to meet all the needs identified in an abuse situation. They seem unwilling or unable to acknowledge that other professionals can be of help and may be able to handle some aspects of the situation better, or more appropriately, than they can. Involvement with a child-abuse team can often help nurses with these attitudes. Through working on a team, the individual nurse learns that the ultimate goal of helping the family can often be achieved. The team can also act as a sounding board or tension reliever for team members. By receiving support and understanding from their professional peers, nurses are then better able to model this constructive type of behavior in their interactions with abusing families.

The community-health nurse is thus in a favorable position to help combat the problem of child abuse. Her knowledge base, her easy access to schools, and the acceptance she enjoys from families as a safer helping person contribute to make her a potentially effective member of a team of professionals dealing with abuse in school-aged children.

References

Ayoub, D., and Pfeifer, D. 1977. An approach to primary prevention: the at-risk program. *Children Today 6*, 14-17.

Bridges, C. 1978. The nurse's evaluation. In B.D. Schmitt, ed. *The child protection team handbook.* New York: Garland STPM Press.

Cross, S. 1978. The public health nurse's role in treatment. In B.D. Schmitt, ed. *The child protection team handbook.* New York: Garland STPM Press.

Cunningham, R. 1979. *Child abuse program, Scarborough Department of Health.* Toronto: Faculty of Nursing, University of Toronto.

Friedman, A., Juntti, M., and Scoblic, M. 1976. Nursing responsibility in child abuse. *Nursing Forum 15*, 95-111.

Josten, L. 1978. Out-of-hospital care for a pervasive family problem—child abuse. *American Journal of Maternal-Child Nursing 3*, 111-116.

Leavell, H.R., and Clark, E.G. 1979. Preventive medicine for the doctor in his community. In R. Cunningham. *Child abuse program, Scarborough Department of Health.* Toronto: Faculty of Nursing, University of Toronto.

Martin, H. 1972. The child and his development. In C.H. Kempe and R. Helfer, eds. *Helping the battered child and his family.* Philadelphia: J.B. Lippincott Co.

Martin, H. 1976. Which children get abused: high risk factors in the child. In H. Martin, ed. *The abused child.* Cambridge, Mass.: Ballinger Publishing Co.

Pollock, D., and Steele, B. 1972. A therapeutic approach to parents. In C.H. Kempe and R. Helfer, eds. *Helping the battered child and his family.* Philadelphia: J.B. Lippincott Co.

Scharer, K. 1978. Rescue fantasies: professional impediments in working with abused families. *American Journal of Nursing 78*, 1483-1484.

Wold, S., and Dagg, N. 1978. School nursing: a framework for practice. *Journal of School Health 48*, 111-114.

14

The Relationship between the Schools and a Multidisciplinary Diagnostic Team

Margaret M. Bailey and
Susan L. Scheurer

Multidisciplinary diagnostic teams have developed in many communities to aid in assessment and intervention with families who have difficult parent-child interaction problems, including child abuse and neglect. The authors of this chapter are members of such a team, which has close ties with the major community resources.

The core team includes a pediatrician, child psychologist, nurse clinician, social worker, and coordinator. The majority of referrals come from Children's Protective Services (PS) and in those cases the P.S. worker is included as a team member. The team does not see all P.S. cases, but only the more difficult or complicated ones. Depending on the needs within individual cases the team also expands to include school personnel, public-health nurses, public and private mental-health therapists, medical personnel, the prosecuting attorney, representatives of the family court, and so on.[1]

Each year the team evaluates approximately 300 children suspected of being abused or neglected, guided by the questions:

1. Is there evidence of abuse or neglect?
2. Is the child safe in the home?
3. If the child is safe in the home, what services does the family need to promote a better parent-child relationship?
4. If the child is not safe what, if anything, can be done to make the home safe?

The team refers the children and families to agencies that can provide appropriate treatment. In addition, the team reviews all cases periodically to determine if treatment occurred and what progress had been made.

School personnel are routinely involved in each of the three major areas of child abuse and neglect. First, recognition: the schools are often concerned about whether a child fits the criteria for abuse or neglect or should be considered as at high risk. Second, assessment: the schools often provide firsthand observations from the school setting, share prior evaluations, and evaluate the child's current functioning. Third, intervention: school resources for the child are very important in treatment planning since well over 50 percent of the children assessed have physical, developmental, or emotional handicaps that require treatment.

In all cases of suspected child abuse and neglect the schools work with P.S. In those situations, where additional help is needed, the schools and P.S. may consult with the diagnostic team. Or the team may initiate contact with the schools regarding a mutual case. Over half of the cases seen yearly by the team have directly involved the schools.

The purposes of this chapter are to

1. Describe in greater detail the working relationship between the team and the schools.
2. Discuss obstacles that block effective community interaction.
3. Suggest the requisites necessary for a successful school program.

The chapter is organized around the areas of recognition, assessment, and intervention in child abuse and neglect, using case presentations and comments for illustration.

Recognition

Schools have extended regular contact with most children from ages five and up.[2] Therefore, if problems of abuse and neglect are present, school personnel are the most likely to identify them.

Case 1. Susie,[3] aged eight, and her sister, Harriet, aged twelve, consistently came to school late and usually dirty. They were shunned by their classmates because of their odor. They did poorly in their school work apparently because of frequent absences. Susie's teacher and school nurse took a special interest and spent extra time with her. During one of those talks, Susie revealed that her aunt's boyfriend had tried to molest her. For the teacher and nurse, this incident crystallized the problems as abuse and neglect.

Comments. Recognizing the existence of abuse and neglect is the critical first step in coming to grips with the problem. Sometimes, as in Susie's case, children confide in school personnel. But at other times, subtle nonverbal cues point out the problems. Abused and neglected children frequently exhibit low self-esteem, joylessness, anxiety, extreme responses to adults' commands, speech and other developmental delays.[4] These indirect signs are not diagnostic of child abuse or neglect, but their presence should function as a warning. The diagnostic team may assist the schools by providing education regarding the physical indicators of abuse and neglect, for example, the typical configuration of belt-mark bruises, as well as common psychological problems and developmental delays of these children.

The next step for the school personnel in the above example was a decision to report this family to Children's Protective Services. The suspicion of child abuse or neglect is sufficient grounds to report. Protective Services' role is to determine whether abuse or neglect actually occurred. For school-system employees, the question of how to report is often a problem. The option of reporting simply as concerned individuals always exists. In addition, most school systems now have guidelines for reporting through the school. Fraser (1977) provides an easily adaptable school-policy model along with an excellent general discussion of child abuse and the educator.

In Susie and Harriet's case, the policy was for the teacher or nurse to contact the school social worker, who in turn contacted the attendance officer. The attendance officer, who specialized in working with troubled families, filed the formal report as required by law. Although sounding cumbersome, the protocol was well disseminated to school personnel. The teacher and nurse knew how to get help. Furthermore, having one person who knew every report of suspected child abuse and neglect in the school system allowed for continuity of cases and development of appropriate school policies. In this situation the attendance officer served as a liaison with P.S. for the school system, which minimized problems in reporting and in getting feedback on cases. Difficulties and differences of opinion about cases may still occur. The diagnostic team may be a useful mediator in such unresolved disputes.

A case like Susie and Harriet's highlights another common problem seen frequently in communities dealing with abuse and neglect. For some people, Harriet and Susie's plight would not be considered suspected abuse or neglect, but simply representative of a certain "life-style." Standards of childrearing vary from family to family. The community as a whole has to determine its minimal criteria for acceptable childrearing. The school system can be a tremendously valuable participant in the process of developing community criteria.[5]

There are significant problems if the schools remain outside the policy-making process. The school's standards may be too high, so that Protective Services repeatedly determines the reports to be unjustified. The opposite may also occur, where the school's standards are too low. For example, the schools may allow teachers to punish children by hitting them with paddles on hands, arms, and buttocks while the Family Court in the same community rules that parents may use physical discipline consisting only of a spanking on the buttocks with the bare hand. In this situation the schools allow teachers to use practices not allowed by parents in the same community. The schools and the family courts are inconsistent.

Refer to table 14-1 for a summary of the school's role in recognition of child abuse and neglect.

Assessment

Once cases of suspected abuse and neglect are recognized and reported, the next step is assessment of the family. Did abuse or neglect occur? Are the children safe in the home? What services do the children and family need? Sometimes the cases are straightforward and Protective Services alone can evaluate the situation. But more often the situations are extremely complicated and require the participation of many professionals to answer the questions.

Table 14-1
Components of an Effective School Program

Requisites	*Common Obstacles*
Recognition	
Basic fund of knowledge regarding child abuse and neglect	Ignorance and/or denial of the problem
Effective working relationship with children's protective services and other community programs dealing with troubled families	Uncoordinated system; scapegoating other agencies when cases fall through the cracks; lack of trust between agencies and professionals
Awareness of and participation in formulating community standards	Reliance on individual values and lack of community coordination.
Assessment	
Documentation of problems, including attendance, school performance, behaviors, and any reports of absence	Lack of policy promoting staff's keeping diaries or logs of concerns
Compilation of school's records; organization of the school's approach to the family	Poor communication among different school programs
Coordination with protective services, a diagnostic team, and other appropriate agencies	Difficulty in sharing control; inability or unwillingness to develop functional policy on confidentiality
Intervention	
Advocate for child's needs with consideration of the family as a whole	Ignore family needs and parents' ability to change
Provision of services for the child.	Lack of community commitment and funding for special services
Coordination of schools's treatment efforts	Failure to identify a case coordinator within the school system
Communication with other treatment agencies	Lack of acceptance of the importance of work with parents and the family as a whole
Method for long-term monitoring of the child's and family's progress	Failure to recognize the need for long-term follow-up of those cases

Case 1. (continued). After receiving the school's report about Susie and Harriet, Protective Services asked the school to collect all relevant records including attendance and school performance. The nurse and teacher were asked to write a verbatim account of Susie's report of attempted molestation. Incidentally, there was no log available of the children's appearance or behavior. The P.S. worker then interviewed the children and parents and assessed the home environment.

Comments. Careful documentation is essential in assessing the severity of abuse and neglect. This point is as true in the schools as it is in medical settings, where particular physical injuries are assessed. In this case P.S. and the schools asked for the diagnostic team's advice on how to interview Susie; the direct services of the team were not necessary at that time.

Case 2. Todd, aged five, began the school year in a regular kindergarten. His teacher quickly recognized he could not do the work and appeared to have significant learning problems. In addition, he frequently came to school with bruises on his upper arm and near his elbow which appeared to be "grab marks." The teacher, through established school channels, reported the family to Protective Services but received no response. She then asked the school social worker to assist Todd's mother in learning better child-management techniques.

The teacher scheduled a conference with Todd's mother to propose that he be evaluated for learning disabilities. Todd's mother flatly refused to consider the possibility that Todd might require special education. Concerned that Todd's educational needs were being neglected, the teacher called together the school social worker, school nurse, and the protective-services worker for a case staffing.

Comments. This teacher's actions were very important for several reasons. First, she did not "forget" about Todd, despite the lack of response to her original report to Protective Services. Second, she also recognized, as more problems became apparent, that this family needed a fuller assessment than she could make, and that the assessment would have to be carefully coordinated to assure the mother's cooperation.

The diagnostic team provided a "buffer" in this case in two ways. First, the team, with the schools, persuaded Protective Services to take Todd's situation seriously. Second, the team provided Todd's mother with a second opinion about Todd's educational needs, and a positive view of school services for him.

Case 3. Lois, aged twelve, was a mildly retarded girl, new to the community and school. She revealed to neighbors that her father regularly engaged in sexual activity with her. The neighbors called the police and Protective Services, who placed her in temporary foster care after the parents denied any problems. Lois was extremely difficult to manage in foster care and in school. The assessment of the situation required, for Lois, physical examination; psychological evaluation and interview regarding the sexual abuse; evaluation of her retardation focused on future educational needs; and ways to help her adjust to foster care.

The assessment of Lois's family required evaluation of family dynamics from interviews and observations; family and individual social histories; psychological assessments of the parents, with emphasis on whether Lois could ever return home with minimal risk of reabuse.

Comments. To obtain this assessment, the Protective-Services worker asked the assistance of the diagnostic team to provide services and especially to coordinate the development of a treatment plan.

The schools provided an evaluation of Lois's learning ability, her coping style, and her relationship with peers. The team provided the other aspects of the assessment. All parties met together to share findings and generate recommendations regarding Lois and her family. This case worked fairly smoothly because the professionals trusted and respected each other's assessments. The school had an important role to play in the assessment as a whole.

The strength of the school's position in such assessments is their advocacy for the child. Often abused and neglected children have significant individual problems that warrant attention. The theory that "helping the parents helps the child" is only partially true. School personnel are in an excellent position to identify and speak up for the children's particular needs.

At the same time, the school is in a unique position to know the child thoroughly, but less likely to have a comprehensive view of the family as a whole. The danger of this position is that recommendations may be made without consideration of the parents' strengths, needs, and their ability to change. In staff meetings, this problem may crystallize around the question of the child's safety in the home. Without a full assessment, removing the children may seem to be the only solution. This kind of controversy is best settled in two ways: first, by the school's awareness of and participating in formulating community standards. Second, each participant in the assessment must recognize the usefulness of pooling everyone's information, in order to generate the most complete evaluation and plan. Table 14-1 summarizes the school's role in assessment.

Intervention

The treatment services offered for families who abuse or neglect their children hinge on a thorough evaluation of the problems leading to the mistreatment of the children. Once the situation is assessed, the schools have a vital, unique role to play in treatment.

Case 1 (continued). The problems identified in Susie and Harriet's family included poor hygiene, lack of adequate supervision by their parents, and reliance on both girls as babysitters for younger siblings during school hours. The attempted sexual assault had occurred when the girls were unsupervised. This family's strengths included strong attachment between mother and children, mother's reliable work history, and mother's willingness to see the problems and accept help.

Comments. In the treatment plan developed for this family, the school personnel provided continuing support and encouragement to the girls; special tutoring to assist them in catching up with their work; guidance regarding hygiene and grooming by the school nurse. Other agencies provided crisis-intervention counseling for Susie and day care for younger siblings. With P.S. the team provided a clear statement of expectations and limits regarding hygiene and school attendance to the mother.

A thorough treatment plan does not end with the provision of services. An additional major component is a method to monitor the success of the plan. In the above example, the schools could monitor progress of the family through records of the girls' attendance and performance, plus the teacher's and nurse's notes on their appearance and behavior. The team convened periodically for reviews with the mother and treatment agencies to assure followthrough.

Case 2 (continued). The problems of Todd's case included his mother's depression, her lack of knowledge of appropriate childrearing techniques, her repeated physical abuse of Todd, her fear of special education for her son (based on her personal experience in school), and Todd's learning disabilities. Medical evaluation indicated Todd had suffered brain damage from blows to the head during infancy. The family's strengths included Todd's mother's strong advocacy for her child and Todd's easygoing nature.

Comments. The school provided Todd's mother with a preliminary visit to the special-education classroom where he was eventually placed, a meeting for all parties concerned to discuss his educational needs,[6] and a social worker to assist Todd's mother in learning and using management techniques developed by his teacher. Additional mental-health services, outside the school system, were provided for Todd's mother.

In this case, because of the multiple school services needed, a coordinated effort was necessary to avoid duplication. The school social worker agreed to provide the required coordination. Careful communication among services also insured that Todd's mother received consistent advice on childrearing rooted in the schoolteacher's actual experiences with him. The diagnostic team provided the schools with information about the success of therapy for Todd's mother.

Case 3 (continued). The assessment of Lois and her family found clear evidence of sexual abuse and that the family needed multiple services from many agencies, including the schools, Family Court, community mental health, and the foster-care agency. Lois was a pleasant, outgoing girl, but the family as a unit had no definable strengths and no ability to protect her. Lois remained in foster care and her foster family functioned as paraprofessionals in the treatment process. Coordinating these agencies was a major task. The diagnostic team remained active in the case to arrange regular reviews of progress and problems for Lois and her family.

Comments. In Lois's case, the schools provided a valuable portion of the intervention plan. However, the major decision-making body became the Family Court, who assumed both jurisdiction and custody over Lois to insure her safety. The diagnostic team arranged regular reviews to share findings and update recommendations with the court worker (see table 14-2 for a summary of the diagnostic team's services to the schools). This process prevented a sense of powerlessness and frustration on the part of other agencies. Although the court retained control, the school and other agencies were able to contribute their opinions and recommendations in an atmosphere of mutual respect. Table 14-2 summarizes the school's role in intervention.

Table 14-2

Services Provided by a Multidisciplinary Team to the Schools

Recognition
1. In-service training in recognizing abuse and neglect
2. Buffer and mediator in unresolved disputes between the school and protective services

Assessment
1. Expertise in multi-problem family assessments
2. Orchestration of the various agencies involved in assessment
3. Mediator between schools and parents

Intervention
1. Identification of a long-term case coordinator
2. Providing a setting where agencies share findings

Summary

The school's role in dealing with the problems of abused and neglected children extends beyond providing services. A complete school program for these children includes recognition and assessment, as well as intervention. The school functions best as an advocate for the special needs of the child, but not to the exclusion of the family. Because of the complexity of these troubled families, the schools benefit from close working ties with a multidisciplinary diagnostic team. In most cases, services and circumstances outside the school system necessitate a continuing coordinated effort among the school, protective services, and other agencies.

Notes

1. The authors are fortunate to be part of a coordinated community effort that deals with child abuse and neglect through assessment, treatment, and education. Helfer (1976) describes this program in detail. Schmitt's (1977)

handbook can serve as a guide for communities in organizing a diagnostic team similar to the one described in this chapter.

2. This chapter addresses only the school-aged child. Many areas, including Michigan, offer extensive services to preschool-aged children. The same process described here for dealing with child abuse and neglect applies to the younger population.

3. All names are fictitious.

4. Martin (1976) describes these children thoroughly and is an excellent reference.

5. Many communities now have regular meetings of representatives from the agencies that deal with child abuse and neglect. The purposes of these meetings often include formulating consistent community policies and protocols. To participate in the development of community standards for childrearing, the schools' staff may attend such meetings. If no such forum exists, the schools may start one.

6. Michigan law provides for such an educational planning and placement committee meeting prior to special-education placement.

References

Fraser, B.G. 1977. *The educator and child abuse.* Chicago, Ill.: National Committee for Prevention of Child Abuse.

Helfer, R.E., and Kempe, H.C. 1976. *Child abuse and neglect: the family and the community.* Cambridge, Mass.: Ballinger Publishing Co.

Martin, H.P. 1976. *The abused child.* Cambridge, Mass.: Ballinger Publishing Co.

Schmitt, B.D. 1978. *The child protection team handbook.* New York: Garland STPM Press.

**Part IV
Current Issues in the Study
and Treatment of Child Abuse**

15 Child-Abuse Law in Canada and the United States

Bernard M Dickens

The capacity of professionals in the school setting to act *in loco parentis* is double-edged; the power of reasonable discipline is countered by the duty to give protective care to children while in the school's charge. Professionalism imports an individual responsibility to maintain skills at the standard which a prudent member of the profession is expected to observe. Recent emphasis upon the school-based professional's role in the detection of child abuse requires all practitioners in schools to become alert to their duty to identify and respond appropriately to grounds for suspecting abuse of the children in their charge. The development of training materials and texts regarding child abuse to sensitize and inform professionals working in schools has raised the standard of care professionals are expected to maintain.

The laws of most jurisdictions require school personnel to observe the health condition of children in attendance, not just to contain any spread of infection from one to another but to safeguard the welfare of each individual child. Learning disorders, inability to concentrate, malnutrition, undernourishment, and comparable conditions, whether or not they immediately affect the educative process, are expected to be identified. Similarly, psychiatric abnormalities may come within the school professional's means of identification, or at least within the range of indications for reasonable suspicion that a need exists for further, more specialized diagnosis.

It cannot yet be said that a school professional failing to identify child abuse or to be suspicious of its presence with the attentiveness and skill expected, and failing to respond appropriately, incurs legal liability to the child for subsequent injury that professional skill and the required response would have prevented. Nevertheless, legal doctrine is firmly in place showing that, at a time not necessarily in the distant future, such liability may be found. North America shares a common-law heritage (except for Quebec and Louisiana), and the potential of its uniform jurisprudence was shown in a 1975 California case, *Landeros* v. *Flood*. This involved a professional, who happened to be a physician, who was held liable to a negligence suit brought on behalf of an abused child. The negligence consisted not so much in failure to appreciate that the child's observed and unexplained injuries might have been inflicted as a result of the deliberate behavior of an adult guardian, but rather in failure to report the suspicions that should have arisen. The physician permitted the child to return home, where further abuse caused the prospect of permanent disability. Professional literature and teaching on diagnosis of injury to young children had recognized the battered-child syndrome some years earlier, and professional liability arose from the defendant's negligent failure to take account of this development and to respond appropriately.

Similarly in the school setting, it has been recently recognized that child abuse, including neglect, may explain a child's poor school performance and behavior problems, the latter perhaps focusing as much upon listlessness and fearfulness as upon mischievousness; the passive, dutiful child may be no less a problem than the child who acts out. Professionals in schools are expected to be alert to this possible explanation of problem behavior, and to react appropriately. At the most basic level, school personnel may be expected to note abnormally frequent or widespread abrasions, bruising, scarring, or comparable markings on a child's body obvious to normal inspection which are not satisfactorily explained. Health personnel in schools may also be expected to note signs of failure to thrive and of emotional distress.

The legal duties *owed by* school personnel are to be vigilant for signs of such expressions, and to respond appropriately. The law must operate by reference to objective criteria of adequately up-to-date knowledge, adequate vigilance and suspicion, and adequate response, since the law has no means to evaluate the subjective human quality of caring. As a normative discipline, the law aims to identify the standards to which school personnel must adhere, by which their performance can be evaluated and self-evaluated. In principle, legal expectations will be based upon the requirements which the different professional groups functioning within schools make of themselves, since the general requirement is that each individual will do what a reasonably prudent competent member of his or her own profession would be expected to do according to the standards of that profession.

No group has exclusive power, however, to set its own legally established standards. If professional negligence were to mean simply falling below internally or privately set standards, professional groups such as physicians, lawyers, and schoolteachers might gain an incentive to set their minimum standards lower than would serve the public interest. Accordingly, the courts acting through a judge or jury reserve for themselves the residual right to find that an individual, who conformed to standards of professional practice, nevertheless fell short of legal expectations, and that a party suffering injury was entitled to a higher standard of professional care than was applied. The converse is not the case, however, since conduct falling below professional standards will axiomatically be below legally required standards. The burden of professionalism is that failure to meet professional standards is unavoidably inculpating, while maintaining minimum standards of the profession is no safeguard against legal liability.

In legal proceedings, the issue of what behavior or response professional standards require in a given situation will be determined by expert evidence, usually called on behalf of all the contending parties to a dispute. Testimony favored by the judge or jury will indicate to the community what standards are acceptable and expected. This means of professional quality control is somewhat sporadic and uneven, however, and legislatures often intervene to give more systematic expression to legal standards. This is particularly so regarding child abuse, since all jurisdictions state what conduct or conditions constitute abuse or neglect of a child, whether a report has to be made, whether a duty to report prevails over other competing interests, such as in parental privacy, and to whom any report may or must be made.

The Concept of Abuse

Legislation addressing abuse, maltreatment, and neglect of children has a common focus, but the fine tuning of particular expression varies from one jurisdiction to another. Professionals must become familiar with the range of factors constituting abuse and/or neglect within their own jurisdiction. Appendixes A and B following this chapter show the range of items covered in the legislation of the American states and Canadian provinces, respectively. A number of items may appear to overlap, but no single jurisdiction includes all of the items tabulated for its country.

There is an obvious sense in which any assault upon or ill-treatment of a child constitutes child abuse, but the term is applied to abuse originating within the relation of parent, or other adult guardian for the time being, and child; that is, between an adult and his "own" child. The concern is with abuse of a child by the person in whose charge the child is, and applies to individual guardians, families, and institutions having factual charge. This is not definite, but supposes a continuous dependent relationship, as opposed to both the episodic involvement with a child of, for instance, a day-care attendant and the nondependent relation between siblings and between a child and its single mother's transient partner. Even in this setting, however, child abuse may occur in the passive sense; that is, the adult guardian is accountable for permitting abuse by the sibling or partner if he fails to act to prevent it.

The concept of abuse is clearly causative; it supposes that the adult guardian has either actively caused or passively permitted the abuse. This poses a problem for professionals required to be protectively vigilant, since when they are suspicious of injury which may have resulted from abuse they may have no reliable means to confirm this cause. The duty of care, however, is a duty to see objective grounds for reasonable suspicion. It is not a duty to be correct in that suspicion. A suspicion arising from reasonable grounds and applied in good faith enjoys legal protection, even when the cause of a child's appearance of abuse is in fact innocent (see below).

The generic concept of child abuse is divisible into active assault and passive neglect, and has both physical and psychological aspects. Active physical assault constitutes the nucleus of child battering and may create visibly obvious indications of bruising, scarring, and fractures. Physical neglect will create different indications, however, perhaps in sores, undernourishment, and hygienic inadequacies of body and clothing. Active psychological injury may result from the child's being under constant reprimand, criticism, and adverse comparison with another child of the family. It may express itself in a poor self-image, lack of confidence, and defeatism. Passive psychological neglect may be disguised behind a supply of material commodities and toys, but may leave the child with a lack of relationships with adults, and affectionless. Particular symptoms of the different forms of abuse or neglect at the different developmental stages of child growth are established by disciplines other than law, of course, but legislation aims to give expression to the specific forms of abuse against which an individual legislature has determined to act.

Definitions of abuse employed in legislation may concentrate, for instance, both upon conditions of children when in unfit company, accommodation, or employment, and upon conduct of parents or analogous guardians. Immoral conduct is almost invariably included in legislated formulae, but there is evidence that this has permitted censorious, oppressive, and intolerant interventions into the homes of the poor and of, for instance, minority-group members. Guidance may be taken from local courts of a jurisdiction to see what forms of unorthodoxy render children in need of protection, liable to supervision in the home, or to removal from their homes and parents. The traditional immoralities, largely focused on sexual relations outside of marriage, are decreasingly found to be disqualifications from childrearing. There is evidence that the concept of abuse requiring intervention by professionals engaged in the school setting may be somewhat more narrowly construed, lest the full license of the law may come to be oppressively employed against parents of harmless but deviant life-styles. This has recently been recognized in, for instance, the province of Ontario. Here, child-welfare legislation defines a child in need of protection, so as to justify public intervention, in traditional form under sixteen of the heads in appendix B, but new provisions in force from 1979 isolate professionally reportable child "abuse" as meaning a condition caused by a child's guardian of (1) physical harm, (2) malnutrition or mental ill-health of a degree that if not immediately remedied could impair growth and development or result in permanent injury or death, or (3) sexual molestation. These conditions are adequately specific and objective in that they may be reasonably identified or suspected by health, educational, or other involved professionals.

Detection

In a legalistic sense, detection of child abuse is a function of its definition, but detection by professionals in schools is a function of their trained skills. Teachers, nurses, and, for instance, social workers have acquired specific abilities they apply to their particular tasks, and must be vigilant to the extent of their expertise and professional capacity. They may receive signs of abuse from different sources and will have trained sensitivities to different forms of expression of victimization. Clearly, no special talent is required to observe bruising and scarring on a child, but a duty may exist to note its frequency and extent. A teacher in routine classroom contact may be expected to note little more of physical manifestations of possible abuse and neglect than the frequency of bruising and scarring, and, for instance, inadequate clothing in severe weather, whereas a nurse with less regular contact may be expected to interpret any single instance of bruising and scarring as possibly being of nonaccidental origin, or to realize that it is unlikely to have been caused by the explanation offered. A teacher may lack a nurse's means to remove clothing for further signs of physical abuse and sexual molestation, although a teacher conducting exercises, games, or giving swimming lessons may gain more opportunities for physical examination than others. While, as a citizen, a teacher enjoys any other individual's right to undertake private investigation of crime at his own risk, the duty of a teacher as such is to involve other available professionals whose skills and legal capacities are more obviously relevant, such as by requesting a school nurse to further investigate the teacher's observations to determine if grounds for suspicion of abuse exist.

Much investigation of possible abuse, such as psychological abuse or physical neglect, requires no physical examination, but only simple questioning, which a teacher and a social worker are entitled to undertake. Children showing abnormal signs, such as exhaustion, may be asked what time they usually go to bed, what household or other tasks they have to perform for their parents or other guardians, and whether they are regularly struck, shouted at, or, for instance, rarely addressed at home by adults. Similarly, children may be asked the cause of visible injuries. School professionals will be aware particularly of younger children's imperfect differentiation between fact and fantasy, and may properly regard many disturbing responses not as proof in themselves of abuse, but as a basis for further enquiry or for reporting concerns to appointed or otherwise suitable authorities for verification. In many cases, children's responses may justify instigating discussions with parents. Accommodating their possible resentment of school personnel's invasion of family privacy is an attribute of professionalism.

Those engaged in schools must be sensitive to the value of parental and domestic privacy and contain any inordinate curiosity about a family's circumstances.

They must be certain to take inquisitorial or referring initiatives only upon appropriate grounds. These may arise spontaneously, for instance, in the course of a child's descriptive play or composition, when some inadvertent disclosures may more clearly generate suspicion than others. When they corroborate pre-existing evidence of domestic irregularity or indicate, for instance, sexual moles-tation, including practices of which the child does not comprehend the sig-nificance, school professionals must not hestitate to initiate inquiries for fear of offending parents. The duty of vigilance is owed to children, as possible victims, and it is to be given priority.

School professionals may have to strive to maintain a duality of perception, however, in acting as if their reasonable suspicions are valid so far as the children are concerned, but invalid regarding the parents or other guardians. They may take instruction from the fact that signs indicating that a child has been delib-erately burned by a cigarette may indeed be authentic indications of cruelty, but the marks may also be infected mosquito bites, which are indistinguishable from cigarette burns without special equipment. One must respond to the child as if they were burns, but respond to the parents as if they were bites in need of attention.

Responses

The point at which a reasonable suspicion of child abuse is verified is a matter of professional judgment, of which training and experience are independently adequate elements; that is, an inexperienced professional should not fail to respond to indications he has been trained to identify when more experienced colleagues may be reluctant to act. Those trained at a time before professional instruction in the field of child abuse was available should not dismiss suspicions founded *on developed intuition.* Pursuit of adequate verification, where it is objectively needed because of the marginal nature of the evidence, may justify reference to peers, senior colleagues, school administrators, or members of related professions working in the same school. Clarification of uncertain evi-dence may be sought by appropriate questioning of the child or his parents, or by physical examination conducted by nursing or other health personnel.

When initial suspicion remains unresolved, after all reasonable and expedi-tious enquiries as may properly be made for purposes of authentication, legisla-tion prescribes the response, which is usually compelled under the threat of penal sanctions. A report of suspicion must be made, with details such as the child's name, address, and ground for suspicion. The report made to an authority will usually be identified by each jurisdiction's legislation, and will probably be a child-welfare agency of government or a comparable quasi-public authority, director of central child-abuse register, local medical officer of health, the police, district attorney, or Crown attorney. Reporting genuine suspicion only to a school principal or other senior officer will not suffice for discharge of the legislated reporting duty.

It must be emphasized that the duty is to report not the proven fact of abuse, but reasonable suspicion. The agency receiving the report will have to assess it, make such further enquiries as it considers proper, and determine upon its own action and the personnel to undertake it. This does not in itself concern the school-based professional, although the agency receiving the report may check back to confirm details of evidence, perhaps with a view to instigating legal proceedings. Further, if such agency maintains a register, it does not necessarily follow that a party reporting will be given details of follow-up activity, and school professionals may be unable to gain access to recorded data to authenticate their suspicions of abuse either before or after a report is made. This will depend, of course, upon the regulations under which the register is operated.

A report made in good faith enjoys full legal protection, under the express terms of legislation and also under the general law. The name of an informant need not be disclosed to a reported child's parents, and if the professional informant does happen to be identified, no legal liability can be established where the report was conscientiously based on reasonable evidence, and accordingly was given in good faith. Mere error of professional judgment falls far short of legal negligence, and attracts no liability in law. Professionals have a legal power to be mistaken, and where a ground for reasonable suspicion exists, a premature report, even when made defensively in order to avoid any risk of liability for nonreporting, is legally defensible.

Where the reported suspicion is proven not to involve abuse in fact, any action for defamation would fail either because legislation precludes such action based on a report made in good faith, or because of the common-law defense of qualified privilege. This protects communications made nonmaliciously by a person with a legal, moral, or social right to give information, including misinformation, to a person with a proper interest to receive it. Thus not only are formal reports protected, but preliminary discussions with colleagues and administrators may also be protected if conducted in reasonable pursuit of clarification and investigation. Similarly, whether the reporter's indication of abuse is sound or not, no question of breach of privacy or of professional confidentiality can usually arise. Legislation again tends to displace common law and otherwise-legislated parental rights and professional obligations of privacy or confidentiality in favor of affording children maximum protection.

The displacement of professional confidentiality serves a double purpose. It indicates to professionals themselves that they have little option about reporting, and cannot invoke confidentiality as a defense for their refusal or failure to report the suspicions they had, or as competent professionals should have had. In addition, however, it invalidates instructions from school heads, municipal departments or boards of education, and similar authorities attempting to circumscribe or regulate reporting by front-line school personnel. The fact that such personnel can disregard such purported instructions with legal impunity does not obviate the need for their express revocation where they exist, however, since they create a harmful obstacle or delay in reporting. A professional cannot succeed in claiming obedience to superior orders as a defense against having disregarded a legislated duty, but may in fact face a career dilemma in seeming to defy such instructions. If they are clearly merely advisory, however, or if they provide a means for passing on a report rather than a means to select which professionally held suspicions will be appropriately reported and which will not, they may be unobjectionable.

Where a narrow definition of compulsorily reportable abuse has been adopted, such as in Ontario (see below), suspicion of need of protection arising from circumstances not so narrowly defined as abusive is obviously not reportable by threat of legal sanction. It may nevertheless remain defensible to report such suspicions, with full protection. In Ontario, for instance, while abuse as narrowly defined must be reported by any person who encounters it in the course of professional or official duties, every person may report a child's being in need of protection, with the same legal protections against suit, for instance, for defamation or breach of confidentiality. This protects neighbors, friends, and every other person deciding on reasonable grounds to take a protective initiative.

Failure to Report

It has been seen that, while no case appears to have been brought, it is conceivable that a school professional whose failure to report suspicion of abuse caused or contributed to preventable injury to a child could be held legally liable to that child for breach of duty. The liability of a school nurse may appear more obvious, both because liability of another health professional has already been recognized by a court, and because a nurse has greater means to investigate and identify battered and otherwise abused children. Other legal liability may be more immediate, however, and more evenly spread among the ranks of school-based professionals.

Legislation imposing a reporting duty has penal sanctions for nonreporting. This may not apply where the basis of nonreporting is nonidentification, since a penalty in the latter case would convert professional incompetence or malpractice into a crime, which is not the intention of such legislation. Disregard or defiance of the legislation upon acquisition of reasonable suspicion, which itself may to a certain extent be objectively determined, will attract penalties of a fine and/or liability to imprisonment. The latter sanction may appear unduly severe, but much legislation creating a number of specific offenses groups them together for designation of penalties, the less severe being governed by the maximum for the more severe; individual cases are resolved, of course, by judicial assessment on their particular facts.

More likely for nurses may be the imposition of professional sanctions. Teachers and social workers have not generally achieved a status of professional self-regulation where they are accountable to their professional peers for offenses of professional misconduct. Nurses tend to bear such accountability, however, and breach of a duty imposed by legislation can scarcely be disregarded by professional disciplinary and licensing authorities. This is a significant means by which self-regulating professions keep faith with the public. Similarly, a nurse failing to identify grounds to suspect child abuse, and thereby escaping criminal liability for nonreporting, may face incompetency charges and jeopardize the right to professional practice. The fact that teachers and social workers may not face comparable proceedings before their peers indicates that they are not organized in the same way as the self-regulating traditional professions. In common with nurses, however, they are liable to dismissal or other disciplinary proceedings by their employers, not least because they may become in breach of their contract of employment by virtue either of incompetence or of failure to comply with collateral legal duties of reporting where required by legislation.

Less formal sanctions may appear less threatening, but in fact they may be the harder to endure because they may offer fewer means of legal challenge and redress, and no opportunity for protection by representations by a labor organization. Condemnation at an inquest conducted by a coroner may be professionally damaging, as may similar condemnation at a judicial inquiry into a child's death thereby proven to have been preventable, even though legal representation may be available at such proceedings. Even where no legal, quasi-legal, or administrative proceedings are taken, adverse criticism by child-welfare agencies and in the news media can follow from professionals disregarding their legal responsibilities, through ignorance, oversight, or obstinacy. It may appear than an historic choice of remaining inactive because of reluctance to become involved may no longer exist. School-based professionals may have no option but to become involved, by legal and social pressures, in saving their young charges from continuing abuse by their permanent guardians.

References

Katz, Sanford. 1978. *When parents fail.* Reproduced in Bernard M. Dickens. Legal responses to child abuse. *Family Law Quarterly 1,* 7–8.

Komar, R., in Bernard M. Dickens. 1978. Legal responses to child abuse in Canada. *Canadian Journal of Family Law 87,* 94–96; Appendix I, 122–125.

Landeros v. *Flood* (1975), 123 Cal. Rptr. 713.

Appendix 15A
United States Tests of
Children in Need of
Protection

A child may be in need of protection:

1. When the child lacks parental care because of its parent's mental or physical disability.
2. When a parent refuses or neglects to provide for a child's needs.
3. When a parent has abandoned a child.
4. When a child's home, by reason of neglect, cruelty, or depravity of its parents, is unfit.
5. When a parent refuses to provide for a child's moral needs.
6. When a parent refuses to provide for a child's mental needs.
7. When a child's best interests are not being met.
8. When a child's environment, behavior, or associations are injurious to it.
9. When a child begs, receives alms, or sings in the street for money.
10. When a child associates with disreputable or immoral people, or lives in a house of ill repute.
11. When a child is found or employed in a bar.
12. When a child's occupation is dangerous or when it is working contrary to the child-labor laws.
13. When a child is living in an unlicensed foster home or has been placed by its parents in a way detrimental to it or contrary to law.
14. When a child's conduct is delinquent as a result of parental neglect.
15. When a child is in danger of being brought up to lead an idle, dissolute, or immoral life.
16. When a mother is unmarried and without adequate provision for the care and support of her child.
17. When a parent, or another with the parent's consent, performs an immoral or illegal act before the child.
18. When a parent habitually uses profane language in front of a child.

Appendix 15B
Canadian Tests of
Children in Need of
Protection

1. A child who is voluntarily surrendered to a child-care agency.
2. An illegitimate child whose mother is unable or unwilling to care for him.
3. A child who is not being properly cared for.
4. A child whose custodian, by reason of illness, infirmity, misfortune, incompetence, or imprisonment, is unable to care for him.
5. A child whose custodian is undergoing imprisonment.
6. A child whose parents are "unfit" to have charge of him.
7. A child whose parents refuse to maintain him.
8. A child who is being allowed to grow up without salutary parental control, and who is tending to become incorrigible, idle, or dissolute.
9. A child who is beyond the control of his parents.
10. A child who is without proper supervision or control.
11. A child under twelve years of age who is unsupervised.
12. A child whose custodian refuses or neglects to provide needed medical or surgical care.
13. A child subjected to emotional or mental neglect, lack of affection, etcetera.
14. A child whose life, health, or morals may be endangered by the custodian's conduct.
15. A child who has been assaulted or ill-treated by the custodian.
16. A child exposed to infection from tuberculosis or from venereal disease where preventative measures are not taken.
17. A child subject to such physical disability as is likely to make him a public charge.
18. A child who is deserted or abandoned by his custodian.
19. A child whose parents have abandoned him to the care of strangers.
20. An orphan who is not being properly cared for.
21. A child who is living in an unfit or improper place.
22. A child who is found in a disorderly house.
23. A child who habitually frequents any tavern, poolhall, or gambling room.
24. A child who has no settled place of abode or who is found sleeping at night in improper accommodation.
25. A child who is associating with unfit or improper persons.
26. A child who is found begging in a public place.
27. A child found to be loitering or vagrant.
28. A child who is engaged in street trades at night.
29. A child who sells newspapers or other objects in a public place.

30. A child who conducts himself immorally.
31. A child who is in possession of obscene pictures, drawings, or printed matter.
32. A child who is employed at night.
33. A child who is guilty of having committed offences.
34. A child whose parent consents or connives in the commission of an offence.
35. A child who habitually absents himself from his home.
36. A child who habitually absents himself from school.
37. A child whose parents refuse to provide an education.
38. A child exhibiting serious character disturbance.

16 Metatheories of Child Abuse

Norman W. Bell

Once upon a time people knew that the earth was the center of the universe. Such was the power of the paradigm they held that their observations lent support to their theory; discordant facts were not seen, or, if seen, dismissed. Heretics such as Galileo had to be shown the error of their ways and made to recant. The struggle to establish a new paradigm of the universe was bitter and long, the costs—political, social, and personal—were great.

The point of this brief glance at the history of science is to emphasize that theory determines facts as much as vice versa. The truth of observations is always relative to the assumptive framework within which observations are made. Nowhere is this problem of the relation of metatheory and observation more acute than in the science of human behavior. For them, the observer is part of what has to be observed. His mental set—his assumptions, his preconceived ideas, his own relationship to the phenomena he observes—structures what is seen and what is not seen (Giovanni, 1974). That which is known is intimately intertwined with the process of knowing and the knower (Dewey and Bentley, 1949; Spiegel, 1971; Spiegel and Bell, 1959).

The Nature of Child Abuse

The relationship between knowing and the known is a salient issue in the study of child abuse. In the past decade and a half there has been an explosion of interest in the phenomenon. The literature has become vast, assembled in bibliographies, reviewed. Some professionals have become specialists on the problem. Workshops, conferences, and seminars are regularly held. Certain findings have been repeated often enough to be passed on and received as true. Laws have been written to combat or control it. Teams have been organized to deal with it. Registries have been established to record it.

Certainly the problem seems real enough. The label itself is sufficiently evocative that one one seems to be in doubt that the phenomenon exists and about what it is. The more closely we look at it the more of it we see; in some places it is said to be epidemic. But what is the it? Or rather, what are the existing conceptions of child abuse, and how do these conceptions guide what we see and how we understand what we see? Perhaps it is worthwhile pausing before the obvious, to see more precisely what it is we are seeing, to identify the perspective from which it is seen, and to reexamine some of the knowledge we have.

This chapter attempts to sketch some existing conceptions of child abuse and to explore some of the areas these conceptions lead us to or lead us away from. Any reexamination of what is obvious and taken for granted may be irritating. The purpose is not to denigrate one or another conception of child abuse, nor to assert that there is one true or superior way of looking at child abuse. If it can show that the obvious is not in all respects so obvious, and the reader sensitized to the notion that the perspectives we bring affect what we see and how we state what we see, the purpose will have been served.

A Legal Conception of Child Abuse

One way of conceiving what child abuse is is to focus on it as a legal category of behavior that is proscribed, and if committed, the perpetrator is punished. Since the status of the child as a person, with rights, is a recent and uncertain field, a clear guide to what constitutes abuse and how it is to be distinguished from accident or legitimate discipline is not clear. The category has come into the law recently, following its establishment as a medical syndrome (Newberger and Bourne, 1979), and has not yet achieved unambiguous definition. In the United States, a California physician risks malpractice action if he fails to report injuries that a teacher in a Miami school can legally inflict (Newberger and Bourne, 1979). Under Canadian law, children may be in need of protection for a wide variety of causes, including frequenting a pool hall, sleeping at night in improper accommodations, selling newspapers in a public place, as well as having been assaulted or ill-treated by the custodian (Dickens, 1980).   The intentions of the law seem clear and laudable, but circular definitions and the subsuming of such diverse conditions does not demarcate clearly a category of action which can be called abuse.

Law is, of course, much more than the statutes which define certain acts as punishable. Law is a social-control mechanism which finds part of its force in the preliminary stages of detection and definition. Child abuse is a special type of crime in that normally the complaint does not come from the victim. Rather it depends largely for its detection on others to suspect that abuse had occurred. The trend in recent law has been to create an obligation for certain professionals to report suspected cases of child abuse, coupled with a protection against liability actions as long as the reporting is done in good faith. As Newberger and Bourne (1979) suggest this touches on the twin dilemmas of family autonomy versus coercive intervention and compassion versus control. The attempts through law to control child abuse appear to impose one kind of definition in an area regarding which there is low consensus and deep ambivalence. Furthermore the law accentuates one aspect of what may be an ongoing relationship (for example, between physician and patient or teacher and child), making it the subject of legal attention. What the implications of such attention are for the relationship, especially since the issue of legal proof will be decided in other ways, and particularly since the beneficial effects of reporting, in terms of good or adequate treatment/control services, are uncertain.

Reporting a suspicion of child abuse does not establish that it has occurred. Verification involves other procedures and often other professionals. The conception that seems to run through legal literature is that the objective establishment of abuse can be attained through the judgment of experts (Dickens, 1976). What cannot be specified in law then comes to rest on the opinion of other non-legal, mainly medical, experts. In some cases the evidence, such as skeletal X-rays, may be conclusive. In the cases where the evidence is less conclusive or may involve the judgment of the effects of passive neglect, the attribution of objectivity to other experts involves definitions and reality which are not easily sustained, and may have consequences for the abuser and the further occurrence of abuse (Marsden, 1978; Newberger and Bourne, 1979).

Within a legal perspective, human actions which are to be proscribed usually must be specified. The law assumes that there are some human actions which can be identified or be isolated from ongoing interaction. It is further assumed that there is a victim, someone who suffers from these human actions, and that the actions can be attributed to an individual or individuals who can be held responsible for having done something or failed to do something (Law Reform Commission of Canada, 1974). Those accused of wrong doing, in turn, have the right to have the charges against them specified and to have their guilt or innocence determined by a defined set of procedures about what is evidence, and how intention and culpability are to be judged. Even though the laws fail to give definitions of what child abuse is and is not—that is, to specify what range or types of actions are to be included within the category "child abuse"—it does suggest it is a type of action in which there is a victim and a victimizer. It also suggests that the intent and the responsibility of the victimizer can be determined. Further, laws specify that when guilt is determined, there are penalties which can be administered against the guilty party.

The vagueness of the law in specifying what child abuse is may be a matter of the lag of law in formulating just what this crime is. Or is may be that the interactions of parents, or other caregivers, and children don't fit well into the mold which the law assumes. Equally possible is the fact that, when the result is assumed to be present—that is, when some minor is perceived as being a victim—the other elements—victimizer, intent, responsibility—will be assumed to exist.

Mental Conceptions of Child Abuse

An alternative conception of child abuse which has become widespread is the notion that child abuse is a disease (Fontana, 1976). Once again it is assumed that something unitary enough to be put into a category exists, and that it can be understood as a form of pathological functioning. The pathology may reside in the parenting individual or the parent-child relationship. As with a legal conception, the assumption is that there is a victim—someone who suffers from the sickness—however, in this conception accent is laid upon pathology rather than upon legal responsibility. Sickness is, of course, by definition undesirable and a state which should be cured by some type of intervention. Just who intervenes and by what means will vary with the formulation of the nature of the sickness, but once again there is a victim and the victim must be helped.

In practical terms, such a conception may be more humane and more effective than a legal conception, but the questions can still be posed as to whether the conception fits reality as commonly perceived and, more important, whether the conception does not structure what will be looked at and what will be seen. Medical, or more properly, sickness, conceptions of child abuse also have the function of explaining the phenomenon and of structuring what should be done about it, in other words, treatment.

One of the difficulties with the sickness conception of child abuse is that it is unclear whether it applies to all cases or only to some cases. If the latter, what are the distinguishing features which would allow a diagnosis of sickness rather than some other assignment of the case to a different class? On this there seems to be considerable dissension with the helping professions. Some writers (Greenland, 1973) seem to suggest that all cases of child abuse stem from a sickness while others hold that the sickness conception only fits a minority of cases (Walters, 1975).

A Social-Construction Conception of Child Abuse

Various investigators have noted that the types of injuries to a child can lead to very different presumptions about the nature of the actions which led up to the inquiry (Walters, 1975; Chatterton, 1976). Chatterton, for example, develops a scenario of a person struck on the street, his nose bleeding, but the violence evokes no action from a nearby policeman. By adding various contextual factors—that the person struck was a child, the striker, his parent; that the child had just endangered himself by stepping into the roadway and nearly being hit by a car; and that the child had been warned by his mother of such danger. What contextual elements are added, he suggests, affects the perception of and response to the event. Gelles (1975) argues in a similar vein that the phenomenon of child abuse must include processes by which it is identified and labeled. Thus the social definitions of the gatekeepers charged with identifying children injured by their caretakers become part of the phenomenon which must be observed. This significant shift of conception to a complex social labeling process shifts the type of theorizing concerning causes and correlates what needs to be observed and what remedial strategies might be undertaken.

Such a shift, or application, of the labeling theory developed by Scheff (1975) to account for mental illness in no way denies that there is an injured child and an injuring caretaker, but it directs our attention to how such actions are perceived and categorized by other actors in the social scene—be they police, social workers, neighbors, or medical personnel. Each such gatekeeper carries some code of what is normal and what is deviant behavior, and, depending on a variety of circumstances, may or may not label the case as one of child abuse or some other type of behavior. What might seem to be a self-evident case of child abuse for some may thus be seen as something different in nature, intention, and consequences by others. A social-labeling perspective would not quarrel with the definitional tendencies (and variations) of particular gatekeepers but would call attention to the fact that such definitions are part of what must be comprehended.

Despite the widening of the lens to include contextual factors, there still seems to remain, within this perspective a conception that there is an agent— a human agent—which acts upon the child. In Gelles's words it has to do with "children injured by their caretakers" (1975).

A Family-System Conception of Child Abuse

A different type of abstraction of what the nature of the phenomenon is can be formed within a system conception: taking clues from formulations about the relation of individual pathology (such as schizophrenia) and the family (Bateson, Jackson, Haley, and Weakland, 1956; Haley, 1959). Within this perspective, it is the familial context which is the subject of attention, and the individual is merely a symptom of the functioning of the family (Watzlawick, Beavin, and Jackson, 1967). The notions of subject and object of action are thus replaced with a unified notion of the transactions within a system (Spiegel and Bell, 1959; Spiegel, 1971). The agent of the transaction would not be the caretaker person but the system itself and its processes. Individual's actions, and their intentions and motives, would not be excluded from consideration but would be seen as system phenomena. Examining the individual phenomena is legitimate but arbitrary, not the whole truth. Another dimension of the truth is brought to light by conceiving of the action as transactions within a system.

This perspective does not seem to have been regularly used in relation to child abuse, but as a tentative definition one might start from the position that child abuse is one type of failure of the control systems in family interactions, a failure in error-activating feedback which brings controls in as preventors of the amplification of deviance beyond the systems control (Maruyama, 1963).

The advantage of this type of perspective is that it makes no presumptions about subject and object, does not lead to seeing causality as lying within individuals and action as flowing unidirectionally from subject to object. Both caretaker and child may then be seen as victims of a process over which neither has exclusive control nor for which one person is responsible. Both may be seen as victims or victimizers. The blame, if such language need be used, rests with system processes. The individual's characteristics (motivations, emotions, intentions) and the nature of his involvement are matters for empirical determination.

Such a conception has, as do all conceptions, difficulties. Our ordinary language, even when used precisely, is based upon a structure of subject acting upon object. It is thus difficult to keep attention consistently focused upon the different kind of abstraction involved in a systems conception. Further, central concepts of system theory, such as boundary, feedback, organization, information, and homeostasis (Buckley, 1967), are as yet difficult to denote in precise terms when they are applied to anything as complex as a family system. However successful they may have been applied to biology and cybernetics their use regarding families is still imprecise (Hoffman, 1971). On the other hand, in the field of mental illnesses and family relationships, a systems perspective has led to many new formulations, insights, and even hypotheses. A systematic application of child abuse might yield similar benefits.

To summarize, it has been suggested in this section that indeed, as Einstein is said to have stated, "It is the theory which decides what we observe." An attempt has been made to sketch a number of different conceptions of what child abuse *is,* and to present how these conceptions contain within them notions of what is to be looked for and seen, and *mutatis mutandis,* how the conceptions contain the seeds of a theory about the causes, and what might reduce child abuse.

Theories of Child Abuse

Theories to explain child abuse are varied. Since these theoretical styles have been written about ably by others (Giovanni, 1974; Walters, 1975), only a brief review is necessary here. *Psychopathological theories* locate the cause of child abuse in the disturbed personality of one or occasionally of both parents. The disturbed personality of the parent, in turn, is usually seen as a result of her or his early socialization. A central proposition (to be examined in more detail below) is that the experience of being abused as a child warps the personality in such a way that the abuse is recreated by the individual when he becomes a parent. Often included in such a formulation is reference to a mechanism of role reversal—the tendency of the parent to expect the child to be (or provide) what the parent ought to be or provide. Thus such parents are seen as holding unrealistic expectations of the child and as trying to derive from the child the respect which the parent has lacked.

Sociocultural theories draw attention to the tolerance, even the encouragement, of violence within our Western culture. When violence is validated as an acceptable way of resolving conflicts or expressing frustration, it will be used to excess by some proportion of the population. Those most likely to resort to violence, especially against children, are those subject to most stress in a stratified society—those beset by poverty, poor housing, low education, uncertain employment, minority-group status, and so on. When their lives are mean, people become mean.

As Giovanni (1974) has pointed out, these theoretical styles tend to get set up as polarities, to become stereotypes which do not correspond with what is observed and formulated in actual studies. She suggests that research can never establish that one theory is right and the other wrong. In part this is because different conceptions underlie the theories and different standards are applied to establish, or deprecate, their validity. Psychological theorists are likely to argue that sociocultural explanations are weak because the result (child abuse) does not occur with great regularity with the cause (poverty, poor housing, and so on) (Spinetta and Rigler, 1972). They see much more cause to accept an explanation in terms of parental deprivation, distorted notions of parenting, and defective character structure. But the same criteria need to be applied to such theorizing, too. How often do the causes (for example, parental deprivation) lead to the result (abuse)? Is the statistical association of the causes and the result greater in a population than the sociocultural causes and the result?

For their part, sociocultural theorists tend to view psychopathological theories with skepticism because they are based on biased, already-identified, clinical samples, are supported by imprecise subjective data, and are cast in frameworks which are easily self-confirming. But it might be asked whether self-confirmation isn't a possibility in their sociocultural theories, even when the data are more measurable. Bias can enter in planning what data to collect as well as what data are being collected and interpreted. Objective questions do not necessarily elicit responses within common frames of references which would make the answers objective (Circourel, 1973).

Some Specific Issues in Child Abuse

The aim of this section is to examine a few more specific issues regarding child abuse and to apply some of the observations made above about conceptions and theories to them. The choice of issues is not systematic; they are merely issues that are current.

"Abused as a Child, Abusing as a Parent"

This proposition about the generational continuity of abuse patterns has attained the status of an article of faith. If substantiated it would provide an important clue to understanding child abuse. If there is a direct transmission of abuse patterns over generations, it would lend some credence to the view that it is individual character, conditioned by individual past experience, which determines the probability of child abuse. If substantiated, the proposition would also have some practical implications. If there is a cycle of abuse, attention to breaking the cycle by strategic interventions (sterilization, counseling, mandatory childrearing training, supervised parenting, and so on) might be justified.

But what is the basis for this widely accepted proposition? The earliest study, and the one most often cited, is that of Kempe and colleagues (Kempe, Silverman, Steele, Droegmueller, and Silver, 1962). In the dramatic and influential article on their study, carried out in 1961, the conclusion seems to grow stronger in the course of the article: ". . . some attacking parents have themselves been subject to *some degree of attack* from their parents [italics added] ; . . . *one of the most important factors to be* found in families where parental assault occurs is to do onto others as you have been done by." Unfortunately the article does not give specific information on how the data were elicited, nor what kind of criteria were used to assess degree of attack.

Another informed observer of the period (Young, 1964) held a quite different view: "There is no evidence yet that any great proportion of abusing parents have themselves been abused as children." Young's vivid portrayal of child abuse was influential but her conclusion was for many years lost in the move to "medicalize" and "legalize" child abuse. It has been suggested (Pfohl, 1977) that professional interests were involved in the medicalization of child abuse. (See also Newberger and Bourne, 1979.) Be that as it may, disconfirming evidence has been slow to appear (Benjamin, 1980), while the assertion of generational continuity continues unabated (Newberger and Bourne, 1979).

This finding, repeated in many clinical studies since, merits examination from two methodological points of view. One is the epidemiological question of whether looking only at cases of positive outcome is a sufficient basis for making etiological statements. Only if comparable reports were not given (or given with lower frequency) by nonabusing parents would the factor be significant. Schematically:

Abusing as a Parent

		Yes	No
		Yes	No
Abused as a Child	Yes	A	B
	No	C	D

Examining only cases in cells A and C will not reveal how many cases fall in cells B and D whether A and B or C and D differ at a level beyond chance. Second, one must wonder what parents being questioned about their responsibility for a child's injuries are likely to recall about their own childhood. We know that currently a very high proportion (95 percent) of parents report using physical punishment on children (Gelles, 1972). Unless there have been dramatic changes over a generation, most parents could remember some degree of attack. When called upon to explain their deviant behavior, would it not seem likely they would recall, as a justificatory mechanism, abuse they suffered themselves?

What is assimilated into a view of the self when one is under the stress of some form of accusation of abuse may not be as serious as the label sounds. In my own interviewing of a few abusive parents I have pushed for details about the "abuse" they suffered, only to find the generational connection evaporating. Pushed for specifics some abusive parents recall that "my father yelled at me a few times," or "I was spanked for something bad I did."

One must also recall that eighty years ago a Viennese psychiatrist consistently heard from adult parents recollections of abuse at the hands of their parents and developed a theory of the traumatic origin of neurosis. Somewhat later Freud was led to revise his theory to allow a place for an intervening variable, the child's sexually motivated infantile wishes. Were the recollections of his patients real psychologically but not necessarily literal? Could the retrospective recollections of abusive parents be subject to such a bending of "fact" to accommodate wishes? What kind of data would be needed to disprove this hypothesis?

"There Always Has Been Child Abuse"

Many books on child abuse include a section on the historical continuity in the abuse of children. Ancient Greeks exposed children to the elements to let them die. In many epochs children were beaten, whipped, cruelly punished, and killed. Even royal offspring, such as Louis XIV, the "Sun King," were severely mistreated in their early youth (Hunt, 1970).

Though the record is far from complete, and may be biased toward positive cases, there can be little doubt that throughout history many children have been mistreated, many innocents slaughtered (Bakan, 1971). But can this be labeled child abuse in the sense we now mean it? If infant mortality is high, and feeding a child a significant economic cost (Shorter, 1976), is the abandonment of a child, perhaps a weakling, equivalent to child abuse in twentieth-century America where, despite considerable deprivation and poor nutrition, the means of survival are available for most? And when people of all ages were regarded as chattel, and men could have a hand cut off for stealing a loaf of bread, does the injurious punishment of a child have the same meaning as contemporary child abuse? Legal codes of past eras often seem extremely harsh, but need to be viewed in the light of the total picture of rights and obligations. "Property," such as slaves, women, and children, conferred extensive rights but also obligations to support and protect that property.

What would seem to be a useful undertaking would be the systematic study of the conceptions of childhood (Aries, 1962) and other age groups in different social classes and the cataloguing of the rights according to individuals from such groups. Only by locating practices in regard to children within the social context of that society at that particular point in time can a balanced posture be gained of how children through the ages have been treated.

Systems of Support and Control

No area holds more frustration and is more puzzling than the one concerning the arrangement of treatment systems for child abuse. Within some conceptions of child abuse what is required seems straightforward. To the extent that child abuse is seen as a legal problem, it seems obvious that what is needed is an adequate detection and control system. To the extent that it is a medical problem, again, one needs good detection procedures, backed up by good information systems so that the previous treatment history of the victim can be quickly and reliably recovered. Beyond the stage of detection and initial contact, both conceptions incline their proponents to develop a set of procedures which are a mixture of control and support—surveillance and help by social workers, treatment by pediatricians and psychiatrists, education and retraining programs, and so on. Based on the summary of Brem (1970), criteria for child-abuse control centers suggest the mixture of procedures which child-abuse experts advocate:

1. Service available on a twenty-four hour basis.
2. Separation of the victim from the abuser and facilities to care of the victim.
3. Reporting of suspected abuse and neglect cases to appropriate social agencies.
4. Coordination of local agencies for case disposition.
5. Recommendations for psychiatric care as needed.
6. Provision of expert witnesses to the courts as needed.
7. Reporting of cases to a central agency.
8. An educational program for professionals and laymen on the problems of child abuse and neglect.

As Hunt (1975) notes, few programs include all these elements but many are striving in that direction. One who has not coped with the problem of developing services for child abuse should not underestimate the difficulties in doing so. At the same time, though, one needs to reflect on some of the features and possible problems inherent in such a system. It is also probably worth noting that there is widespread dissatisfaction with systems of treatment which exist, and their effectiveness is far from demonstrated. But let us note some of the assumptions and implications "built into" such a list of program elements:

1. It is assumed that child abuse can be identified by a "control center."
2. It assumes that there is a victim and that there are (parent) victimizers.
3. It assumes that there is no conflict between the operators of control and treatment, either in the "control center" or in social agencies. The possibilities of role conflicts are not (explicitly) recognized. What does it do to the physician's relationship with his patient if he is put into the role of being a reporter of abuse and a witness in court? What happens when social workers try to give help and at the same time are responsible for reporting to court authorities on a case?
4. It assumes that the power over cases should be in the hands of professionals. It is they who detect, treat, report, and testify. But there is a widespread opinion, particularly in self-help groups, that professionals have no monopoly in understanding and that their ways of assuming power over people is counterproductive. A recent report from Ontario noted that "models are numerous but most of them experience fundamental problems in establishing sound, workable, and continuing collaboration between and among professionals and non-professionals. Until and unless these relationships can be made productive, service will probably continue to flounder" (Ministry of Community and Social Services, 1976, p. 25).
5. It assumes that the power to coordinate separate and autonomous agencies exists or can be created by the child-abuse center. No legislative mandate to exercise such coordination exists, and how it might be implemented even if it did exist is not clear. Short of having budgetary and administrative control over different operations, coordination is at best a difficult matter. To attempt coordination among organizations linked to different hosts (governmental ministries, voluntary associations, municipal governments, and so on), having different ideologies and different professions, is an undertaking of great proportions.

The situation is further complicated by the existence of self-help groups in the community. Such groups have their own views of the nature and control of child abuse, views which are at some point in conflict with the views, or at least practices, of legal and medical authorities. Assertions of expertise, for instance by medical authority, and assumption of responsibility, often seem to be counterproductive.

As if the problem of coordinating diverse agencies with different professional ideologies and lay self-help groups were not enough, there seems to be an additional stumbling block. A small series of interviews with practitioners in the field of child abuse suggested a lack of consensus about the abilities and procedures, even within a single professional group. The mutually shared assumption of competence often characteristic of a professional group seemed to be lacking in relation to child abuse. At the same time the work was viewed as frustrating and difficult. The professionals in the field seemed thus to be saying, "This is hard, unrewarding, and unpleasant work. People doing it burn out quickly. I don't like it, but I don't want anyone else to do it." Perhaps this impression overstates the case, and it is based on a small number of interviews in one metropolitan area, but such an impression comes through clearly in the interviews.

Students of organizations which deal with a range of complex problems in the human-services area and have available only a range of "soft technologies" are likely to recognize such problems as familiar. Whenever work involves a large component of human judgment, is guided by inexact theories strongly influenced by beliefs, and is difficult to assess in terms of results, the organization of that work tends to be unstable and problematic (Perrow, 1965).

In short, the organization of treatment services in the area of child abuse presents a number of problems which seem not to have been overcome to date. There are many assumptions built into the thinking about treatment systems, and various actual or potential conflicts built into existing approaches. In common with other human services, such as mental health, rehabilitation, parole, or mental retardation services, the problems of organizing a coherent treatment system are complex, subject to swings between centralized and decentralized, professional and lay, technological and humanistic directions.

To Register or Not to Register

A good deal of emphasis has been placed on the creation of child-abuse registries. Most jurisdictions in Canada and the United States have founded such registries. On the face of it, the existence of a register seems to be a valuable idea. Surprisingly, there seems to be no literature documenting that such registers produce results which can be specified. Their use of a part of the criminal-justice system seems to be minor; the frequency of charges and convictions is low. If they are effective in reducing repeat abuse this has yet to be documented. Few believe that they give any reliable reflection of the extent of child abuse as a social problem.

It can be argued that, on the contrary, registers impede understanding and effective coping with the problem of child abuse. Central registries require clear, objective definitions and may thereby lead to a false appreciation of the nature of the problem. Walters (1975) has noted some of the respects in which the (United States) National Standards Form for the reporting of child abuse is inadequately designed to ascertain the "entire population of abuses," is "biased toward middle-class values," and is likely to yield unreliable data. In addition, registers, however well intentioned they may be, present a potential for abuse of civil rights. Even when provisions are made to remove unconfirmed or disconfirmed cases from a register, the consequences at the level of attitudes of local workers, and authorities are not so easily expunged. So pervasive is the negative feeling about the parents of the abused child that it is difficult to eliminate the possibility that such feelings could be strengthened by the reporting, with negative effects on treatment (Newberger and Bourne, 1979).

In the final analysis the effects of registers need to be assessed in terms of their usefulness in reducing risks for the child and advancing treatment services for families. Some careful study of the effects of registering cases of suspected child abuse would seem to be in order. In any event, registers as a form of access to information can never be a substitute for better communication among those involved in the treatment of child abuse.

Summary

This chapter has tried to examine child abuse as a social phenomenon, examining how people see and formulate ideas and feelings about this type of parent-child behavior. An attempt was made to point out that all practices involve the construction of conceptions of nature, causes, and responses. The emphasis was placed on the view that conceptions function as preconceptions, that theories shape what facts are observed and formulated.

In regard to more articulate theories of child abuse it has been suggested that the existing theories tend to talk past each other and to suggest that a more inclusive, systems-oriented theory would offer some advantages.

Finally some comment was offered on a few issues of some concern to the field of child abuse. In so doing, the interest was not in undermining theory and practice in the treatment of child abuse, but rather to reexamine some of the conventional knowledge to the end of broadening and deepening our understanding of the very real human problem of child abuse.

References

Aries, P. 1962. *Centuries of childhood.* New York: Knopf.

Bakan, D. 1971. *Slaughter of the innocents.* Toronto: C.B.C. Learning Systems.

Bateson, G., Jackson, D.D., Haley, J.J., and Weakland, J.H. 1956. Toward a theory of schizophrenia. *Behavioral Science 1,* 251-264.

Benjamin, M. 1980. Abused as a child, abusive as a parent: practitioners beware. In R. Volpe, M. Breton, and J. Mitton, eds. *The maltreatment of the school-aged child.* Lexington, Mass.: LexingtonBooks, D.C. Heath and Co.

Brem, J. 1970. Child abuse control centers: a prospect for the academy? *Pediatrics 45*(5): 894-895.

Buckley, W. 1967. *Sociology and modern systems theory.* Englewood Cliffs, N.J.: Prentice-Hall.

Chatterton, M.R. 1976. The social contexts of violence. In M. Borland, ed. *Violence in the family.* Manchester: Manchester University Press.

Circourel, A. 1973. *Theory and method in a study of Argentine fertility.* New York: Wiley.

Dewey, J., and Bentley, A.F. 1949. *Knowing and the known.* Boston: Beacon Press.

Dickens, B. 1976. *Legal issues in child abuse.* Toronto: Centre of Criminology, University of Toronto.

Dickens, B. 1980. Child-abuse law in Canada and the United States. In R. Volpe, M. Breton, and J. Mitton, eds. *The maltreatment of the school-aged child.* Lexington, Mass.: LexingtonBooks, D.C. Heath and Co.

Fontana, V.J. 1976. *Somewhere a child is crying.* New York: Mentor.

Gelles, R.J. 1972. *The violent home.* Beverly Hills, Calif.: Sage Pub.

Gelles, R.J. 1975. The social construction of child abuse. *American Journal of Orthopsychiatry 45,* 363-371.

Giovanni, J.M. 1974. *Research in child abuse: a way of seeing is a way of not seeing.* Paper presented at the National Symposium on Child Abuse: "Child Abuse: Present and Future," Chicago.

Greenland, C. 1973. *Child abuse in Ontario.* Toronto: Ministry of Community and Social Services.

Haley, J. 1959. The family of the schizophrenic: a model system. *Journal of Nervous and Mental Diseases 125,* 357-374.

Hoffman, L. 1971. Deviation-amplifying process in natural groups. In J. Haley, ed. *Changing families.* New York: Grune & Stratton.

Hunt, D. 1970. *Parents and children in history.* New York: Basic Books.

Hunt, M. 1975. *Child abuse and neglect: a report on the status of research.* Washington, D.C.: U.S. Department of Health, Education and Welfare.

Kempe, C.H., Silverman, F.N., Steele, B.F., Droegmueller, W., and Silver, H.K. 1962. The battered child syndrome. *Journal of the American Medical Association 181*(1): 17-24.

Law Reform Commission of Canada. 1974. *Criminal law: strict liability.* Working Paper #2. Ottawa: Information Canada.

Marsden, D. 1978. Sociological perspectives on family violence. In J.P. Martin, ed. *Violence and the family.* New York: Wiley.

Maruyama, M. 1963. The second cybernetics: deviation-amplifying mutual causative processes. *American Scientist 51,* 164-179.

Ministry of Community and Social Services. 1976. *Inter-professional seminar on child abuse.* Toronto: Ministry of Community and Social Services, p. 25.

Newberger, E.H., and Bourne, R. 1979. The medicalization and legalization of child abuse. In R. Bourne and E.H. Newberger, eds. *Critical perspectives on child abuse.* Lexington, Mass.: LexingtonBooks, D.C. Heath and Co.

Perrow, C. 1965. Hospitals: technology structure and goals. In J. March, ed. *Handbook of organizations*. Chicago: Rand-McNally.

Pfohl, S. 1977. The discovery of child abuse. *Social Problems 24*(3): 310–323.

Scheff, T. 1975. *Labelling madness*. Englewood Cliffs, N.J.: Prentice-Hall.

Shorter, E. 1976. *The making of the modern family*. New York: Basic Books.

Spiegel, J.P. 1971. *Transactions*. New York: Science House.

Spiegel, J.P., and Bell, N.W. 1959. The family of the psychiatric patient. In S. Arieti, ed. *American handbook of psychiatry*. New York: Basic Books, Vol. 1.

Spinetta, J.J., and Rigler, D. 1972. The child-abusing parent: a psychological review. *Psychological Bulletin 77*, 296–304.

Walters, D.R. 1975. *Physical and sexual abuse of children: causes and treatment*. Bloomington: Indiana University Press.

Watzlawick, P., Beavin, H.H., and Jackson, D.D. 1967. *Pragmatics of human communication*. New York: Norton.

Young, L. 1964. *Wednesday's child: a study of child neglect and abuse*. New York: McGraw Hill, 1964.

17 Abused as a Child, Abusive as a Parent: Practitioners Beware

Michael Benjamin

Within any culture, certain ideas gradually come to be accepted as self-evident. Subsequently these ideas may be held tenaciously, often contrary to available evidence. Within Western culture, such an idea is "that the environment in the early years exerts a disproportionate and irreversible effect on a rapidly developing organism, compared with the potential for later environmental influences (Clarke and Clarke, 1976, p. ix).

This model of human development is founded upon three fundamental assumptions: (1) that the consequences of early experience are, for all intents and purposes, irreversible; (2) that antecedent experience as opposed to proximate events has the status of causal primacy; and (3) that the direction of effect is unidirectional, from parent to child, and not vice versa.

Collectively, these assumptions have profoundly influenced the course, substance, and direction of much research in the behavioral and the social sciences. This is especially true in the study of child abuse. In this context, there is widespread acceptance of the notion that early childhood experience involving abuse is etiologically related to abusive behavior in adulthood. Essentially, the proposition "Abused as a child, abusive as a parent" has achieved the status of an article of faith (Bell, 1977), affirmed by each succeeding review of the literature (for example, Belsky, 1978).

Empirical validation of the notion that patterns of abuse can be transmitted across generations would be of singular importance. If patterns of abuse can be transmitted, then it is individual personality development, conditioned by early experience, which determines whether or not abuse will occur. In practice, it would demand that practitioners give serious attention to a range of intervention strategies aimed at interrupting the "cycle of violence" (for example, counseling, mandatory childrearing training, supervised parenting, licensing for parenthood, sterilization; Bell, 1977).

However, serious doubts remain concerning the validity of the intergenerational-transmission proposition. Data accumulated over the past decade lead some investigators to argue that the assumptions upon which the proposition is founded are spurious (for example, Clarke and Clarke, 1976). In view of the importance of this issue, the present chapter seeks to critically reevaluate the validity of both the intergenerational transmission proposition as well as the assumptions upon which it is founded.

The chapter will be organized as follows: first, the data upon which the intergenerational transmission hypothesis is grounded will be examined. This will reveal an unacceptably high level of inconsistency in recent reports. Next, the theoretical bases of the proposition will be evaluated. Finally, an alternative, more dynamic perspective on abuse, derived from General Systems Theory, will be outlined, emphasizing that all abusive family members contribute to and are trapped in the dysfunctional interactional process which constitutes abuse.

Abused as a Child, Abusive as a Parent: The Evidence

Of the many explanations of abuse now available in the literature, three are especially prominent: the sociocultural, the psychopathological, and the social-interactional perspectives. Of these, only the last two are relevant in the present context and so will be discussed below.

For proponents of the social-interactional approach, early childhood mal-treatment—one of four factors regarded as etiologically significant—is seen to have special importance. Kempe and Kempe (1978, pp. 12–13) make this clear when they state that "a priori we assume that physical abuse and neglect imply the presence of some emotional abuse, but the opposite may not always be true. . . . It seems to us that the tenacity with which parents cling to their parent-ing behavior owes its strength to the threat to survival they themselves ex-perience in the time before marriage. . . ." For proponents of the social inter-actional approach, then, early experience is a necessary but not a sufficient condition for abuse.

Alternatively, proponents of the psychopathological approach, typically relying on psychoanalytic theory, argue that the fundamental cause of abuse is personality disorder in one or, more rarely, both abusive parents (Spinetta and Rigler, 1972). Such disorder is thought to originate "in childhood around at-tempts to defend against experience of emotional conflict and stress [that is, abuse and/or emotional deprivation] and that these types of psychopathology become relatively crystallized in the elementary-school years. In the absence of treatment, it is believed that the defensive styles, and the resulting warp or malfunction of personality, will endure into adulthood and will be expressed as adult symptomatology given adult experience of conflict or stress" (Kohlberg, LaCrosse, and Ricks, 1972, p. 1217). Thus abuse is thought to be causally re-lated to specific types of early experience; in the absence of such experience, abuse is believed to be most improbable.

Steele (1978, p. 293), for example, argues that after initial neglect and/or abuse, "through the rest of his life, [the abusive parent] tends under stress to regress to the earliest pattern and, if involved in childcare, will repeat in the in-fant the treatment he himself received. . . . In order [for violence against small children] to become so embedded in the individual's mind and unleashed so automatically . . . in later years, it must have been transmitted by the parents during the first three years of the individual's life" (1978, p. 296).

For proponents of the psychopathological approach, then, adverse early experience is both a necessary and a sufficient condition for abuse.

If correct, both of the aforementioned formulations should lead to the expectation that an overwhelming proportion of abusive parents should consistently and reliably report early childhood maltreatment. Available empirical data, however, do not support this expectation. In fact, there is little agreement among investigators as to the proportion of abusive parents who report such adverse experience. Flynn (1970) reported two cases of severe abuse in which the parents in question explicitly denied childhood abuse. Similarly, Silver, Dublin, and Lourie (1969) found that of thirty-four abusive parents interviewed, only 11.8 percent claimed childhood maltreatment (see also Gil, 1970, p. 108; Justice and Justice, 1976, pp. 92–93; Fergusson, Fleming, and O'Neill, 1972). Somewhat higher results were reported by Scott (1973b), who found childhood abuse in 41.9 percent of the twenty-nine cases of fatal baby battering he examined. In no instance, however, has any investigator reported a sample of abusive parents 100 percent positive for early childhood abuse.

When the criteria of atypical childhood socialization are broadened to include emotional deprivation, emotional abuse, and/or the witness of intrafamilial violence, the figures rise sharply. Steele and Pollock (1974) found that all of the sixty abusive parents they interviewed reported either physical or emotional abuse as a child. These findings, however, are unique; most investigators report that anywhere from 40 to 90 percent of their samples of abusive parents exhibit some form of atypical childhood socialization (Justice and Justice, 1976, pp. 92–93; Ounsted, Oppenheimer, and Lindsay, 1974; Scott, 1973a).

Taken together, the inconsistency of these findings lends support to Kadushin's (1974, cited in Jayaratne, 1977) conclusion that "there is little valid evidence to support the theory that abusive parents were themselves abused as children" (see also Smith, 1976; Young, 1964). These data also imply that at least some proportion of abusive parents received a relatively normal upbringing (Rutter, 1979).

Theoretical Issues

As stated in the introduction, the notion that patterns of abusive behavior can be transmitted intergenerationally is rooted in three fundamental assumptions. In what follows below, each of these assumptions is critically examined in turn. In each case, available evidence unequivocally suggests that they do not stand up to close scrutiny.

Reversibility of Effects: Outcome Studies

The notion that the effects of early experience are irreversible leads to the following expectations: first, that there should be a one-to-one correlation between antecedent experience and proximate (that is, adult) outcome—early exposure to parental maltreatment should produce readily discernible psychological deficits in adulthood; and second, that there should be a direct relationship between the degree of atypical childhood socialization and the degree of observed deficit in adulthood. Recent empirical studies, using a range of methodological techniques, fail to support either expectation.

Koluchova (1972, 1976) presents a rare case study of a pair of identical twin boys subjected to severe and prolonged deprivation. Over a five-and-a-half-year period, starting at eighteen months of age, the boys grew up in almost total isolation, living in an unheated closet or locked up for long periods in a cellar. They slept on the floor on polyethylene sheets, were regularly beaten severely by their father (in front of witnesses), were inadequately fed, and were totally excluded from any kind of relationship with any of their family members.

At the time of their discovery, at age seven, they had the appearance of three year olds. They were hardly able to walk, had only rudimentary speech, were unable to understand the meaning or function of pictures, and suffered severe rickets. Psychological testing revealed IQs of about 40.

Returned to the Boys Home, at the age of nine they were given out for adoption to a pair of middle-aged sisters who were able to accept them as "natural and loved children." Over the next two years, their IQs jumped to 95 and 93, respectively. By age fifteen their IQs had reached 100 and the author suggests that their delayed development may not yet have been complete. In terms of social behavior and personality development, they were judged to be normal, average teenagers.

Based on these findings, Koluchova (1976, p. 65) concludes that "in cases of severe deprivation, originating at an early age, the therapeutic prognosis has usually been considered poor. But the above mentioned case of deprived children, together with others that are still being observed, prove that even gross damage, previously considered irreversible, can be remedied."

Similar results were reported by Kagan (1976) in a comparative study of the cognitive and perceptual development of a group of rural Guatemalan children and a group of American children. At one year of age, the cognitive development of the Guatemalan children was judged to be three to twelve months behind that of their American counterparts. As a result of parental treatment, frequent illness, lack of experiental variety, and mild malnutrition, the Guatemalan children were quiet, unsmiling, minimally alert, motorically passive, temperamentally passive, realtively retarded in their tendency to reach for attractive objects they watched being hidden, and were at least thirteen months of age before they reacted to a stranger with apprehension of crying. In contrast, the American children were highly vocal, smiling, alert, and active.

In order to determine whether these deficits persisted into adolescence, two different groups of Guatemalan and American children, aged ten, were compared. Tests showed virtually no difference between the two groups with respect to perceptual analysis, perceptual interference, recall, and recognition memories.

Considering these and other data, Kagan (1976, p. 121) concludes that "the total corpus of information implies that the young animal retains an enormous capacity for change in early patterns of behavior and cognitive competence, especially if the initial environment is seriously altered. The data offer no firm support for the popular belief that certain events during the first years of life produce irreversible consequences in either human or infrahuman infants."

Taken together, the findings of the above studies strongly support the conclusion of Kohlberg et al. that "the evidence for irreversible effects of early childhood trauma is extremely slight. Early childhood maternal deprivation, parental mistreatment, separation, incest, all seem to have much slighter effects upon adult adjustment . . . than anyone seems to [have] anticipate[d] " (1972, p. 1271).

For the practitioner, these conclusions suggest at least four implications. First, early-experience data may provide an unreliable basis for diagnostic decision-making. The diagnosis of child abuse typically depends on the identification of one or more discrepancies between the nature of the presented injuries and the parents' accounts of these injuries. In cases of severe abuse, such discrepancies are usually readily discernible. The majority of cases, however, involve much less dramatic injuries; available evidence is frequently ambiguous and thus demands a subjective judgment on the part of the practitioner. In this context, information concerning parental early-childhood maltreatment—whether revealed as part of an anamnestic interview or contained in preexisting medical records—may just tip the scale in favor of a "positive" diagnosis. Data presented above, then, indicate that such a conclusion may be unwarranted and that a "presumption of health" is more in order (cf. Ryan, 1971, pp. 145-146).

Second, it suggests that practitioners should be much more cautious in drawing a causal link between antecedent experience and proximate events. Practitioners are trained to seek information about early-childhood experience where adult behavioral deviance exists. Typically, such data are readily forthcoming and a causal link is then said to exist between the two periods. With respect to child abuse, for example, Dr. Mullany (1975, cited in Silverman, 1978, p. 41) states quite baldly that "today's battered babies are tomorrow's killers. A mind brutalized in infancy may seek revenge in adulthood through apparently inexplicable, meaningless crimes of violence." (See also Piers, 1978, 117; Steele, 1976.)

This kind of logic is a non sequitur, for it ignores the probability that later experiences were also deviant (Clarke and Clarke, 1976, p. 19). One could just as easily argue on these grounds that the cumulative effects of atypical child-rearing are responsible for adult outcome, or that later experience is prepotent.

Third, practitioners, as well as investigators, frequently made the faulty assumption that correlational data necessarily imply causation (Walters, 1975, p. 30). To the extent that specific antecedent events are consistently and reliably correlated with specific proximate events, a causal linkage may be suggested. Such findings would certainly provide the basis for more intensive investigation.

With respect to child abuse, however, practitioners all too frequently observe a correlation between a set of nonspecific events loosely referred to as "emotional deprivation," and a broad range of dysfunctional adult outcomes, only one of which may include abuse. Such evidence simply cannot provide the grounds for imputing a causal connection. In this sense, Fontana's (1975, p. 2285) categorical statement that "prolonged maternal deprivation" can "cause" a variety of adult disorders including "hostility, alcoholism, drug addiction, sexual maladjustment, and inadequate maternal behavior" fundamentally misconstrues the nature of correlational data. Since the same antecedent condition is alleged to have given rise to a multiplicity of outcomes, it follows that some additional unspecified factor(s) must be introduced to account for this variability. In short, these kinds of data diminish the explanatory importance of early-childhood experience and direct the attention of the practitioner to proximate events.

Finally, the practitioners' traditional focus on antecedent events may unwittingly reduce their therapeutic effectiveness (Vernon, 1964, cited in Clarke and Clarke, 1976, p. 259). The practitioners' concern with antecedent events may be perceived by the patient as a welcome relief from having to discuss current problems. Consequently, both the practitioner and the client may inadvertently act as mutual reinforcers in "discovering" anomalies in the patients' early life. For the practitioner, such discoveries are consistent with their professional expectations. For the client, such discoveries may provide a means whereby they may either be absolved of responsibility for proximate events ("It wasn't my fault! My mother did the same thing to me when I was a kid.") or at least justification found for what is perceived as deviant behavior (see Meisleman, 1978, p. 196). In the process, however, the practitioners' attention is invariably drawn away from the fact that the anomalies in question are *both* proximate as well as antecedent events. Consequently, an opportunity will have been missed or at least delayed for effective therapeutic intervention in prevailing proximate life circumstances.

Reversibility of effect: Compensatory interactional processes

To the extent that antecedent experience has causal primacy, one would expect the current rate of child abuse to be determined by childhood maltreatment of the parents in question. However, the previous two sections suggest that there need be no necessary relationship between childhood experience and adult outcome. A more useful explanation is that a supportive relationship, either in childhood or later in life, may compensate for any ill effects of childhood maltreatment. Specifically, it may be argued that: (1) individual development is fundamentally characterized by resilience and plasticity; (2) the effective operation of those features of development requires a close, intimate, and enduring relationship with a significant other; (3) the occurrence of such a relationship may fully or partially compensate for early environmental adversity; (4) the compensatory effects of such a relationship are not diminished if it occurs in adulthood; (5) the effects of such a relationship are not confined to individuals within any specific role position, but rather the supportive quality of the relationship per se is what appears to be salient (Freud & Dan, 1951 cited in Clarke & Clarke, 1976: 69–70).

If correct, this formulation has two implications: First, it suggests that the practitioner pay particular attention to the proximate interactional characteristics of families suspected of abuse. Second, it suggests that the practitioner seriously consider employing a compensatory relationship as a therapeutic modality.

The Bidirectionality of Parent-Child Relations

The assumptions that (1) the direction of effect in parent-child interaction is consistently from parent to child and (2) children are relatively passive and malleable continue to predominate in the socialization literature. Despite the fact that various authors have, from time to time, called attention to the paucity of research into child effects (Nowlis, 1952; Sears, 1951), a unidirectional orientation pervades the work of most investigators (Bell, 1971). As Bell and Harper (1977, p. ix) note, "[the bidirectional] orientation is still overshadowed by a massive literature directed almost entirely to the effects of adults on children. The new perspective has excited much interest . . . but the tide of more traditional, unidirectional thought has yet to be stemmed." Indeed, in the vast socialization literature, only two books are currently available specifically concerned with the bidirectionality of parent-child relations (Bell and Harper, 1977; Lewis and Rosenblum, 1974).

These conclusions have several implications for the practitioner. First, they suggest that practitioners viewing parent-child relations from a traditional perspective frequently confuse cause and effect (Clarke and Clarke, 1976, p. 13). To the extent that the child is the agent of much of his own learning, early experience may produce particular effects which, acting upon his later environment, may result in reinforcing feedback. Such experience, in turn, acts to prolong the effects of early learning. Thus the child may unwittingly create his own difficulties. An obvious case in point is the child who learns to associate love and affection with violence. Accordingly, the abused child, by consistently and repeatedly provoking his parent(s) (see Collins, 1978, p. 97), acts to precipitate subsequent incidents of abuse. To attribute such behavior to the child's early experience alone is to fundamentally misconstrue the reciprocal nature of the interactional process that underlies it.

Second, and perhaps more important, the evidence suggests that therapeutic modalities focusing on individual family members will seldom show desired results over time and may even be counterproductive. Family interactional processes evolve slowly and consequently tend to exhibit considerable stability over time. Conversely, families tend to actively resist efforts at therapeutic destabilization. By focusing on individual family members, intervention may either render another member symptomatic or may produce remission of symptomatic behavior only to have it recur once the patient is reintroduced into a family structure which has, after all, not received the benefit of therapy (see Rees, Oudendijk, and Spanje, 1978). Moreover, by singling out a family member by labeling him an "abusive parent," intervention may eliminate whatever marginal flexibility the family may previously have had prior to contact.

This discussion leads to an alternative conceptualization of abuse. Specifically the family unit per se can be viewed as the "patient" requiring therapy. This may initially entail a marked shift in perspective for those practitioners trained to see abuse in terms of an offender-victim dichotomy. However, to the extent that relations among family members are truly reciprocal, as the data presented above suggest, it must be recognized that all abusive family members actively contribute to the dysfunctional interactional process in which they are trapped and from which they all suffer accordingly.

Child Abuse: An Alternative Perspective

The thrust of the previous sections has been to suggest that a perspective which focuses on individual attributes as these are affected by antecedent experience is both too linear and too static to encompass the complexity of the phenomenon of child abuse. Rather, what seems to be required is an alternative perspective whose orientation is both non-linear and process oriented. General Systems Theory (GST) embodies such a perspective.

GST may be described as a scientific exploration of wholes (that is, systems) and wholeness (Bertalanffy, 1968, p. 37). Whereas traditional models seek to isolate the elements of any given phenomenon—on the premise that knowledge of these components constitutes knowledge of the whole—GST focuses not only on these components but on their interrelations as well. Accordingly, a system may generally be defined as any set of two or more elements whose pattern of reciprocal interaction remains relatively stable through time despite considerable variability in its environment (Hall and Fagen, 1956; Weiss, 1969).

This perspective involves shifting conceptually from substantial to relational entities. Whereas traditional models posit particular entities (that is, individuals) as the ultimate furnishings of the world, proponents of GST attempt to describe classes of entities (for example, family systems) "forming ordered structures of events" (Laszlo, 1972, p. 25). Consequently, the focus of concern is the family system per se: the behavior of one of its individual members is thought to reflect the functioning of the larger system of which they are a part. Symptomatic behavior on the part of an abusive parent is thus interpreted as one aspect of the operation of a dysfunctional family system. Moreover, the traditional offender-victim dichotomy no longer applies; action is no longer seen to flow unidirec-tionally from parent to child. Rather, all family members necessarily participate in the offense, either directly or indirectly, and all are victimized by it; in short, all family members are part of a larger family system process over which none has exclusive control.

This perspective holds a diverse set of implications for the future study and treatment of child abuse. It suggests, for example, that the relationship between antecedent experience and proximate behavior is, at best, indirectly causal (Benjamin, 1977, p. 109). Within family systems, the effect of any initial event at a given point in time is significantly diffused by the reciprocal nature of the relationship among members. Such causal diffusion continues as increasing numbers of interactional processes intervene through time between the initial event and some proximate state of the system. Consequently, the current state of any family system can only be explained in terms of ongoing interactional processes. This suggests that the diagnostic and treatment concerns of the practitioner should be directed at the current state of abusive family dynamics rather than the antecedent experience of any one of its members.

Further, it suggests to the investigator that the application of system con-cepts (homeostasis, feedback, equifinality, nonsummativity, and so on: see Buckley, 1967) to the phenomenon of child abuse may provide the basis for developing new explanatory formulations from which testable hypotheses may be derived. While efforts to apply GST to the area of abuse remain rare in the literature (Straus, 1973; Benjamin, 1978; Grodner, 1978; Levitt, 1978), its fruitful use in other areas of study (for example, mental disorders: see Wynne, 1978) holds out the promise that it may yet yield similar benefits with respect to the study of child abuse.

It also suggests the need for studies involving the direct observation of on-going interactional processes in abusive and nonabusive families. While rare, several such studies have recently been reported in the literature (Burgess, Kimball, and Burgess, 1978; Burgess and Conger, 1977; Hyman and Parr, 1978), with impressive results. Unfortunately, these studies have to date been exclusive-ly descriptive and thus atheoretical. This is puzzling, as this research design is optimally suited to testing theoretically derived hypotheses. In an effort to remedy this situation, an experimental study of child abuse aimed at testing hypotheses derived from GST has recently been initiated by Benjamin (1978).

Finally, a GST perspective has important implications for the diagnosis and treatment of abusive families. With respect to the former, this perspective pro-vides a useful tool for the identification of abuse, real or potential. At present, detection of abuse is a complex matter, relying on hospital-based samples on the subjective judgment by practitioners of the appropriateness of the parental explanation of child injuries. Such judgments are even more ambiguous in nonhospital settings, in the absence of sophisticated technical aids. Consequently, suspected abuse cases reported to child protective agencies have a high disconfirmation rate. Examination of family-interaction processes (Benjamin, 1978) may provide an independent means of identifying abuse and would apply equally to the hospital-based practitioner as well as to the practitioner on a home visit (Dean, MacQueen, Mitchell, and Kempe, 1978). Similarly, it may yield a reliable means of identifying families at risk for abuse, even in the absence of other hard evidence to warrant such suspicion.

With respect to treatment, a GST perspective implies that short-term intervention may be inadequate. In multi-child abusive families, removal of the abused child may simply shift abuse to another child. In cases where removal is only temporary, this suggests the need for continual monitoring of family-interaction processes in order to determine that those patterns generative of abuse (Benjamin, 1978) have abated or been interrupted prior to the return of the child in question. In cases where removal is permanent, it should not be assumed that the problem has been eliminated, but rather that the family requires long-term follow-up. Such contract would serve not only to protect any remaining siblings, but even those as yet unborn.

Moreover, the GST perspective implies that certain intervention strategies appear more appropriate than others. So long as child abuse is conceptualized as an individual problem, based on personality disorder and rooted in antecedent experience, then intervention strategies geared to alter individual functioning (for example, individual psychotherapy) will be the treatment modality of choice. Recognition, however, that abuse represents a dysfunctional family-interaction process necessarily requires that intervention strategies be employed that are designed to reorganize and restructure family systems (for example, family therapy).

The notion that childhood maltreatment is causally related to later parental abusive behavior is widely accepted. However, critical examination of the assumptions underlying this belief suggests that they are not supported by available data. Furthermore, data bearing directly on this issue are highly inconsistent. If this analysis is correct, it follows that the assertion that the majority of abused children will necessarily have a negative outcome as adults is logically indefensible.

Accordingly, it has been argued that the perspective represented by proponents of the intergenerational-transmission proposition is inadequate to the complexity of the phenomenon of child abuse.

References

Avery, N.A. 1975. Treatment of families in protective services. In N.B. Ebeling and D.A. Hill, eds. *Child abuse: intervention and treatment.* Acton, Mass.: Pub. Sci. Group.

Baher, E., Hyman, C., Jones, C., Jones, R., Kerr, A., and Mitchell, R. 1976. *At risk: an account of the work of the battered child research department, NSPCC.* London: Routledge & Kegan Paul.

Bandura, A. 1978. Learning and behavioral theories of aggression. In I.L. Kutash, L.B. Schlesinger, and Associates, eds. *Violence; perspectives on murder and aggression.* San Francisco: Josey-Bass.

Bell, N.W. 1977. *Child abuse:—some sociological perspectives.* Unpublished manuscript, Department of Sociology, University of Toronto, Toronto, Ontario.

Bell, R.Q. 1960. Retrospective and prospective views of early personality development. *Merrill-Palmer Quarterly 6,* 131-144.

Bell, R.Q. 1968. A reinterpretation of the direction of effects in studies of socialization. *Psychological Bulletin 75,* 81-95.

Bell, R.Q. 1971. Stimulus control of parent or caretaker behavior of offspring. *Developmental Psychology 4,* 63-72.

Bell, R.Q., and Harper, L.V. 1977. *Child effects on adults.* Hillsdale, N.J.: Lawrence Erlbaum.

Belsky, J. 1978. Three theoretical models of child abuse: a critical review. *Child Abuse & Neglect 2*(1): 37-49.

Bender, B. 1976. Self-chosen victims: scapegoating behavior sequential to battering. *Child Welfare 55,* 417-422.

Benjamin, M. 1977. *A comparative analysis of three explanatory models of mental disorder and a preferred focus of explanation.* Unpublished M.A. thesis, Department of Sociology, Concordia University, Montreal, Quebec.

Benjamin, M. 1978. *Child abuse and family interaction processes: a general systems theory formulation.* Unpublished manuscript, Department of Sociology, University of Toronto, Toronto, Ontario.

Berdie, J., Baizerman, M., and Lourie, I.S. 1977. Violence towards youth: themes from a workshop. *Children Today 6*(2): 7-10, 35.

Bertalanffy, L. von. 1968. *General systems theory: foundations, development, applications* (rev. ed.). New York: Braziller.

Blumberg, M.L. 1974. Psychopathology of the abusing parent. *American Journal of Psychotherapy 28,* 21-29.

Brekstad, A. 1966. Factors influencing the reliability of anamnestic recall. *Child Development 37,* 603-612.

Buckley, W. 1967. *Sociology and modern systems theory.* Englewood Cliffs, N.J.: Prentice-Hall.

Burgess, R.L., and Conger, R.D. 1977. *Family interaction in abusive, neglectful and normal families.* Paper presented at the Annual Meeting of the Society for Research in Child Development.

Burgess, J.M., Kimball, W.H., and Burgess, R.L. 1978. *Family interaction as a function of family size.* Paper presented at the Annual Meeting of the Southeastern Conference on Human Development.

Clarke, A.M., and Clarke, A.D.B., eds. 1976. *Early experience: myth and evidence*. London: Open Books.

Collins, M.C. 1978. *Child abuser: a study of child abusers in self-help group therapy*. Littleton, Mass.: PSG Publishers.

Dean, J.G., MacQueen, I.A.G., Mitchell, R.G., and Kempe, C.H. 1978. Health visitor's role in prediction of early childhood injuries and failure to thrive. *Child Abuse & Neglect 2*(1): 1-17.

Doane, J.A. 1978. Family interaction and communication deviance in disturbed and normal families: a review of research. *Family Processes 17*, 357-376.

Fergusson, D.M., Fleming, J., O'Neill, D.P. 1972. *Child abuse in New Zealand* Wellington, New Zealand; Research Division, Department of Social Welfare.

Ferreira, A.J. 1963. Family myth and homeostasis. *Archives of General Psychiatry 9*, 457-463.

Flynn, W.R. 1970. Frontier justice: a contribution to the theory of child battery. *American Journal of Psychiatry 127*, 375-379.

Fontana, V.J. 1975. Child maltreatment and battered child syndromes. In A.F. Freedman, H.I. Kaplan, and B.J. Sadoch, eds. *Comprehensive textbook of psychiatry*. 2nd Ed., Vol. 2. Baltimore, Md.: Williams & Wilkins.

Fosson, A.R., and Kaak, O. 1977. *Child abuse and neglect case studies*. Flushing, N.Y.: Medical Examiner Publishers.

French, A.P. 1977. *Disturbed children and their families*. New York: Human Science Press.

Friday, N. 1977. *My mother, my self*. New York: Dell.

Galdston, R. 1975. Preventing the abuse of little children: the parent's center project for the study of prevention of child abuse. *American Journal of Orthopsychiatry 45*, 372-381.

Garbarino, J., and Jacobson, N. 1978. Youth helping youth in cases of maltreatment of adolescents. *Child Welfare 57*, 505-510.

Garmezy, N., and Streitman, S. 1974. Children at risk: the search for the antecedents of schizophrenia. Part I. Conceptual models and research methods. *Schizophrenia Bulletin 8*, 14-90.

Gelles, R.J. 1978*a*. Violence against children in the United States. *American Journal of Orthopsychiatry 48*, 580-592.

Gelles, R.J. 1978*b*. Methods for studying sensitive family topics. *American Journal of Orthopsychiatry 48*, 408-424.

George, C., and Main, M. 1979. Social interaction of young abused children: approach, avoidance, and aggression. *Child Development 50*, 306-318.

Gil, D.G. 1970. *Violence against children: physical child abuse in the United States*. Cambridge, Mass.: Harvard University Press.

Goode, W. 1969. Violence among intimates. In D.J. Mulvihill and M.M. Tumin, eds. *Crimes of violence*. Vol. 13, Appendix 19. Washington, D.C.: U.S. Government Printing Office.

Grodner, B. 1978. Prevention of child abuse and neglect: thoughts on a family system approach. In M.L. Lauderdale, R.N. Anderson, and S.E. Cramer, eds. *Child abuse and neglect: issues on innovation and implementation.* Conference on Child Abuse and Neglect, April 17-20, 1977, Vol. 1. Washington, D.C.: U.S. Department of H.E.W.

Haggard, E.A., Brekstad, A., and Skad, A.G. 1960. On the reliability of the anamnestic interview. *Journal of Abnormal and Social Psychology 61,* 311-318.

Hall, A.D., and Fagen, R.E. 1956. The definition of system. *General Systems Yearbook 1,* 18-28.

Harlow, H.F., and Harlow, M.K. 1965. The effect of rearing conditions on behavior. In J. Money, ed. *Sex research: new developments.* New York: Holt, Rinehart & Winston.

Hefner, L.T. 1962. Reliability of maternal reports on child development. Unpublished Ph.D. thesis, University of Michigan.

Hefner, L.T., and Mednick, S.A. 1969. Reliability of developmental histories. *Pediatrics Digest 11,* 28-39.

Hyman, C.A., and Parr, R. 1978. A controlled video observational study of abused children. *Child Abuse & Neglect 2*(4), 217-222.

Jayaratne, S. 1977. Child abusers as parents and children: a review. *Social Work 22,* 5-9.

Jayaswal, S.R., and Stott, L.H. 1955. Persistence and change in personality from childhood to adulthood. *Merrill-Palmer Quarterly 1,* 47-56.

Justice, B., and Justice, R. 1976. *The abusing family.* New York: Human Science Press.

Kagan, J. 1976. Resilience and continuity in psychological development. In A.M. Clarke and A.D.B. Clarke, eds. *Early experience: myth and evidence.* London: Open Books.

Kaufman, I. 1975. The physically abused child. In N.B. Ebeling and D.A. Hill, eds. *Child abuse: intervention and treatment.* Acton, Mass.: Pub. Sci. Group.

Kempe, R.S., and Kempe, C.H. 1978. *Child abuse.* Cambridge, Mass.: Harvard University Press.

Klaus, M.H., and Kennell, J.H., eds. 1976. *Maternal-infant bonding.* St. Louis: Mosby.

Kohlberg, L., LaCross, J., and Ricks, D. 1972. The predictability of adult mental health from childhood behavior. In B.D. Wolman, ed. *Manual of child psychopathology.* New York: McGraw-Hill.

Koluchova, J. 1972. Severe deprivation in twins: a case study. *Journal of Child Psychology and Psychiatry 13,* 107-114.

Koluchova, J. 1976. A report on the further development of twins after severe and prolonged deprivation. In A.M. Clarke and A.D.B. Clarke, eds. *Early experience: myth and evidence.* London: Open Books.

Laszlo, E. 1972. *Introduction to systems philosophy: toward a new paradigm of contemporary thought*. New York: Harper & Row.

Levitt, J.M. 1978. A family system approach to treatment of child abuse. In M.L. Lauderdale, R.N. Anderson, and S.E. Cramer, eds. *Child abuse and neglect: issues on innovation and implementation*. Proceedings of the Second Annual National Conference on Child Abuse and Neglect, April 17-20, 1977, Vol. 1. Washington, D.C.: U.S. Department of H.E.W.

Lewis, M., and Rosenblum, L.A., eds. 1974. *The effects of the infant on its caregiver*. New York: Wiley.

MacFarlane, J.W. 1964. Perspectives on personality consistency and change from the guidance study. *Vita Humana 7*, 115-126.

Martin, H.P., Beezley, P., Conway, E.F., and Kempe, C.H. 1974. The development of the abused child. Part I. A review of the literature. *Advances in Pediatrics 21*, 25-44.

McGraw, M., and Molloy, L.B. 1941. The pediatric anamnesis: inaccuracies in eliciting developmental data. *Child Development 12*, 255-265.

Mednick, S.A., and Shaffer, J.B.P. 1963. Maternal retrospective reports in child rearing research. *American Journal of Orthopsychiatry 33*, 457-461.

Meiselman, K.D. 1978. *Incest: a psychological study of causes and effects with treatment recommendations*. San Francisco: Jossey-Bass.

Milowe, I.D., and Lourie, R.S. 1964. The child's role in the battered child syndrome. *Journal of Pediatrics 65*, 1079-1081.

Mischel, W.1970. Sex-typing and socialization. In P.H. Mussen, ed. *Carmichael's manual of child psychology*. 3rd Ed. New York: Wiley.

Nowlis, V. 1952. The search for significant concepts in a study of parent-child relations. *American Journal of Orthopsychiatry 22*, 286-299.

Ounsted, C., Oppenheimer, R., and Lindsay, J. 1974. Aspects of bonding failure: the psychopathology and psychotherapeutic treatment of families of battered children. *Developmental Medicine and Child Neurology 16*, 447-456.

Piers, M.W. 1978. *Infanticide*. New York: Norton.

Pyles, M.K., Stolz, H.R., and MacFarlane, J.W. 1935. The accuracy of maternal reports on birth and developmental data. *Child Development 6*, 165-176.

Rees, R. Van, Oudendijk, N., and Spanje, M. van. 1978. The Triangle (sociotherapeutical institute). *Child Abuse and Neglect 2*(4): 207-215.

Robbins, L.C. 1963. The accuracy of parental recall of aspects of child development and child rearing practices. *Journal of Abnormal and Social Psychology 66*, 261-270.

Rutter, M. 1979. Maternal deprivation, 1972-1978: new findings, new concepts, new approaches. *Child Development 50*, 283-305.

Ryan, W. 1971. *Blaming the victim*. New York: Vintage.

Scott, P.D. 1973*a*. Parents who kill their children. *Medicine, Science, and the Law 13*, 120-126.

Scott, P.D. 1973*b*. Fatal battered baby cases. *Medicine, Science, and the Law 13*, 197-206.

Sears, R.R. 1951. A theoretical framework for personality and social behavior. *American Psychologist 6*, 476-482.

Silver, L.B., Dublin, C.C., and Lourie, R.S. 1969. Does violence breed violence? Contributions from a study of the child abuse syndrome. *American Journal of Psychiatry 126*(3): 404-407.

Silverman, P. 1978. *Who speaks for the children?* Don Mills, Ont.: Musson.

Skolnick, A. 1978. The myth of the vulnerable child. *Psychology Today 11*(9): 56-65.

Smith, S.M. 1976. The battered child syndrome—some research aspects. *Psychiatric Journal of the University of Ottawa 4*, 158-164.

Spinetta, J.J., and Rigler, D. 1972. The child-abusing parent: a psychological review. *Psychological Bulletin 77*, 296-304.

Steele, B.F. 1976. Violence within the family. In R.E. Helfer & C.H. Kempe, eds. *Child abuse and neglect*. Cambridge, Mass.: Ballinger, 1976.

Steele, B.F. 1978. The child abuser. In I.L. Kutash, S.B. Kutash, L.B. Schlesinger, and Associates, eds. *Violence: perspectives on murder and aggression*. San Francisco: Jossey-Bass.

Steele, B.F., and Pollack, C.B. 1974. A psychiatric study of parents who abuse infants and small children. In R.F. Helfer and C.H. Kempe, eds. *The battered child*. 2nd Ed. Chicago: University of Chicago Press.

Steinmetz, S.K. 1977. *The cycle of violence: assertive, aggressive, and abusing family interaction*. New York: Praeger.

Straus, M.A. 1971. Some social antecedents of physical punishment: a linkage theory interpretation. *Journal of Marriage and the Family 33*, 658-663.

Straus, M.A. 1973. A general systems theory approach to a theory of violence between family members. *Social Science Information 12*, 105-125.

Straus, M.A. 1978. Wife beating: how common and why? *Victim 2*, 443-458.

Thomas, A., Chess, S., and Birch, H.G. 1970. The origin of personality. *Scientific American 223*, 102-109.

Tonge, W.L., James, D.S., and Hillam, S.M. 1975. Families without hope: a controlled study of 33 problem families. *British Journal of Psychiatry Special Publication #11*. Ashford, Kent: Headley Bros.

Walters, D.R. 1975. *Physical and sexual abuse of children: causes and treatment*. Bloomington: Indiana University Press.

Warme, B., and Thomas, S. 1978. Wednesday's parents and the role of the paraprofessional. In M.A.B. Gammon, ed. *Violence in Canada*. Toronto: Methuen.

Weiss, P.A. 1969. The living system: determinism stratified. In A. Koestler and J.R. Smythies, eds. *Beyond Reductionism*. New York: Macmillan.

Wenar, C. 1963. The reliability of developmental histories. *Psychosomatic Medicine 25*, 505-509.

Wenar, C., and Coulter, J.B. 1962. A reliability study of developmental histories. *Child Development 33*, 453–462.

Wright, H.F. 1967. *Recording and analyzing child behavior.* New York: Harper & Row.

Wynne, L.C. 1978. Family interaction: an alternative starting point for evaluating risk of psychosis. In E.J. Anthony, C. Koupernik, and C. Chiland, eds. *The child in his family: vulnerable chidren.* Vol. 4, New York: Wiley.

Yarrow, L.J. 1961. Maternal deprivation: toward an empirical and conceptual re-evaluation. *Psychological Bulletin, 1961, 58,* 459–490.

Yarrow, M.R., Campbell, J.D., and Burton, R.V. 1964. Reliability of maternal retrospection: a preliminary report. *Family Processes 3,* 207–218.

Yarrow, M.R., Campbell, J.D., and Burton, R.V. 1968. *Child rearing: an inquiry into research and methods.* San Francisco: Jossey-Bass.

Yarrow, M.R., Campbell, J.D., and Burton, R.V. 1970. Recollections of childhood: a study of the retrospective method. *Monograph Soc. Res. Child Development 35*(3): Serial No. 138.

Yarrow, M.R., Waxler, C.Z., and Scott, P.M. 1971. Child effects on adult behavior. *Developmental Psychology 5,* 300–311.

Young, L. 1964. *Wednesday's child: a study of child neglect and abuse.* New York: McGraw-Hill.

Index

Abbot, J.L., 29

Abuse: assessment, 148–150. *See also* identification; causes, 177–179, 187–202. *See also* theories; as disease, 173–174; drug, 52; impersonators, 55–56; incidence, 45; treatment of, 117. *See also* intervention; types of abuse, 45. *See also* adolescent abuse, emotional abuse, institutional abuse, neglect, physical abuse, and sexual abuse

Abused child: academic achievement of, 22–24, 99; battle fatigue of, 102; compared to prisoner of war, 91–107; compensating relationships, 131–132, 192–193; coping with pain, 95–96; degradation of, 101; described before and after treatment, 23; development of, 20–21; effects of maltreatment, 3, 19–26; feeling different, 97; feeling guilt, 100; fear of rejection, 97–98; friendships, 98–99; learning problems, 20–21; need for love, 98; outrage, 101–102; perceptions of abuse, 91–107; pressures on, 101–102; problems of communication, 99–100; problems with concentration, 99; provoking behavior, 11–17; reactions to leaving home, 104–106; relationship to parents, 91–107; role as victim in sexual abuse, 51; survival tactics of, 93. *See* identification of abuse. *See also* indicators of abuse

Abused as a child, abusive as a parent, 177–179, 187–202

Abusive families: characteristics, 30–33

Abusive parents, 11; characteristics, 31, 47–48; childhood experiences of, 189; perceptions of child, 14–15; psychopathology of, 48; "sick but slick", 93–94, 102; social

isolation, 31–32; unrealistic expectations of children, 32; power oriented discipline, 32–33

Adolescent abuse, 7, 24, 69–78; incidence, 134; intervention, 72; patterns, 70–72; physical punishment, 69–78; uncertainty in identification, 70–72

Anderson, R.J., 118

Appolini, T., 29

Aries, P., 180

Ayoub, D., 138

Bailey, M.M., 5, 145–153

Baizerman, M., 69, 70

Bakan, D., 121, 122, 179

Baker, J.M., 133

Bates, R.P., 7, 45–56

Bateson, G., 175

Battered child syndrome, 11, 49–50

Beavin, H.H., 175

Beckhard, R., 113

Behavior of school-aged children, 12–13

Bell, N.W., 9, 171–185, 187

Bell, R.Q., 193

Belsky, J., 11, 187

Benjamin, M., 9, 131, 187–202

Bensel ten, R.W., 111

Bentley, A.F., 171

Berdie, J., 69, 70, 111

Bertalanffy von, L., 194–195

Bidirectionality of child-parent relations, 193–194

Billingsley, A., 30

Blager, F., 20

Blair, A.W., 16

Boriskin, J.A., 14

Boulding, K.E., 129

Bourne, R., 172, 173, 178, 183

Bowlby, J., 62

Bowles, D., 133

Bowles, S., xi

Brassard, J., 129
Brem, J., 180
Breton, M., 6, 111–121, 122
Bridges, C., 140
Brill, N.L., 113–122
Broadhurst, D.B., 3, 4, 5, 19–26, 116, 117
Buck, C., 24
Buckley, W., 176, 195
Burgess, A.W., 7, 79–89
Burgess, J.M., 195
Burgess, R.L., 11, 12, 195
Burston, N., 134
Burton, W.H., 16
Bybee, R., 24, 25, 69, 70, 72

Caffey, J., 45
Campbell, D.T., 129
Caplan, G., 114, 130
Chatterton, M.R., 174
Child-abuse control centers, 180–181
Child-abuse registries, 182–183; Canada, 182
Child-abuse team. See child-protection team
Child-protection team, 4, 6, 111, 115, 116, 117; assessing abuse, 148–150; collaboration, 5; coordinating, 5, 6, 112; leading, 113; reporting to, 117; role in prevention, 115–116; treating abuse, 117. See also interdisciplinary groups; working with natural helping network, 115–118
Child molester, 79–80
Child rearing, 12; power oriented, 32–33; use of punishment and guilt, 76
Child-abuse registry, 46, 163, 182–183; civil rights and privacy, 182–183
Christiansen, J., 4, 21
Circourel, A., 177
Clark, E.G., 137
Clarke, A.D.B., 187, 191, 192, 193
Clarke, A.M., 187, 191, 192, 193
Cochran, M., 129

Coles, R., 76
Collins, A.H., 113, 119, 129, 132
Collins, M.C., 193
Collmer, C.W., 11, 12, 30
Conger, R.D., 195
Cooke, T.P., 29
Cross, S., 141
Crouter, A., 132, 134
Cunningham, R., 137
Cutler, C., 131
Cycle of abuse. See intergenerational transmission of abuse

Dagg, N., 140
D'Agostino, P.A., 3, 27–41
Dan, S., 193
Davis, L.G., 112
Dean, J.G., 131–196
Detection of abuse. See identification of abuse
Development of the school-aged child, 12–13, 187
Dewey, J., 171
Diagnosis of abuse. See identification of abuse. See also indicators of abuse
Dickens, B., 8, 152–173
Dinkmeyer, D.C., 29
Discipline and abuse, 69–78
Drews, K., 3, 4, 116
Droegemueller, W., 45, 178
Dublin, C.C., 189

Easton, F., 112
Education: family life, 39; life enhancing-development obstructing, xi
Eells, D.R., 29
Einstein, A., 176
Elmer, E., 11, 121
Emotional abuse (neglect), 7; defined, 59–68; effects on child, 52–53; legal definition, 66–67
Erikson, E.H., 12, 62
Erlanger, H.B., 75
Explanations of abuse. See theories of abuse

Fagen, R.E., 194
Failure to thrive. *See* emotional abuse
Family: abusive, 193; coalitions, 28–
    29; interaction, 14; isolation, 47,
    131; medicine, 15; support systems,
    130–132; systems, 175–176
Fanshel, D., 133
Fergusson, D.M., 189
Filipczak, J., 29, 36
Fisher, B., 69, 70
Fleming, J., 189
Flynn, W.R., 189
Foley, F.W., 121
Fontana, V.J., 11, 45, 173, 192
Forrer, S.E., 112
Forward, S., 24
Foster care, 133–134, 139
Fox, P., 4
Fraser, B.G., 147
Freud, A., 193
Freud, S., 64, 179
Friedman, R.M., 3, 27–41, 130, 131,
    137
Friedrick, W.N., 14
Fromm, E., xi
Fuller, L., 75

Gale, P., 112
Galileo, G., 171
Garbarino, J., 5, 30, 70, 73, 111,
    129–136
Gelles, R.J., 11, 73, 174, 175, 179
Gershenfeld, M., 123
Gesmonde, J., 60
Giannangelo, D.M., 39
Gil, D.G., ix–xii, 3, 11, 14, 30, 73,
    111, 116, 189
Gintis, H., xi
Giovanni, J.M., 30, 171, 176, 177
Gold, R., 133
Gordon, W.I., 123
Gottlieb, B., 129
Gourash, N., 129
Gray, J., 131
Greenland, C., 174
Gregg, G.S., 11
Griggs, S.A., 112

Grodner, B., 195
Groth, N., 7

Haley, J., 175
Hall, A.D., 194
Halperin, M., 22
Harper, L.V., 193
Helfer, R.E., 11, 30, 46, 48, 121, 131,
    152
High risk: child, 11–17, 47; char-
    acteristics of child, 48; parents,
    47–48
Hobbes, T., 64
Hoffman, L., 176
Holmes, S., 113
Holt, J., 64
Horowitz, M.J., 105
Howe, R.J., 123
Howell, D.A., 20
Hunt, D., 179
Hunt, M., 180
Humbition, 76
Hyman, C.A., 195

Identification of abuse: assessment by
    teams, 116, 148–150; detection,
    161–162; diagnosis, 45–56; inter-
    viewing, 49; intuition, 162; inves-
    tigation, 161–162; team, 146–148;
    verificiation, 173. *See also* indica-
    tors of abuse
Indicators of abuse, 19–20, 49–55,
    85, 97, 161
Institutional abuse, ix–xii
Interdisciplinary problem-solving
    groups, 121–128; composition,
    122; principles for organizing,
    122–124; tasks of, 124–126; train-
    ing of, 126–127
Intergenerational transmission of
    abusive behavior, 177–179, 187–
    202
Intervention, 24, 102–103, 115–118,
    129–136, 150–152, 162–164
Investigation of abuse. *See* identifica-
    tion of abuse
Isolation of abusive parents, 47, 131

Jackson, D.D., 175
Jacobson, N., 129, 134
Jayaratne, S., 189
Johnson, A.W., 93
Johnson, G., 14
Jones, F.D., 93
Josten, L., 141
Juntti, M., 137
Justice, B., 189
Justice, R., 189

Kadushin, M., 189
Kagan, J., 190, 191
Kane, R.A., 113
Karnes, M.B., 29
Kaufman, W., 76–77
Kempe, C., 11, 21, 30, 45, 48, 121,
    131, 178, 188, 196
Kempe, R.S., 21, 188
Kent, J.T., 22–24
Killilea, M., 114
Kimball, W.H., 195
Kline, D.F., 3, 4, 20, 21
Kohlberg, L., 188, 191
Koluchova, J., 190
Kristal, H.I., 121
Kyte, A., 113

LaCrosse, J., 188, 191
Landsberger, B.H., 29
La Pouse, R., 13
Larkin, C., 75
Larrick, N., 29
Laszlo, E., 194
Lauderdale, M., 4, 8, 117
Laurie, I.S., 65, 66, 67
Leavell, H.R., 137
Lebsack, J., 3
Lee, B., 6, 111, 113, 121–128
Legislation dealing with child abuse:
    American and Canadian, 157–172;
    conflicts within, 75; definitional
    problems, 159–160, 172–173;
    public opinion, 75; protection for
    those reporting abuse, 69, 163–
    164; social change, 172; vagueness
    of, 173

Levitt, J.M., 195
Libbey, P., 7, 24, 25, 69–78
Lieber, L.L., 133
Lindsay, J., 189
Lissovoy de, V., 5, 11–17
Lordeman, A., 29, 30, 38
Lourie, I.S., 20, 69, 70, 71
Lourie, R.S., 14, 189

MacQueen, A.G., 196
Mahler, M.S., 62
Maltreated child. See abused child
Marcuse, H., 64
Marsden, L., 173
Martin, H.P., 4, 11, 19, 20, 22, 47, 48,
    117, 131, 138, 140, 153
Maruyama, M., 175
Marx, K., 64
Maurer, A., 11
McCaffrey, M., 24
McCatheren, R., 75
McEvoy, J., 75
McEwen, M.K., 112
McIntire, W.G., 29
Meares, P.A., 112
Meiselman, K.D., 192
Milowe, J.D., 14
Mitchell, M., 196
Mitton, J., 7, 137–143
Models of abuse. See theories of abuse
Monk, M.A., 13
Moore, E.M., 29
Morse, C.W., 45
Morse, H.R., 14
Mullany, P., 191
Murdock, C.J., 111, 117
Murdock, G., 4

Napier, R.N., 123
Natural helping networks, 112–113,
    115, 117, 129–136
Neglect, 64–65, 138, 160; effects on
    school-aged child, 19–26, emotional,
    52–68; guardian, 54, incidence, 45;
    nutritional, 53; theories of, 11–12;
    types of, 45
Newberger, E.H., 172, 173, 178, 183

Nicholson, M., 4, 117
Nowlis, V., 193
Nurse: acceptance of, 140–142; community health role, 7, 137–143; detection of abuse, 54–55; emotional conflicts of, 142; home visits, 138, 139, 141; relationship to teachers, 139–140; rescue fantasy, 142; role in dealing with abuse, 138–140

O'Neill, D.P., 189
Oppenheimer, R., 189
Oudendijk, N., 194
Ounsted, C., 189

Parens patriae, 60, 66
Parke, R.D., 11, 12, 30
Pancoast, D.L., 113, 119, 129, 132
Parents: bidirectionality of relations with child, 193–194; child-rearing skill, 141; high risk, 47–48; involvement in school activities, 29–30; support systems, 37–38; role in rape prevention, 88–89
Parr, R., 195
Patterson, P.G.R., x, 7, 59–68
Payne, D.C., 29
Pellegrino, J., 29
Perrow, C., 182
Peterson, D.R., 13
Pfeifer, D., 138
Pfohl, S., 77, 178
Piers, M.W., 191
Pollock, C., 48, 189
Pollock, D., 138
Pound, R., 75
Powell, T.J., 113
Prevention: child-abuse team, 115–116; primary, 137, 138; secondary, 138; tertiary, 139–140
Privacy, 161–162
Problem-solving groups, 121–128. *See* child-abuse teams
Professional response: confidentiality, 163–164; duties, 157–159; emotional reaction to abuse, 121;

incompetence, 164–165; legal responsibilities, 157–158; rescue fantasy, 142; standards of, 157–159
Physical abuse, 45–56; pain, 95–96; punishment of adolescents, 69–78

Raber, S., 134
Rape. *See* sexual abuse
Redl, F., 12, 13
Rees van, R., 194
Reese, S.C., 38
Reporting abuse: child-abuse teams, 117; errors in judgement, 117; legislation surrounding, 172–173; penalties for failure, 164–165; reasonable suspicion, 4, 159–160, 162–163, 173; under-reporting, 46
Ricks, D., 188, 191
Riessman, F., 114
Rigler, D., 11, 48, 177, 188
Rock, M., 131
Rosenblum, L.A., 193
Rozansky, P., 20
Rubin, L., 113
Russel, R., 134
Rutter, M., 189
Ryan, W., 191

Saunders, S., 133
Sayre, J.W., 121
Scheff, T., 175
Scharer, K., 142
Scheinfeld, D., 133
Scheurer, S.L., 145–153
Schmitt, B.D., 152
Schmuck, R.A., 29–30
School-aged child. *See* development
School personnel: assumptions about parents, 33–34; collaborating, 12; dealing with abuse, 33–36, 84–87; relating to families, 27–28; training, 38, 116
Schooling: abusive and arbitrary, ix; impact on families, 27–41, meaning to families, 27–28

School's role: child-abuse teams, 145–153; coordinating, 111–120; providing feedback to families, 38; identification, 3, 24, 145; natural helping networks, 133–135; outreach, 36–37; parent education, 138–139; placement of abused children, 21–22; prevention, 89; providing resources, 37; reporting, 163–164; treatment, 117
Scoblic, M., 137
Scott, P.D., 189
Sears, R.R., 193
Self esteem, 7, 9
Self-help groups, 181–182; abused children, 134–135; mothers, 138; parents, 133
Sexual abuse, 50–52, 79–89, 160; child's experience, 83; identification, 84–85; impact on child, 51–52; incest, 24; incidence, 83; investigation, 85–87; protecting child, 86–87; rape, 51, 87–89; reporting, 50–51; sadism, 82–83
Sgroi, S.M., 85–87
Sheridan, J., 16
Sherman, D., 129, 132
Shorter, E., 179
Silver, H.K., 45, 178
Silver, L.B., 189
Silverman, F.N., 45, 178
Silverman, P., 191
Smith, S.M., 189
Social networks, 129. See also natural helping systems
Social worker, 7, 111–121, 122
Solomon, G., 105
Spanje van, M., 194
Special education, 21–22
Spiegel, J.P., 171, 175
Spinetta, J.J., 11, 48, 177, 188
Stark, R., 75
Steele, B.F., 45, 48, 138, 178, 188, 189, 191
Stocking, S.H., 131
Straus, M.A., 14, 73, 195
Sullivan, H.S., 62

Support systems 29, 129–136, 180–182. See natural helping networks. See also social networks

Tagg, P., 112
Tannenbaum, D., 129
Teachers, 6–7, 15–16; home visits, 16; identification, 11
Theories of abuse, 11–12, 171–185, 188–189; causal models, 11–12, 177–179, 187–202; ecological, 11–17, 132; metatheories, 171–185; psychological, 11, 52, 173–174, 176, 188–189; socio-cultural, xi, 12–14, 32, 175, 176–177, 188; systems, 9, 12, 28, 29, 175–176, 194–196
Thomas, M., 116
Thompson, M.G., x, 7, 59–68
Treatment of abuse: child-protection teams, 117; compensatory relationships, 193; emotional neglect, 65–66; natural helping networks, 129–136; organization, 182
Tuck, S., 133

Vernon, P., 192
Volpe, R., ix, 3–10, 112

Wald, M., 74, 75, 76
Walters, D.R., 51, 174, 176, 182, 191
Watzlawick, P., 175
Weakland, J.H., 175
Weiss, P.A., 194
Whiting, L., 59, 66, 67
Wise, H., 113
Wold, S., 140
Wood, F., 75
Wright, L., 94
Wynne, L.C., 195

Young, L., 32, 54, 178, 189

Zehrbach, R.R., 79
Zemdegs, J., 3, 91–107
Zingarella, E.S., 121

About the Editors

Richard Volpe is currently an Associate Professor, Educational Psychology, Institute of Child Study, Faculty of Education, University of Toronto. He is also a member of the Department of Educational Theory, School of Graduate Studies, University of Toronto. He received the Ph.D. from the University of Alberta in social psychology and was a Laidlaw Foundation, Postdoctoral Fellow at Toronto's Hospital for Sick Children and the Clarke Institute of Psychiatry. His recent publications deal with the interrelation of theory and practice, human development, and child abuse. Currently he is doing research on the prediction of adult adaptation on the basis of childhood records.

Margot Breton received the Bachelor of Arts degree from the College Bourgeoys, Université de Montréal, and the Master of Social Work degree from McGill University. Her first teaching post was at the École de Service Social, Université de Montréal. Currently she is an Assistant Professor, Faculty of Social Work, University of Toronto. Her publications are in the areas of group work consultation and child abuse.

Judith Mitton, R.N., B.N., M.Sc. (A) graduated from the Moncton Hospital School of Nursing, Moncton, New Brunswick, and attended McGill University, Montréal, Québec, where she received both the Baccalaureate and the Master's degrees. She is presently an Assistant Professor on the Nursing Faculty, University of Toronto, Toronto, Ontario. Professor Mitton has held a variety of clinical nursing and teaching positions, with her primary interest and publications in the area of care of children and their families.

About the Contributors

Margaret M. Bailey, Ph.D., Staff Psychologist at the Ingham County Mental Health Center in Lansing, Michigan.

Robert P. Bates, M.D., Pediatrician and Director of the Child Abuse Program at the Hospital for Sick Children, Toronto, Ontario.

Norman W. Bell, Ph.D., Professor of Sociology and Associate Professor of Psychiatry at the University of Toronto, Toronto, Ontario.

Michael Benjamin, M.A., Ph.D. candidate in the Department of Sociology at the University of Toronto, Toronto, Ontario.

Margot Breton, M.S.W., Assistant Professor, Faculty of Social Work, University of Toronto.

Diane D. Broadhurst, M.L.A., Educational Consultant at the Help Resource Project, Baltimore, Maryland.

Ann Wolbert Burgess, R.N., D.N.Sc., Professor and Director of Research, Boston University School of Nursing, Boston, Massachusetts.

Paul A. D'Agostino, A.C.S.W., Executive Director, Community Council on Child Abuse and Neglect, Inc., Tampa, Florida.

Bernard M. Dickens, Ph.D., LL.D., Professor of Law at the University of Toronto, Toronto, Ontario.

Robert M. Friedman, Ph.D., Associate Professor and Adolescent Project Director at the Florida Mental Health Institute, Florida Department of Health and Rehabilitative Services, Tampa, Florida.

James Garbarino, Ph.D., Associate Professor of Human Development, College of Human Development, Pennsylvania State University, University Park, Pennsylvania.

Nicholas Groth, Ph.D., Director of the Sex Offender Program at the Connecticut Correctional Institution, Somers, Connecticut.

Bill Lee, M.S.W., Assistant Professor at the School of Social Work, McMaster University, Hamilton, Ontario.

Patricia Libbey, B.Sc., M.A.T., Ph.D. candidate in the School of Psychology, at the University of Minnesota, Minneapolis, Minnesota.

Vladimir de Lissovoy, Ph.D., Professor of Child Development and Family Relations at the College of Human Development, Pennsylvania State University, University Park, Pennsylvania.

Judith Mitton, R.N., M.Sc.(A), Assistant Professor, Faculty of Nursing, University of Toronto.

Paul G.R. Patterson, M.D., F.R.C.P.(C), Director of Child and Family Center at the War Memorial Children's Hospital, London, Ontario.

Susan L. Scheurer, M.D., Assistant Professor in the Department of Human Development at Michigan State University, East Lansing, Michigan.

Michael G.G. Thompson, M.D., F.R.C.P.(C), Executive Director of the West End Creche, Child and Family Center, Toronto, Ontario.

Richard Volpe, Ph.D., Associate Professor, Educational Psychology, Institute of Child Study, Faculty of Education, University of Toronto.

Janice Zemdegs, R.N., N.P., Nurse Practitioner, McMaster Family Practice Clinic, Hamilton, Ontario.